Frommer's®

PORTABLE

Acapulco, Ixtapa & Zihuatanejo

4th Edition

by Lynne Bairstow

Here's what critics say about Frommer's:

"Amazingly easy to use. Very portable, very complete."

—*Booklist*

"Detailed, accurate, and easy-to-read information for all price ranges."

—*Glamour Magazine*

Wiley Publishing, Inc.

Published by:

WILEY PUBLISHING, INC.
111 River St.
Hoboken, NJ 07030-5774

ISBN-13: 978-0-7645-8976-8
ISBN-10: 0-7645-8976-8

Editor: Stephen Bassman
Production Editor: Bethany J. André
Photo Editor: Richard Fox
Cartographer: Tim Lohnes
Production by Wiley Indianapolis Composition Services

For information on our other products and services or to obtain technical support, please contact our Customer Care Department within the U.S. at 800/762-2974, outside the U.S. at 317/572-3993 or fax 317/572-4002.

Wiley also publishes its books in a variety of electronic formats. Some content that appears in print may not be available in electronic formats.

Manufactured in the United States of America

5 4 3 2 1

Contents

List of Maps

ABOUT THE AUTHOR

Lynne Bairstow has lived in Puerto Vallarta for most of the past 13 years and has written about Mexico for the *New York Times*, *Los Angeles Times*, *Private Air* magazine, *Luxury Living* magazine, and other publications. In 2000, Lynne was awarded the Pluma de Plata, a top honor granted by the Mexican government to foreign writers, for her work in the Frommer's guidebook to Puerto Vallarta. She is appreciative of the invaluable contribution of her research assistant, **Alejandra Macedo,** for her work on this book.

AN INVITATION TO THE READER

In researching this book, we discovered many wonderful places—hotels, restaurants, shops, and more. We're sure you'll find others. Please tell us about them, so we can share the information with your fellow travelers in upcoming editions. If you were disappointed with a recommendation, we'd love to know that, too. Please write to:

Frommer's Portable Acapulco, Ixtapa & Zihuatanejo, 4th Edition
Wiley Publishing, Inc. • 111 River St. • Hoboken, NJ 07030-5774

AN ADDITIONAL NOTE

Please be advised that travel information is subject to change at any time—and this is especially true of prices. We therefore suggest that you write or call ahead for confirmation when making your travel plans. The authors, editors, and publisher cannot be held responsible for the experiences of readers while traveling. Your safety is important to us, however, so we encourage you to stay alert and be aware of your surroundings. Keep a close eye on cameras, purses, and wallets, all favorite targets of thieves and pickpockets.

FROMMER'S STAR RATINGS, ICONS & ABBREVIATIONS

Every hotel, restaurant, and attraction listing in this guide has been ranked for quality, value, service, amenities, and special features using a **star-rating system.** In country, state, and regional guides, we also rate towns and regions to help you narrow down your choices and budget your time accordingly. Hotels and restaurants are rated on a scale of zero (recommended) to three stars (exceptional). Attractions, shopping, nightlife, towns, and regions are rated according to the following scale: zero stars (recommended), one star (highly recommended), two stars (very highly recommended), and three stars (must-see).

In addition to the star-rating system, we also use **seven feature icons** that point you to the great deals, in-the-know advice, and unique experiences that separate travelers from tourists. Throughout the book, look for:

Finds	Special finds—those places only insiders know about
Fun Fact	Fun facts—details that make travelers more informed and their trips more fun
Kids	Best bets for kids—advice for the whole family
Moments	Special moments—those experiences that memories are made of
Overrated	Places or experiences not worth your time or money
Tips	Insider tips— great ways to save time and money
Value	Great values—where to get the best deals

The following **abbreviations** are used for credit cards:

| AE | American Express | DISC | Discover | V | Visa |
| DC | Diners Club | MC | MasterCard | | |

FROMMERS.COM

Now that you have the guidebook to a great trip, visit our website at **www. frommers.com** for travel information on more than 3,000 destinations. With features updated regularly, we give you instant access to the most current trip-planning information available. At Frommers.com, you'll also find the best prices on airfares, accommodations, and car rentals—and you can even book travel online through our travel booking partners. At Frommers. com, you'll also find the following:

- Online updates to our most popular guidebooks
- Vacation sweepstakes and contest giveaways
- Newsletter highlighting the hottest travel trends
- Online travel message boards with featured travel discussions

Planning Your Trip to Southern Pacific Mexico

This chapter tells you everything you need to know before you go: customs and passport requirements, currency details, package tours, getting there, getting around, and more.

1 The Region at a Glance

Though Pacific Mexico may be uniform in its exotic, tropical beaches and jungle scenery, the resorts along this coast couldn't be more varied in personality. From high-energy seaside cities to pristine, primitive coves, this is the Mexico that first lured vacationers around the globe.

Spanish conquistadors were attracted to this coast for its numerous sheltered coves and protected bays from which they set sail to the Far East. Years later, Mexico's first tourists found the same elements appealing, but for different reasons—they were seeking escape in the warm sunshine, and stretches of blue coves nicely complemented the heady tropical landscape of the adjacent coastal mountains.

Time at the beach is generally the top priority for most travelers to this part of Mexico. Each of the beach towns detailed in this book is capable of satisfying your sand-and-surf needs for a few days, or even a week or more. You could also combine several coastal resorts into a single trip, or mix the coastal with the colonial, say, with visits to both Puerto Escondido and Oaxaca City, or Acapulco and Taxco.

The resorts have distinct personalities, but you get the requisite beach wherever you go, whether you choose a city that offers virtually every luxury imaginable or a rustic town providing little more than basic (but charming) seaside relaxation.

Over the years, a diverse selection of resorts has evolved in the area. Each is distinct, yet together they offer an ideal attraction for almost any type of traveler. The region encompasses the country's oldest, largest, and most decadent resort, **Acapulco,** one-time playground of Hollywood's biggest celebrities. Of all the resorts, Acapulco has the best airline connections, the broadest range of late-night

Mexico

UNITED STATES

Tijuana
Mexicali
Ensenada
BAJA
CALIFORNIA
NORTE
San
Quintin
Puerto
Penasco
Nogales
Ciudad
Juárez
SONORA
Guerrero
Isla Negro
Cedros
Hermosillo
CHIHUAHUA
Ojinaga
Chihuahua
Santa
Rosalia
Mulegé
Cuidad
Obregón
Cuauhtémoc
COAHUILA
BAJA
CALIFORNIA
SUR
Loreto
Delicias
Monclova
Hidalgo
del Parral
Los
Mochis
SINALOA
Culiacán
DURANGO
Torreón
Saltillo
La Paz
Sea of Cortés
Durango
Fresnillo
San José
del Cabo
Todos Santos
Cabo San Lucas
Mazatlán
ZACATECAS
Zacatecas
San
Luis
Potosí
San Blas
Tuxpan
Tepic
NAYARIT
AGUASCALIENTES
Aguascalientes
León
*Islas
Marias*
Puerto Vallarta
Guadalajara
Guanajuato
GUANA-
JUATO
JALISCO
Lake Chapala
Morelia
Barra de Navidad
Uruapan
Colima
Pátzcuaro
Manzanillo
COLIMA
MICHOACAN
Lázaro
Cárdenas
**Zihuatanejo
& Ixtapa**
(Chapter 3)

PACIFIC
OCEAN

UNITED STATES

Piedras Negras

Nuevo Laredo

Monterrey

NUEVO
LEÓN

Matamoros

Gulf of Mexico

TAMAULIPAS

Ciudad Victoria

Ciudad Mante

Tampico

SAN LUIS
POTOSÍ

San Miguel
de Allende

QUERÉTARO

Tuxpan

HIDALGO

Poza Rica

Papantla

Querétaro

Pachuca

Mexico City

Xalapa

*Bay of
Campeche*

Cuernavaca
(Chapter 5)

TLAXCALA

Tlaxcala

Veracruz

MORELOS

PUEBLA

Puebla

Orizaba

Taxco
(Chapter 5)

Tehuacán

Catemaco

VERACRUZ

GUERRERO

Oaxaca

Acapulco
(Chapter 2)

OAXACA

Salina
Cruz

Puerto Escondido
(Chapter 4)

Puerto
Ángel
(Chapter 4)

Huatulco
(Chapter 4)

*Gulf of
Tehuantepec*

Río Lagartos

*Isla
Mujeres*

Progreso

Valladolid

Cancún

Celestún

Mérida

Cozumel

YUCATÁN

Playa del
Carmen

Campeche

*Punta
Allen*

QUINTANA
ROO

CAMPECHE

Bacalar

*Majahual
Peninsula*

Escárcega

Chetumal

TABASCO

Villahermosa

Coatzacoalcos

Palenque

BELIZE

Tuxtla
Gutiérrez

San Cristóbal
de las Casas

*Caribbean
Sea*

CHIAPAS

Comitán

GUATEMALA

HONDURAS

Tapachula

EL
SALVADOR

entertainment, the most savory dining, and the widest range of accommodations—from hillside villas and luxury resort hotels to modest inns on the beach and in the city center.

The resort of **Ixtapa** and its neighboring seaside village, **Zihuatanejo,** offer beach-bound tourist attractions, but on a smaller, newer, and less hectic scale than Acapulco. They attract travelers for their complementary contrasts—sophisticated high-rise hotels in one, plus the local color and leisurely pace of the other. To get here, many people fly into Acapulco, then make the 4- to 5-hour trip north (by rental car or bus).

South of Acapulco, along the Oaxacan Coast, lie the small, laid-back beach towns of **Puerto Escondido** and **Puerto Angel,** both on picturesque bays bordered by relaxed communities. The region's newest resort community, **Bahías de Huatulco,** couples an unspoiled, slow-paced nature with the kind of modern infrastructure and luxurious facilities you'd find in the country's crowded, overdeveloped megaresorts. Nine bays encompass 36 beaches—many are isolated stretches of pure white sand—and countless inlets and coves. Huatulco has become increasingly known for its eco-tourism attractions; you won't find much in the way of shopping or nightlife, but for most visitors, the clear blue waters and quiet, restful beaches are reason enough to come.

From Acapulco a road leads inland to **Taxco,** a colonial city that clings to the side of a mountain and is famed for its hundreds of silver shops. And verdant **Cuernavaca,** known as the land of eternal spring, has gained a reputation for exceptional spa facilities, while also boasting a wealth of cultural and historic attractions.

The whole region is graced with a stunning coastline and tropical mountains. Outside the urban centers, however, paved roads are few, and these two states remain among Mexico's poorest, despite decades-long influx of U.S. tourist dollars (and many other currencies).

2 Visitor Information

The **Mexico Hotline** (© 800/44-MEXICO) is an excellent source for general information; you can request brochures on the country and get answers to the most commonly asked questions. If you have a fax, Mexico's Ministry of Tourism also offers extensive written information on a variety of topics from general destination information to accommodations (the service lists 400 hotels), shopping, dining, sports, sightseeing, festivals, and nightlife. Call the same number above, and they can fax you a listing of what is available.

More information (15,000 pages' worth, they say) about Mexico is available on the Mexican Tourist Promotion Council's website: www.visitmexico.com.

The **U.S. State Department** (© 202/647-5225 for travel information and Overseas Citizens Services) offers a **Consular Information Sheet** on Mexico, with a compilation of safety, medical, driving, and general travel information gleaned from reports by official U.S. State Department offices in Mexico. You can also request the Consular Information Sheet by fax (© 202/647-3000). The State Department is also on the Internet: Check out **http://travel.state.gov** and click on International Travel for Consular Information Sheets, Travel Warnings, and Regional Information (with *Tips for Travelers to Mexico*).

Destination: Mexico—Red Alert Checklist

- Has the **U.S. State Department** (http://travel.state.gov) issued any travel advisories regarding Mexico?
- Do you have your passport or official ID? If traveling in a coastal area, did you pack insect repellent? Sunblock? A hat? Sunglasses? A sweater or jacket?
- Do you need to book tour, restaurant, or travel reservations in advance?
- Did you make sure attractions and activities that interest you are operating? Some attractions, such as seasonal nature tours, sell out quickly. (Mexico is considered at low risk for a terrorist attack; few event schedule changes or building closings have been instituted.)
- If you purchased traveler's checks, have you recorded the check numbers and stored the documentation separately from the checks?
- Did you pack your camera and an extra set of camera batteries, and purchase enough film?
- Do you have a safe, accessible place to store money?
- Did you bring emergency drug prescriptions and extra glasses and/or contact lenses?
- Do you know your daily ATM withdrawal limit?
- Do you have your credit card personal identification numbers (PINs)?
- If you have an e-ticket, do you have documentation?
- Do you know the address and phone number of your country's embassy?

The **Centers for Disease Control Hotline** (𝄢 **800/311-3435** or 404/639-3534) is another source for medical information affecting travelers to Mexico and elsewhere. The centers' website, **www.cdc.gov**, provides lengthy information on health issues for specific countries. The Web page with health information for travelers to Mexico and Central America is **www.cdc.gov/travel/camerica.htm**. The U.S. State Department offers medical information for Americans traveling abroad at **http://travel.state.gov**. This site provides general information and a list of air ambulance services and international travel insurance providers.

MEXICAN GOVERNMENT TOURIST OFFICES

Mexico has foreign tourist offices (MGTO) in the United States and Canada. They include the following:

United States: Chicago, IL (𝄢 **312/606-9252**); Houston, TX (𝄢 **713/772-2581**); Los Angeles, CA (𝄢 **310/282-9112**); Miami, FL (𝄢 **310/282-9112**); New York, NY (𝄢 **212/308-2110**); and the Mexican Embassy Tourism Delegate, 1911 Pennsylvania Ave., Washington, DC 20005 (𝄢 **202/728-1750**). The MGTO offices have been combined with Mexican Consulate offices in the same cities, providing one central source for official information on Mexico.

Canada: 1 Place Ville-Marie, Suite 1931, Montreal, Quebec H3B 2C3 (𝄢 **514/871-1052**); 2 Bloor St. W., Suite 1502, Toronto, Ontario M4W 3E2 (𝄢 **416/925-0704**); and 999 W. Hastings, Suite 1110, Vancouver, British Columbia V6C 2W2 (𝄢 **604/669-2845**). The Embassy is located at 1500-45 O'Connor St., Ottawa, Ontario K1P 1A4 (𝄢 **613/233-8988;** fax 613/235-9123).

3 Entry Requirements & Customs

For information on how to get a passport, go to the "Fast Facts: Mexico" section, later in this chapter—the websites listed provide downloadable passport applications as well as the current fees for processing passport applications. For an up-to-date country-by-country listing of passport requirements around the world, go to the "Foreign Entry Requirements" Web page of the U.S. State Department at **http://travel.state.gov**.

DOCUMENTS

All travelers to Mexico are required to present **proof of citizenship,** such as an original birth certificate with a raised seal, a valid passport, or naturalization papers. Those using a birth certificate should also have current photo identification, such as a driver's license or official

ID. If the last name on the birth certificate is different from your current name, bring a photo identification card *and* legal proof of the name change, such as the original marriage license or certificate. *Note:* Photocopies are *not* acceptable.

The best ID is a passport.

You must carry a **Mexican Tourist Permit (FMT),** the equivalent of a tourist visa, which Mexican border officials issue, free of charge, after proof of citizenship is accepted. Airlines generally provide the necessary forms aboard your flight to Mexico. The FMT is more important than a passport, so guard it carefully. If you lose it, you may not be permitted to leave until you can replace it—a bureaucratic hassle that can take anywhere from a few hours to a week.

The FMT can be issued for up to 180 days. Sometimes officials don't ask but just stamp a time limit, so be sure to say "6 months," or at least twice as long as you intend to stay. If you decide to extend your stay, you may request that additional time be added to your FMT from an official immigration office in Mexico.

Note that children under age 18 traveling without parents or with only one parent must have a notarized letter from the absent parent or parents authorizing the travel.

LOST DOCUMENTS

To replace a **lost passport,** contact your embassy or nearest consular agent (see "Fast Facts: Mexico," later in this chapter). You must establish a record of your citizenship and also fill out a form requesting another Mexican Tourist Permit if it, too, was lost. Without the **tourist permit** you can't leave the country, and without an affidavit affirming your passport request and citizenship, you may have problems at Customs when you get home. So it's important to clear everything up *before* trying to leave. Mexican Customs may, however, accept the police report of the loss of the tourist permit and allow you to leave.

CUSTOMS ALLOWANCES

When you enter Mexico, Customs officials will be tolerant as long as you have no illegal drugs or firearms. You're allowed to bring in two cartons of cigarettes, or 50 cigars, plus 1 kilogram (2.2 lb.) of smoking tobacco. The liquor allowance is two 1-liter bottles of anything, wine or hard liquor; you are also allowed 12 rolls of film. A laptop computer, camera equipment, and sporting equipment (golf clubs, scuba gear, a bicycle) that could feasibly be used during your stay are also allowed. The underlying guideline is: Don't bring anything that looks like it's meant to be resold in Mexico.

Returning **U.S. citizens** who have been away for at least 48 hours are allowed to bring back, once every 30 days, $800 worth of merchandise duty-free. You'll be charged a flat rate of 4% duty on the next $1,000 worth of purchases. Any dollar amount beyond that is dutiable at whatever rates apply. On mailed gifts, the duty-free limit is $200. Be sure to have your receipts or purchases handy to expedite the declaration process. *Note:* If you owe duty, you are required to pay on your arrival in the United States, either by cash, personal check, government or traveler's check, or money order, and in some locations, a Visa or MasterCard.

To avoid having to pay duty on foreign-made personal items you owned before you left on your trip, bring along a bill of sale, insurance policy, jeweler's appraisal, or receipts of purchase. Or you can register items that can be readily identified by a permanently affixed serial number or marking—think laptop computers, cameras, and CD players—with Customs before you leave. Take the items to the nearest Customs office or register them with Customs at the airport from which you're departing. You'll receive, at no cost, a Certificate of Registration, which allows duty-free entry for the life of the item.

With some exceptions, you cannot bring fresh fruits and vegetables into the United States. For specifics on what you can bring back, download the invaluable free pamphlet *Know Before You Go* online at **www.cbp.gov**. (Click on "Travel," and then click on "Know Before You Go! Online Brochure.") Or contact the **U.S. Customs & Border Protection (CBP),** 1300 Pennsylvania Ave., NW, Washington, DC 20229 (© **877/287-8667**) and request the pamphlet.

For a clear summary of **Canadian** rules, write for the booklet *I Declare,* issued by the **Canada Customs and Revenue Agency** (© **800/461-9999** in Canada, or 204/983-3500; www.ccra-adrc. gc.ca). Canada allows its citizens a C$750 exemption, and you're allowed to bring back duty-free one carton of cigarettes, 1 can of tobacco, 40 imperial ounces of liquor, and 50 cigars. In addition, you're allowed to mail gifts to Canada valued at less than C$60 a day, provided they're unsolicited and don't contain alcohol or tobacco (write on the package "Unsolicited gift, under $60 value"). All valuables should be declared on the Y-38 form before departure from Canada, including serial numbers of valuables you already own, such as expensive foreign cameras. Note: The $750 exemption can be used only once a year and only after an absence of 7 days.

U.K. citizens returning from **a non-E.U. country** have a customs allowance of: 200 cigarettes; 50 cigars; 250 grams of smoking tobacco; 2 liters of still table wine; 1 liter of spirits or strong liqueurs (over 22% volume); 2 liters of fortified wine, sparkling wine, or other liqueurs; 60cc (ml) perfume; 250cc (ml) of toilet water; and £145 worth of all other goods, including gifts and souvenirs. People under 17 cannot have the tobacco or alcohol allowance. For more information, contact HM Customs & Excise at ✆ **0845/010-9000** (from outside the U.K., 020/8929-0152), or consult their website at www.hmce.gov.uk.

The duty-free allowance in **Australia** is A$400 or, for those under 18, A$200. Citizens can bring in 250 cigarettes or 250 grams of loose tobacco, and 1,125 milliliters of alcohol. If you're returning with valuables you already own, such as foreign-made cameras, you should file form B263. A helpful brochure available from Australian consulates or Customs offices is *Know Before You Go.* For more information, call the **Australian Customs Service** at ✆ **1300/363-263,** or log on to www.customs.gov.au.

The duty-free allowance for **New Zealand** is NZ$700. Citizens over 17 can bring in 200 cigarettes, 50 cigars, or 250 grams of tobacco (or a mixture of all three if their combined weight doesn't exceed 250g); plus 4.5 liters of wine and beer, or 1.125 liters of liquor. New Zealand currency does not carry import or export restrictions. Fill out a certificate of export, listing the valuables you are taking out of the country; that way, you can bring them back without paying duty. Most questions are answered in a free pamphlet available at New Zealand consulates and Customs offices: *New Zealand Customs Guide for Travellers, Notice no. 4.* For more information, contact **New Zealand Customs,** The Customhouse, 17–21 Whitmore St., Box 2218, Wellington (✆ **04/473-6099** or 0800/428-786; www.customs.govt.nz).

GOING THROUGH CUSTOMS

Mexican Customs inspection has been streamlined. At most points of entry, tourists are requested to press a button in front of what looks like a traffic signal, which alternates on touch between red and green signals. Green light and you go through without inspection; red light and your luggage or car may be inspected briefly or thoroughly. If you have an unusual amount of luggage or an oversized piece, you may be subject to inspection despite the traffic signal routine.

4 Money

The currency in Mexico is the Mexican **peso.** Paper currency comes in denominations of 20, 50, 100, 200, 500, and 1,000 pesos. Coins come in denominations of 1, 2, 5, 10, and 20 pesos and 20 and 50 **centavos** (100 centavos equal 1 peso). The current exchange rate for the U.S. dollar is around 11 pesos; at that rate, an item that costs 11 pesos would be equivalent to US$1.

Getting **change** continues to be a problem in Mexico. Small-denomination bills and coins are hard to come by, so start collecting them early in your trip and continue as you travel. Shopkeepers everywhere seem always to be out of change and small bills; that's doubly true in a market.

Many establishments that deal with tourists, especially in coastal resort areas, quote prices in dollars. To avoid confusion, they use the abbreviations "Dlls." for dollars and "M.N." (*moneda nacional,* or national currency) for pesos. All dollar equivalencies in this book were based on an exchange rate of 11 pesos per dollar.

EXCHANGING MONEY

The rate of exchange fluctuates a tiny bit daily, so you probably are better off not exchanging too much of your currency at once. Don't forget, however, to have enough pesos to carry you over a weekend or Mexican holiday, when banks are closed. In general, avoid carrying the US$100 bill, the bill most commonly counterfeited in Mexico, and therefore the most difficult to exchange, especially in smaller towns. Because small bills and coins in pesos are hard to come by in Mexico, the US$1 bill is very useful for tipping.

Exchange houses *(casas de cambio)* are generally more convenient than banks because they have more locations and longer hours; the rate of exchange may be the same as a bank or only slightly lower. *Note:* Before leaving a bank or exchange-house window, always count your change in front of the teller before the next client steps up.

Large airports have currency-exchange counters that often stay open whenever flights are arriving or departing. Though convenient, these generally do not offer the most favorable rates.

A hotel's exchange desk commonly pays less favorable rates than banks; however, when the currency is in a state of flux, higher-priced hotels are known to pay *higher* than bank rates, in their effort to attract dollars.

Money Matters

The **universal currency sign ($)** is used to indicate pesos in Mexico. The use of the symbol in this book, however, denotes U.S. currency.

The bottom line: It pays to shop around, but in almost all cases, you receive a better exchange by changing money first, then paying for goods or services, rather than by paying with dollars directly to an establishment.

BANKS & ATMs

Banks in Mexico are rapidly expanding and improving services. They tend to be open weekdays from 9am until 5pm, and often for at least a half-day on Saturday. In larger resorts and cities, they can generally accommodate the exchange of dollars (which used to stop at noon) anytime during business hours. During times when the currency is in flux, a particular bank may not exchange dollars, so check before standing in line. Some, but not all, banks charge a service fee of about 1% to exchange traveler's checks. However, you can pay for most purchases directly with traveler's checks at the establishment's stated exchange rate. Don't even bother with personal checks drawn on a U.S. bank—the bank will wait for your check to clear, which can take weeks, before giving you your money.

Travelers to Mexico can easily withdraw money from **ATMs** (automated teller machines) in most major cities and resort areas. The U.S. State Department has an advisory against using ATMs in Mexico for safety reasons, stating that they should be used only during business hours, but this pertains primarily to Mexico City, where crime remains a significant problem. In most resorts in Mexico, the use of ATMs is perfectly safe—just use the same precautions you would at any ATM. Universal bank cards (such as the Cirrus and PLUS systems) can be used. This is a convenient way to withdraw money and avoid carrying too much with you at any time. The exchange rate is generally more favorable than that at a currency house. Most machines offer Spanish/English menus and dispense pesos, but some offer the option of withdrawing dollars. The **Cirrus** (© 800/424-7787; www.mastercard.com) and **PLUS** (© 800/843-7587; www.visa.com) networks span the globe; look at the back of your bank card to see which network you're on, then call or check online for ATM locations at your destination. Be sure you know your personal identification number (PIN) before you leave home and be sure to find out your daily withdrawal limit before you depart. Also keep in mind that many banks impose a fee every time a card is used at a different bank's ATM, and that fee can be higher for international transactions (up to $5 or more) than for domestic ones (where they're rarely more than $1.50). On top of this, the bank from which you withdraw cash may charge its own fee. To compare banks' ATM fees within the U.S., use www.bankrate.com. For international withdrawal fees, ask your bank.

You can also get cash advances on your credit card at an ATM. Keep in mind that credit card companies try to protect themselves from theft by limiting the funds someone can withdraw outside their home country, so call your credit card company before you leave home. And keep in mind that you'll pay interest from the moment of your withdrawal, even if you pay your monthly bills on time.

TRAVELER'S CHECKS

Traveler's checks are something of an anachronism from the days before the ATM made cash accessible at any time. Traveler's checks used to be the only sound alternative to traveling with dangerously large amounts of cash. They were as reliable as currency, but, unlike cash, could be replaced if lost or stolen.

These days, traveler's checks are less necessary because most cities have 24-hour ATMs that allow you to withdraw small amounts of cash as needed. However, keep in mind that you will likely be charged an ATM withdrawal fee if the bank is not your own, so if you're withdrawing money every day, you might be better off with traveler's checks—provided that you don't mind showing identification every time you want to cash one.

Tips   A Few Words About Prices

The peso's value continues to fluctuate—at press time, it was roughly **11 pesos to the dollar**. Also note that Mexico has a **value-added tax of 15%** (*Impuesto de Valor Agregado,* or IVA; pronounced "*ee*-vah") on most everything, including restaurant meals, bus tickets, and souvenirs. Always ask to see a printed price sheet and always ask if the tax is included.

You can get traveler's checks at almost any bank. **American Express** offers denominations of $20, $50, $100, $500, and (for cardholders only) $1,000. You'll pay a service charge ranging from 1% to 4%. You can also get American Express traveler's checks over the phone by calling ℂ **800/221-7282;** Amex gold and platinum cardholders who use this number are exempt from the 1% fee.

Visa offers traveler's checks at Citibank locations nationwide, as well as at several other banks. The service charge ranges between 1.5% and 2%; checks come in denominations of $20, $50, $100, $500, and $1,000. Call ℂ **800/732-1322** for information. AAA members can obtain Visa checks without a fee at most AAA offices or by calling ℂ **866/339-3378. MasterCard** also offers traveler's checks. Call ℂ **800/223-9920** for a location near you.

If you choose to carry traveler's checks, be sure to keep a record of their serial numbers separate from your checks in the event that they are stolen or lost. You'll get a refund faster if you know the numbers.

CREDIT CARDS

Credit cards are a safe way to carry money: They also provide a convenient record of all your expenses, and they generally offer relatively good exchange rates. You can also withdraw cash advances from your credit cards at banks or ATMs, provided you know your PIN. If you've forgotten yours, or didn't even know you had one, call the number on the back of your credit card and ask the bank to send it to you. It usually takes 5 to 7 business days, though some banks will provide the number over the phone if you tell them your mother's maiden name or some other personal information.

Keep in mind that when you use your credit card abroad, most banks assess a 2% fee above the 1% fee charged by Visa or Master-Card or American Express for currency conversion on credit charges. But credit cards still may be the smart way to go when you factor in things like exorbitant ATM fees and higher traveler's check exchange rates (and service fees).

In Mexico Visa, MasterCard, and American Express are the most accepted cards. You'll be able to charge most hotel, restaurant, and store purchases, as well as almost all airline tickets, on your credit card. You generally can't charge gasoline purchases in Mexico. You can get cash advances of several hundred dollars on your card, but there may be a wait of 20 minutes to 2 hours.

Charges will be made in pesos, then converted into dollars by the bank issuing the credit card. Generally you receive the favorable bank rate when paying by credit card. However, be aware that some establishments in Mexico add a 5% to 7% surcharge when you pay with a credit card. This is especially true when using American Express. Many times, advertised discounts will not apply if you pay with a credit card.

5 When to Go

SEASONS

Mexico has two principal travel seasons: high and low. **High season** begins around December 20 and continues to Easter, although in some places high season can begin as early as mid-November. **Low season** begins the day after Easter and continues to mid-December; during low season, prices may drop 20% to 50%. In beach destinations popular with Mexican travelers, such as Acapulco, the prices will revert back to high season during the months of July and August, the traditional national summer vacation period.

Mexico has two main climate seasons as well: **rainy** (May to mid-Oct) and **dry** (mid-Oct through Apr). The rainy season can be of little consequence in the dry, northern region of the country. The Pacific coastal region typically receives tropical showers, which begin around 4 or 5pm and last a few hours. Though these rains can come on suddenly and be quite strong, they usually end just as fast and cool off the air for the evening. **Hurricane season** particularly affects the southern Pacific coast, especially from June through October. However, if no hurricanes strike, the light, cooling winds, especially from September through November, can make it a perfect time to more comfortably explore the area. Most of coastal Mexico experiences temperatures in the 80s in the hottest months.

MEXICO CALENDAR OF EVENTS

January

New Year's Day (Año Nuevo). National holiday. Parades, religious observances, parties, and fireworks welcome in the new year everywhere. In traditional indigenous communities, new tribal leaders are inaugurated with colorful ceremonies rooted in the pre-Hispanic past. January 1.

Three Kings Day (Día de Reyes), nationwide. Commemorates the Three Kings' bringing of gifts to the Christ Child. Children receive gifts, much like on Christmas in the United States, and families eat a special *Rosca de Reyes* cake, with a small Christ child doll inside. Whoever receives the doll in his or her piece must host a tamales-and-*atole* party the next month. January 6.

February

Candlemass (Día de la Candelaria), nationwide. Music, dances, processions, food, and other festivities lead up to a blessing of seed and candles in a tradition that mixes pre-Hispanic and European traditions marking the end of winter. All those who attended the Three Kings Celebration reunite to share *atole* and tamales at a party hosted by the recipient of the doll found in the Rosca. February 2.

Constitution Day (Día de la Constitución). This national holiday is in honor of the current Mexican constitution, signed in 1917 as a result of the revolutionary war of 1910. It's celebrated through small parades. February 5.

Carnaval. Carnaval takes place the 3 days preceding Ash Wednesday and the beginning of Lent. Transportation and hotels are packed, so it's best to make reservations 6 months in advance and arrive a couple of days ahead of the beginning of celebrations.

Ash Wednesday. The start of Lent and time of abstinence. It's a day of reverence nationwide, but some towns honor it with folk dancing and fairs.

March

Benito Juárez's Birthday. National holiday. Small hometown celebrations countrywide, especially in Juárez's birthplace—Guelatao, Oaxaca. March 21.

April

Holy Week. Celebrates the last week in the life of Christ from Palm Sunday through Easter Sunday with somber religious processions almost nightly, spoofing of Judas, and reenactments of specific biblical events, plus food and craft fairs. Special celebrations are held in Taxco. Businesses close during this traditional week of Mexican national vacations. Make reservations early and avoid weekend travel. Early April.

May

Labor Day, nationwide. Workers parade countrywide and everything closes. May 1.

Holy Cross Day (Día de la Santa Cruz). Workers place a cross on top of unfinished buildings and celebrate with food, bands, folk dancing, and fireworks around the work site. May 3.

Cinco de Mayo. A national holiday that celebrates the defeat of the French at the Battle of Puebla. May 5.

Feast of San Isidro. The patron saint of farmers is honored with a blessing of seeds and work animals. May 15.

June

Navy Day (Día de la Marina), celebrated in all coastal towns with naval parades and fireworks. June 1.

Corpus Christi, celebrated nationwide. Honors the Body of Christ (the Eucharist) with religious processions, Masses, and food. Festivities include performances of *voladores* (flying pole dancers) beside the church and at the ruins of El Tajín. Dates vary.

Día de San Pedro (St. Peter and St. Paul's Day), nationwide. Celebrated wherever St. Peter is the patron saint, and honors anyone named Pedro or Peter. June 29.

July

The Guelaguetza Dance Festival, Oaxaca. One of Mexico's most popular events. Villagers from the seven regions around Oaxaca gather in the city's amphitheater and dress in traditional costumes with "dancing" masks. The celebration goes back to pre-Hispanic times to the fertility goddess for a plentiful corn harvest. Very popular internationally; make advance reservations. June 21 to 28.

August

Assumption of the Virgin Mary. Celebrated throughout the country with special masses and in some places with processions. August 20 to 22.

September

Independence Day. Celebrates Mexico's independence from Spain. A day of parades, picnics, and family reunions throughout the country. The schedule of events is the same in every village, town, and city across Mexico, following that of the capital: At 11pm on September 15, the president of Mexico gives the famous independence *grito* (shout) from the National Palace in Mexico City. People crowd into the central plaza to hear it and to watch the traditional fireworks display that follows. A parade follows the following morning. September 15 to 16.

October

Oaxaca's Ninth Annual Food of the Gods Festival. Oaxaca, Oaxaca. A culinary exploration of the indigenous cultures of Oaxaca. Known globally for its culinary creativity, Oaxaca is the birthplace of chocolate. More information on this weeklong event is available at www.food-of-the-gods-festival.com. October 2 to 9.

Día de la Raza ("Ethnicity Day" or Columbus Day). Commemorates the fusion of the Spanish and Mexican peoples. October 12.

November

Day of the Dead. What's commonly called the Day of the Dead is actually 2 days: All Saints' Day—honoring saints and deceased children—and All Souls' Day, honoring deceased adults. Relatives gather at cemeteries countrywide, carrying candles and food, often spending the night beside graves of loved ones. Weeks before, bakers begin producing bread formed in the shape of mummies or round loaves decorated with bread "bones." Decorated sugar skulls emblazoned with glittery names are sold everywhere. Many days ahead, homes and churches erect special altars laden with Day of the Dead bread, fruit, flowers, candles, favorite foods, and photographs of saints and of the deceased. On the 2 nights, children dress in costumes and masks, often carrying mock coffins and pumpkin lanterns, into which they expect money will be dropped, through the streets. Cemeteries around Oaxaca are well known for their solemn vigils and some for their Carnaval-like atmosphere. November 1 to 2.

Revolution Day. Commemorates the start of the Mexican Revolution in 1910 with parades, speeches, rodeos, and patriotic events. November 20.

National Silver Fair, Taxco. A competition of Mexico's best silversmiths and some of the world's finest artisans. There are exhibits, concerts, dances, and fireworks. Check local calendars or call ✆ **800/44-MEXICO** for details. Late November to early December.

December

Feast of the Virgin of Guadalupe. Throughout the country the patroness of Mexico is honored with religious processions, street fairs, dancing, fireworks, and masses. It is one of Mexico's most moving and beautiful displays of traditional culture. The Virgin of Guadalupe appeared to a young man, Juan Diego, in December 1531, on a hill near Mexico City. He convinced the bishop that he had seen the apparition by revealing his cloak, upon which the Virgin was emblazoned. Every village celebrates this day, often with processions of children dressed as Juan Diego and with *charreadas* (rodeos), bicycle races, dancing, and fireworks. December 12.

Christmas Posadas. On each of the 9 nights before Christmas, it's customary to reenact the Holy Family's search for an inn, with door-to-door candlelit processions in cities and villages nationwide. You may see them especially in Taxco. December 15 to 24.

Christmas. Mexicans extend this celebration and leave their jobs often beginning 2 weeks before Christmas all the way through New Year's. Many businesses close, and resorts and hotels fill up. Significant celebrations take place on December 23. In Oaxaca it's the "Night of the Radishes," with displays of huge carved radishes. On the evening of December 24 in Oaxaca, processions culminate on the central plaza.

Festival of the Radishes (Festival de los Rabanos), Oaxaca. Local artisans and sculptors set up stalls around the main square to display their elaborate pieces of art—made entirely from radishes! Balloons and birds crafted from local flowers add even more color. December 23.

New Year's Eve. As in the rest of the world, you'll find parties, fireworks, and plenty of noise. Special festivities take place at Tlacolula, near Oaxaca, with commemorative mock battles for good luck in the new year. December 31.

6 Insurance, Health & Safety

INSURANCE

TRAVEL INSURANCE AT A GLANCE

Check your existing insurance policies and credit card coverage before you buy travel insurance. You may already be covered for lost luggage, canceled tickets, or medical expenses. The cost of travel insurance varies widely, depending on the cost and length of your trip, your age and health, and the type of trip you're taking, but expect to pay between 5% and 8% of the vacation itself.

If you'll be driving in Mexico, see "Getting There: By Car" and "Getting Around: By Car," later in this chapter, for information on **collision** and **damage** and **personal accident insurance.**

TRIP-CANCELLATION INSURANCE

Trip-cancellation insurance helps you get your money back if you have to back out of a trip, if you have to go home early, or if your travel supplier goes bankrupt. Allowed reasons for cancellation can range from sickness to natural disasters to the State Department declaring your destination unsafe for travel. Insurers usually won't cover vague fears, though, as many travelers discovered who tried to cancel their trips in October 2001 because they were wary of flying after the September 11 terrorist attacks. In this unstable world, trip-cancellation insurance is a good buy if you're getting tickets well in advance—who knows what the state of the world, or of your airline, will be in 9 months? Insurance policy details vary, so read the fine print—and make sure that your airline or cruise line is on the list of carriers covered in case of bankruptcy. A good resource is **"Travel Guard Alerts,"** a list of companies considered high-risk by Travel Guard International (see website below). Protect yourself further by paying for the insurance with a credit card—by law, consumers can get their money back on goods and services not received if they report the loss within 60 days after the charge is listed on their credit card statement.

Note: Many tour operators, particularly those offering trips to remote or high-risk areas, include insurance in the cost of the trip or can arrange insurance policies through a partnering provider, a convenient and often cost-effective way for the traveler to obtain insurance. Make sure the tour company is a reputable one, however: Some experts suggest you avoid buying insurance from the tour or cruise company you're traveling with, saying it's better to buy from a "third party" insurer than to put all your money in one place.

For more information, contact one of the following recommended insurers: **Access America** (© 866/807-3982; www.accessamerica. com); **Travel Guard International** (© 800/826-4919; www.travel guard.com); **Travel Insured International** (© 800/243-3174; www. travelinsured.com); or **Travelex Insurance Services** (© 888/457-4602; www.travelex-insurance.com).

MEDICAL INSURANCE

For travel overseas, most health plans (including Medicare and Medicaid) do not provide coverage, and the ones that do often require you to pay for services upfront and reimburse you only after you return home. Even if your plan does cover overseas treatment, most out-of-country hospitals make you pay your bills upfront, and send you a refund only after you've returned home and filed the necessary paperwork with your insurance company. As a safety net, you may want to buy travel medical insurance, particularly if you're traveling to a remote or high-risk area where emergency evacuation is a possible scenario. If you require additional medical insurance, try **MEDEX Assistance** (© 410/453-6300; www.medexassist.com) or **Travel Assistance International** (© **800/821-2828;** www.travel assistance.com; for general information on services, call the company's Worldwide Assistance Services, Inc., at © **800/777-8710**).

LOST-LUGGAGE INSURANCE

On domestic flights, checked baggage is covered up to $2,500 per ticketed passenger. On international flights (including U.S. portions of international trips), baggage coverage is limited to approximately $9.07 per pound, up to approximately $635 per checked bag. If you plan to check items more valuable than the standard liability, see if your valuables are covered by your homeowner's policy, get baggage insurance as part of your comprehensive travel-insurance package, or buy Travel Guard's "BagTrak" product. Don't buy insurance at the airport, as it's usually overpriced. Be sure to take any valuables or irreplaceable items with you in your carry-on luggage, as many valuables (including books, money, and electronics) aren't covered by airline policies.

If your luggage is lost, immediately file a lost-luggage claim at the airport, detailing the luggage contents. For most airlines, you must report delayed, damaged, or lost baggage within 4 hours of arrival. The airlines are required to deliver luggage, once found, directly to your house or destination free of charge.

Keep in mind that in these uncertain times, insurers no longer cover some airlines, cruise lines, and tour operators. *The bottom line:* Always, always check the fine print before you sign; more and more policies have built-in exclusions and restrictions that may leave you out in the cold if something goes awry.

STAYING HEALTHY

In most of Mexico's resort destinations, health care meeting U.S. standards is now available. Mexico's major cities are also known for their excellent health care, although the facilities available may be more sparse, and equipment older than what is available at home. Prescription medicine is broadly available at Mexico pharmacies; however, be aware that you may need a copy of your prescription, or obtain a prescription from a local doctor. This is especially true in the border towns, such as in Tijuana, where many Americans have been crossing into Mexico specifically for the purpose of purchasing lower-priced prescription medicines.

Contact the **International Association for Medical Assistance to Travelers (IAMAT)** (© **716/754-4883,** or 416/652-0137 in Canada; www.iamat.org) for tips on travel and health concerns in the countries you're visiting, and lists of local, English-speaking doctors. The United States **Centers for Disease Control and Prevention** (© **800/311-3435;** www.cdc.gov) provides up-to-date information on health hazards by region or country and offers tips on food safety.

Over-the-Counter Drugs in Mexico

Antibiotics and other drugs for which you'd need a prescription to buy in the States are available over the counter in Mexican pharmacies. Mexican pharmacies also carry a limited selection of common over-the-counter cold, sinus, and allergy remedies.

COMMON AILMENTS

Mosquitoes and **gnats** are prevalent along the coast. Insect repellent *(repelente contra insectos)* is a must, and it's not always available in Mexico. If you'll be in these areas, bring a repellent along that contains the active ingredient DEET. Avon's Skin So Soft also works extremely well. Another good remedy to keep the mosquitoes away is to mix citronella essential oil with basil, clove, and lavender essential oils. If you're sensitive to bites, pick up some antihistamine cream from a drugstore at home.

Most visitors won't ever see a scorpion *(alacrán)*. But if you're stung by one, go immediately to a doctor. In Mexico you can buy scorpion toxin antidote at any drugstore; it is an injection and it costs around $25. This is a good idea if you plan on going camping to a remote area where medical assistance can be several hours away.

MORE SERIOUS DISEASES

You shouldn't be overly concerned about tropical diseases if you stay on the normal tourist routes and don't eat street food. However, both dengue fever and cholera have appeared in Mexico in recent years. Talk to your doctor or a medical specialist in tropical diseases about any precautions you should take. You can also get medical bulletins from the U.S. State Department and the Centers for Disease Control (see "Visitor Information," earlier in this chapter). You can protect yourself by taking some simple precautions: Watch what you eat and drink; don't swim in stagnant water (ponds, slow-moving rivers, or wells); and avoid mosquito bites by covering up, using repellent, and sleeping under mosquito netting. The most dangerous areas seem to be on Mexico's west coast, away from the big resorts, which are relatively safe.

EMERGENCY EVACUATION

In extreme medical emergencies, a service from the United States will fly people to American hospitals. **Global Lifeline** (© **888/554-9729,** or 01-800/305-9400 in Mexico) is a 24-hour air ambulance.

SAFETY
CRIME

I have lived and traveled in Mexico for over a decade, have never had any serious trouble, and rarely feel suspicious of anyone or any situation. You will probably feel physically safer in most Mexican cities and villages than in any comparable place at home. However, crime in Mexico has received attention in the North American press over the past several years. Many feel this unfairly exaggerates the real dangers, but it should be noted that crime rates, including taxi robberies,

 What to Do If You Get Sick

It's called "travelers' diarrhea" or *turista,* the Spanish word for "tourist": the persistent diarrhea, often accompanied by fever, nausea, and vomiting, that used to attack many travelers to Mexico. The U.S. Public Health Service recommends the following measures for preventing travelers' diarrhea:

- *Drink only purified water.* This means tea, coffee, and other beverages made with boiled water; canned or bottled carbonated beverages and water; or beer and wine. Most restaurants with a large tourist clientele use only purified water and ice.
- *Choose food carefully.* In general, avoid salads, uncooked vegetables, and unpasteurized milk or milk products (including cheese). However, salads in a first-class restaurant, or one serving a lot of tourists, are generally safe to eat. Choose food that is freshly cooked and still hot. Peelable fruit is ideal. Don't eat undercooked meat, fish, or shellfish.

In addition, something as simple as clean hands can go a long way toward preventing turista.

Because **dehydration** can quickly become life-threatening, the Public Health Service advises that you be especially careful to replace fluids and electrolytes (potassium, sodium, and the like) during a bout of diarrhea. Do this by drinking Pedialyte, a rehydration solution available at most Mexican pharmacies, or glasses of natural fruit juice (high in potassium) with a pinch of salt added. Or you can also try a glass of boiled pure water with a quarter-teaspoon of sodium bicarbonate (baking soda) added.

kidnappings, and highway carjackings, have risen in recent years. The most severe problems have been concentrated in Mexico City, where even long-time foreign residents will attest to the overall lack of security. If in Mexico City, avoid ostentatious displays of wealth (no fine jewelry), and take taxis only dispatched from official sites *(sitios).* Isolated incidents have also occurred in Ixtapa, and even the traditionally tranquil Puerto Escondido. See "Visitor Information," earlier in this chapter, for information on how to access the latest **U.S. State Department advisories.**

A good rule of thumb is that you can generally trust people whom you approach for help, assistance, or directions—but be wary of anyone who approaches you offering the same. The more insistent they are, the more cautious you should be. But you are much more likely to meet kind and helpful Mexicans than you are to encounter those set on thievery and deceit.

BRIBES & SCAMS

As you travel in Mexico, you may encounter several types of **scams,** which are typical throughout the world. One involves some kind of a **distraction** or feigned commotion. While your attention is diverted, a pickpocket makes a grab for your wallet. In another common scam, an **unaccompanied child** pretends to be lost and frightened and takes your hand for safety. Meanwhile the child or an accomplice plunders your pockets. A third involves **confusing currency.** A shoeshine boy, street musician, guide, or other individual might offer you a service for a price that seems reasonable—in pesos. When it comes time to pay, he or she tells you the price is in dollars, not pesos. Be very clear on the price and currency when services are involved.

Bribes are another matter and can land you in deeper trouble. If you believe a bribe is being requested by a police officer, here are a few tips on dealing with the situation. Even if you speak Spanish, don't utter a word of it to Mexican officials. That way you'll appear innocent, all the while understanding every word.

When you are crossing the border, should the person who inspects your car ask for a tip, you can ignore this request—but understand that the official may suddenly decide that a complete search of your belongings is in order. If faced with a situation where you feel you're being asked for a *propina* (literally, "tip"; colloquially, "bribe"), how much should you offer? Usually $3 to $5 or the equivalent in pesos will do the trick. Many tourists have the impression that everything works better in Mexico if you "tip"; however, in reality, this only perpetuates the *mordida* attitude. If you are pleased with a service, feel free to tip, but you shouldn't tip simply to attempt to get away with something illegal or inappropriate, whether it is crossing the border without having your car inspected or not getting a ticket that's deserved.

Whatever you do, **avoid impoliteness;** under no circumstances should you insult a Latin American official. Mexico is ruled by extreme politeness, even in the face of adversity. Stand your ground, but do it politely.

7 Tips for Travelers with Special Needs

FOR FAMILIES

Children are considered the national treasure of Mexico, and Mexicans will warmly welcome and cater to your children.

Before leaving, you should check with your doctor to get advice on medications to take along. Disposable diapers cost about the same in Mexico but are of poorer quality. You can get high-quality brands, but you'll pay. Gerber's baby foods are sold in many stores. Dry cereals, powdered formulas, baby bottles, and purified water are all easily available in midsize and large cities or resorts.

Cribs, however, may present a problem; only the largest and most luxurious hotels provide them. However, rollaway beds to accommodate children staying in the room with parents are often available. Child seats or high chairs at restaurants are common, and most restaurants will go out of their way to accommodate the comfort of your child. Consider bringing your own car seat, as they are not readily available for rent in Mexico.

Familyhostel (© **800/733-9753;** www.learn.unh.edu/family hostel) takes the whole family, including kids ages 8 to 15, on moderately priced domestic and international learning vacations. Lectures, field trips, and sightseeing are guided by a team of academics.

Recommended family travel Internet sites include **Family Travel-Forum** (www.familytravelforum.com), a comprehensive site that offers customized trip planning; **Family Travel Network** (www.familytravelnetwork.com), an award-winning site that offers travel features, deals, and tips; **Traveling Internationally with Your Kids** (www.travelwithyourkids.com), a comprehensive site offering sound advice for long-distance and international travel with children; and **Family Travel Files** (www.thefamilytravelfiles.com), which offers an online magazine and a directory of off-the-beaten-path tours and tour operators for families.

FOR GAY & LESBIAN TRAVELERS

Mexico is a conservative country, with deeply rooted Catholic religious traditions. Public displays of same-sex affection are rare and still considered shocking for men, especially outside of urban or resort areas. Women in Mexico frequently walk hand in hand, but anything more would cross the boundary of acceptability. However, gay and lesbian travelers are generally treated with respect and should not experience any harassment, assuming the appropriate regard is given to local culture and customs.

The International Gay and Lesbian Travel Association (IGLTA) (© **800/448-8550** or 954/776-2626; www.iglta.org) is the trade association for the gay and lesbian travel industry, and offers an online directory of gay- and lesbian-friendly travel businesses; go to their website and click on "Members."

Many agencies offer tours and travel itineraries specifically for gay and lesbian travelers. **Above and Beyond Tours** (© **800/397-2681;** www.abovebeyondtours.com) is the exclusive gay and lesbian tour operator for United Airlines. **Now, Voyager** (© **800/255-6951;** www. nowvoyager.com) is a well-known San Francisco–based gay-owned and operated travel service. **Olivia Cruises & Resorts** (© **800/631-6277;** www.olivia.com) charters entire resorts and ships for exclusive lesbian vacations and offers smaller group experiences for both gay and lesbian travelers.

FOR TRAVELERS WITH DISABILITIES

Mexican airports are upgrading their services, but it is not uncommon to board from a remote position, meaning you either descend stairs to a bus that ferries you to the plane, which you board by climbing stairs, or you walk across the tarmac to your plane and ascend the stairs. Deplaning presents the same problem in reverse.

Escalators (and there aren't many in the country) are often out of order. Stairs without handrails abound. Few restrooms are equipped for travelers with disabilities; when one is available, access to it may be through a narrow passage that won't accommodate a wheelchair or a person on crutches. Many deluxe hotels (the most expensive) now have rooms with bathrooms for people with disabilities. Those traveling on a budget should stick with one-story hotels or hotels with elevators. Even so, there will probably still be obstacles somewhere. Generally speaking, no matter where you are, someone will lend a hand, although you may have to ask for it.

Many travel agencies offer customized tours and itineraries for travelers with disabilities. **Flying Wheels Travel** (☎ 507/451-5005; www.flyingwheelstravel.com) offers escorted tours and cruises that emphasize sports and private tours in minivans with lifts. **Access-Able Travel Source** (☎ 303/232-2979; www.access-able.com) offers extensive access information and advice for traveling around the world with disabilities. **Accessible Journeys** (☎ 800/846-4537 or 610/521-0339; www.disabilitytravel.com) caters specifically to slow walkers and wheelchair travelers and their families and friends.

Organizations that offer assistance to disabled travelers include **MossRehab** (www.mossresourcenet.org), which provides a library of accessible-travel resources online; **SATH (Society for Accessible Travel & Hospitality)** (☎ 212/447-7284; www.sath.org; annual membership fees: $45 adults, $30 seniors and students), which offers a wealth of travel resources for all types of disabilities and informed recommendations on destinations, access guides, travel agents, tour operators, vehicle rentals, and companion services; and the **American Foundation for the Blind (AFB)** (☎ 800/232-5463; www.afb.org), a referral resource for the blind or visually impaired that includes information on traveling with Seeing Eye dogs.

FOR SENIORS

Mexico is a popular country for retirees. For decades, North Americans have been living indefinitely in Mexico by returning to the border and recrossing with a new tourist permit every 6 months. Mexican immigration officials have caught on, and now limit the maximum time in the country to 6 months within any year. This is to encourage even partial residents to comply with the proper documentation.

Some of the most popular places for long-term stays are Cuernavaca, Morelos, and Oaxaca.

AIM, Apdo. Postal 31-70, 45050 Guadalajara, Jalisco, Mexico, is a well-written, candid, and very informative newsletter for prospective retirees. Subscriptions are $18 to the United States and $21 to Canada. Back issues are three for $5.

Sanborn Tours, 2015 South 10th St., P.O. Drawer 519, McAllen, TX 78505-0519 (☎ 800/395-8482), offers a "Retire in Mexico" Guadalajara orientation tour.

Mention the fact that you're a senior citizen when you make your travel reservations. Although all of the major U.S. airlines except America West have cancelled their senior discount and coupon book programs, many hotels still offer discounts for seniors.

Members of **AARP** (formerly known as the American Association of Retired Persons), 601 E St. NW, Washington, DC 20049 (© 888/687-2277; www.aarp.org), get discounts on hotels, airfares, and car rentals. AARP offers members a wide range of benefits, including *AARP: The Magazine* and a monthly newsletter. Anyone over 50 can join.

Many reliable agencies and organizations target the 50-plus market. **Elderhostel** (© 877/426-8056; www.elderhostel.org) arranges study programs for those ages 55 and over (and a spouse or companion of any age) in the U.S. and in more than 80 countries around the world. Most courses last 5 to 7 days in the U.S. (2–4 weeks abroad), and many include airfare, accommodations in university dormitories or modest inns, meals, and tuition. **ElderTreks** (© 800/741-7956; www.eldertreks.com) offers small-group tours to off-the-beaten-path or adventure-travel locations, restricted to travelers 50 and older. **INTRAV** (© 800/456-8100; www.intrav.com) is a high-end tour operator that caters to the mature, discerning traveler, not specifically seniors, with trips around the world that include guided safaris, polar expeditions, private-jet adventures, and small-boat cruises down jungle rivers.

FOR SINGLES

Mexico may be an old favorite for romantic honeymoons, but it's also a great place to travel on your own without really being or feeling alone. Although offering an identical room rate regardless of single or double occupancy is slowly becoming a trend in Mexico, many of the hotels mentioned in this book still offer singles at lower rates.

Mexicans are very friendly, and it's easy to meet other foreigners. But if you don't like the idea of traveling alone, then try **Travel Companion Exchange,** P.O. Box 833, Amityville, NY 11701 (© 800/392-1256 or 631/454-0880), which brings prospective travelers together. Members complete a profile, then place an anonymous listing of their travel interests in the newsletter. Prospective traveling companions then make contact through the exchange. Membership costs $99 for 6 months or $159 for a year. They also offer an excellent booklet on avoiding theft and scams while traveling abroad, for $3.95.

FOR WOMEN

As a female traveling alone, I can tell you firsthand that I feel safer traveling in Mexico than in the United States. But I use the same common-sense precautions I use traveling anywhere else in the world and am alert to what's going on around me.

Mexicans in general, and men in particular, are nosy about single travelers, especially women. If taxi drivers or anyone else with whom you don't want to become friendly ask about your marital status, family, for example, my advice is to make up a set of answers (regardless of the truth): "I'm married, traveling with friends, and I have three children."

Saying you are single and traveling alone may send out the wrong message about availability. Movies and television shows exported from the United States have created an image of sexually aggressive North American women. If bothered by someone, don't try to be polite—just leave or head into a public place.

Check out the award-winning website **Journeywoman** (www. journeywoman.com), a "real life" women's travel information network where you can sign up for a free e-mail newsletter and get advice on everything from etiquette and dress to safety; or the travel guide *Safety and Security for Women Who Travel* by Sheila Swan and Peter Laufer (Travelers' Tales, Inc.), offering common-sense tips on safe travel.

FOR STUDENTS

Because Mexicans consider higher education more a luxury than a birthright, there is no formal network of student discounts and programs. Most Mexican students travel with their families rather than with other students, so student discount cards are not commonly recognized.

However, more hostels have entered the student travel scene. The **Mexican Youth Hostel Network,** or Red Mexicana de Albergues Juveniles (www.remaj.com), offers a list of hostels that meet international standards in Mexico City, Cuernavaca and surrounding areas, Oaxaca, and Veracruz. The **Mexican Youth Hostel Association,** or Asociación Mexicana de Albergues Juveniles (www.hostels.com./en/mx.html), offers a list of hostels in Mexico City, Puerto Escondido, and other cities in Mexico.

If you're a student planning to travel outside the U.S., you'd be wise to arm yourself with an **International Student Identity Card (ISIC),** which offers substantial savings on rail passes, plane tickets, and entrance fees. It also provides you with basic health and life insurance and a 24-hour help line. The card is available for $22 from **STA Travel** (© **800/781-4040** in North America; www.sta.com or www.statravel.com), the biggest student travel agency in the world. If you're no longer a student but are still under 26, you can get an **International Youth Travel Card (IYTC)** for the same price from the same people, which entitles you to similar discounts.

8 Getting There

BY PLANE

The airline situation in Mexico is rapidly improving, with many new regional carriers offering scheduled service to areas previously not served. In addition to regularly scheduled service, charter service direct from U.S. cities to resorts is making Mexico more accessible.

THE MAJOR INTERNATIONAL AIRLINES

The main airlines operating direct or nonstop flights from the United States to points in Mexico include **Aerocalifornia** (© 800/237-6225), **Aeromexico** (© 800/237-6639; www.aeromexico.com), **Air France** (© 800/237-2747; www.airfrance.com), **Alaska Airlines** (© 800/426-0333; www.alaskaair.com), **America West** (© 800/235-9292; www.americawest.com), **American Airlines** (© 800/433-7300; www.aa.com), **Continental** (© 800/231-0856; www.continental.com), **Frontier Airlines** (© 800/432-1359; www.frontierairlines.com), **Mexicana** (© 800/531-7921; www.mexicana.com), **Northwest/KLM** (© 800/225-2525; www.nwa.com), **Taca** (© 800/225-2272; www.taca.com), **United** (© 800/241-6522; www.ual.com), and **US Airways** (© 800/428-4322; www.usairways.com).

The main departure points in North America for international airlines are Atlanta, Chicago, Dallas/Fort Worth, Denver, Houston, Los Angeles, Las Vegas, Miami, New York, Orlando, Philadelphia, Phoenix, Raleigh/Durham, San Antonio, San Francisco, Seattle, Toronto, and Washington, D.C.

GETTING THROUGH THE AIRPORT

With the federalization of airport security, security procedures at U.S. airports are more stable and consistent than ever. Generally, you'll be fine if you arrive at the airport **1 hour** before a domestic flight and **2 hours** before an international flight; if you show up late, tell an airline employee and she'll probably whisk you to the front of the line.

Bring a **current, government-issued photo ID** such as a driver's license or passport. Keep your ID at the ready to show at check-in, the security checkpoint, and sometimes even the gate. (Children under 18 do not need government-issued photo IDs for domestic flights, but they do for international flights to most countries.)

In 2003, the TSA phased out **gate check-in** at all U.S. airports. And **e-tickets** have made paper tickets nearly obsolete. Passengers with e-tickets can beat the ticket-counter lines by using airport **electronic kiosks** or even **online check-in** from their home computers.

Online check-in involves logging on to your airline's website, accessing your reservation, and printing out your boarding pass—and the airline may even offer you bonus miles to do so! If you're using a kiosk at the airport, bring the credit card you used to book the ticket or your frequent-flier card. Print out your boarding pass from the kiosk and simply proceed to the security checkpoint with your pass and a photo ID. If you're checking bags or looking to snag an exit-row seat, you will be able to do so using most airline kiosks. Even the smaller airlines are employing the kiosk system, but always call your airline to make sure these alternatives are available. Note that at press time, these check-in services were not available at Mexico's airports, so plan on checking in the old-fashioned way—by standing in line. **Curbside check-in** is also a good way to avoid lines, although a few airlines still ban curbside check-in; call before you go.

Federalization has stabilized **what you can carry on** and **what you can't.** The general rule is that sharp things are out, nail clippers are okay, and food and beverages must be passed through the X-ray machine—but that security screeners can't make you drink from your coffee cup. Bring food in your carry-on rather than checking it, as explosive-detection machines used on checked luggage have been known to mistake food (especially chocolate, for some reason) for bombs. Travelers in the U.S. are allowed one carry-on bag, plus a "personal item" such as a purse, briefcase, or laptop bag. Carry-on hoarders can stuff all sorts of things into a laptop bag; as long as it has a laptop in it, it's still considered a personal item. The Transportation Security Administration (TSA) has issued a list of restricted items; check its website (www.tsa.gov/public/index.jsp) for details.

BY CAR

Driving is not the cheapest way to get to Mexico, but it is the best way to see the country. Even so, you may think twice about taking your own car south of the border once you've pondered the bureaucracy that affects foreign drivers here. One option is to rent a car for touring around a specific region once you arrive in Mexico. Rental cars in Mexico are now generally new, clean, and very well maintained. Although pricier than in the United States, discounts are often available for rentals of a week or longer, especially when arrangements are made in advance from the United States. (See "Car Rentals," later in this chapter, for more details).

If, after reading the section that follows, you have any additional questions or you want to confirm the current rules, call your nearest Mexican consulate, or the Mexican Government Tourist Office. To check on road conditions or to get help with any travel emergency while in Mexico, call © **01-800/903-9200** or 55/5250-0151 in Mexico City. Both numbers are staffed by English-speaking operators.

In addition, check with the **U.S. State Department** (see "Visitor Information," earlier in this chapter) for their warnings about dangerous driving areas.

CAR DOCUMENTS

To drive your car into Mexico, you'll need a **temporary car-importation permit,** which is granted after you provide a required list of documents (see below). The permit can be obtained through Banco del Ejército *(Banjercito)* officials, who have a desk, booth, or office at the Mexican Customs *(Aduana)* building, after you cross the border into Mexico.

The following strict requirements for border crossing were accurate at press time:

- **A valid driver's license,** issued outside of Mexico.
- **Current, original car registration and a copy of the original car title.** If the registration or title is in more than one name and not all the named people are traveling with you, a notarized letter from the absent person(s) authorizing use of the vehicle for the trip is required; have it ready just in case. The registration and your credit card (see below) must be in the same name.
- **A valid international major credit card.** With a credit card, you are required to pay only a $23 car-importation fee. The credit card must be in the same name as the car registration. If you do not have a major credit card, you must post a bond or make a deposit equal to the value of the vehicle. Check cards are not accepted.
- **Original immigration documentation.** This is either your tourist permit (FMT) or the original immigration booklet, FM2 or FM3, if you hold more permanent status.
- **A signed declaration promising to return to your country of origin with the vehicle.** Obtain this form *(Carta Promesa de Retorno)* from AAA or Sanborn's before you go, or from Banjercito officials at the border. There's no charge. The form does not stipulate that you must return by the same border entry through which you entered.

• **Temporary Importation Application.** By signing this form, you state that you are only temporarily importing the car for your personal use and will not be selling it. This is to help regulate the entry and restrict the resale of unauthorized cars and trucks. Vehicles in the U.S. are much less expensive and for years were brought into Mexico for resale. Make sure the permit is cancelled when you return to the U.S.

If you receive your documentation at the border, Mexican officials will make two copies of everything and charge you for the copies. For up-to-the-minute information, a great source is the Customs office in Nuevo Laredo, or *Módulo de Importación Temporal de Automóviles, Aduana Nuevo Laredo* (© **867/712-2071**).

Important reminder: Someone else may drive, but the person (or relative of the person) whose name appears on the car-importation permit must *always* be in the car. (If stopped by police, a non-registered family member driving without the registered driver must be prepared to prove familial relationship to the registered driver—no joke.) Violation of this rule subjects the car to impoundment and the driver to imprisonment, a fine, or both. You can drive a car with foreign license plates only if you have a foreign (non-Mexican) driver's license. You do not need an international driver's license in Mexico.

MEXICAN AUTO INSURANCE

Liability auto insurance is legally required in Mexico. U.S. insurance is invalid; to be insured in Mexico, you must purchase Mexican insurance. Any party involved in an accident who has no insurance may be sent to jail and have his or her car impounded until all claims are settled. This is true even if you just drive across the border to spend the day. U.S. companies that broker Mexican insurance are commonly found at the border crossing, and several quote daily rates.

You can also buy car insurance through **Sanborn's Mexico Insurance,** P.O. Box 52840, 2009 S. 10th, McAllen, TX 78505-2840 (© **956/686-3601;** fax 800/222-0158 or 956/686-0732; www. sanbornsinsurance.com). The company has offices at all U.S. border crossings. Its policies cost the same as the competition's do, but you get legal coverage (attorney and bail bonds if needed) and a detailed mile-by-mile guide for your proposed route. Most of Sanborn's border offices are open Monday through Friday, and a few are staffed on Saturday and Sunday. **AAA** auto club also sells insurance.

RETURNING TO THE UNITED STATES WITH YOUR CAR

You *must* return the car documents you obtained when you entered Mexico when you cross back with your car, or at some point within 180 days. (You can cross as many times as you wish within the 180 days.) If the documents aren't returned, heavy fines are imposed ($250 for each 15 days late), your car may be impounded and confiscated, or you may be jailed if you return to Mexico. You can return the car documents only to a Banjercito official on duty at the Mexican Customs *(Aduana)* building *before* you cross back into the United States. Some border cities have Banjercito officials on duty 24 hours a day, but others do not; some do not have Sunday hours. On the U.S. side, Customs agents may or may not inspect your car from top to bottom.

BY SHIP

Numerous cruise lines serve Mexico. Possible trips might cruise from California down to ports of call on the Pacific Coast. Several cruise-tour specialists arrange substantial discounts on unsold cabins if you're willing to take off at the last minute. One such company is **The Cruise Line,** 150 NW 168 St., North Miami Beach, Miami, FL 33169 (© **800/777-0707** or 305/521-2200).

BY BUS

Greyhound-Trailways or its affiliates (© **800/229-9424;** www.greyhound.com) offer service from around the United States to the Mexican border, where passengers disembark, cross the border, and buy a ticket for travel into the interior of Mexico. At many border crossings there are scheduled buses from the U.S. bus station to the Mexican bus station.

9 Package Tours for the Independent Traveler

Package tours are not the same thing as escorted tours. Package tours are simply a way to buy the airfare, accommodations, and other elements of your trip (such as car rentals, airport transfers, and sometimes even activities) at the same time and often at discounted prices—kind of like one-stop shopping. Packages are sold in bulk to tour operators—who resell them to the public at a cost that usually undercuts standard rates.

> ### ⎛Tips Before You Book a Package
>
> - **Read the fine print.** Make sure you know *exactly* what's included in the price you're being quoted, and what's not.
> - **Know what you're getting yourself into—and if you can get yourself out of it.** Often, packagers will offer trip cancellation insurance (for around $25–$30), which will return your payment if you need to change your plans.

The best deals usually coincide with high season—from mid-December to April—when demand is at its peak, and companies are more confident about filling planes. You might think that package rates would be better during low season, when room rates and airfares plunge. But the key is air access, which is much easier during the winter. Packages vary widely, with some companies offering a better class of hotels than others. Some offer the same hotels for lower prices. Some offer flights on scheduled airlines, while others book charters. In some packages, your choices of accommodations and travel days may be limited. Each destination usually has some packagers that are better than the rest because they buy in even bigger bulk. Not only can that mean better prices, but it also can mean more choices.

WHERE TO BROWSE

- One specialist in Mexico vacation packages is **www.mexicotravelnet.com**, an agency that offers most of the well known travel packages to Mexico beach resorts, plus offers last-minute specials.
- Check out **www.2travel.com** and find a page with links to a number of the big-name Mexico packagers, including several of those listed here.
- For last-minute air-only or package bargains, check out **Vacation Hot Line** (www.vacationhotline.net). Once you find your deal, you'll need to call to make booking arrangements. This service offers packages from the popular Apple and Funjet vacation wholesalers.
- Several big **online travel agencies**—Expedia, Travelocity, Orbitz, Site59, and Lastminute.com—also do a brisk business in packages.

RECOMMENDED PACKAGERS

- **Aeromexico Vacations** (© 800/245-8585; www.aeromexico. com) offers year-round packages to Acapulco, Ixtapa/Zihuatanejo, and others, with more than 100 resorts in a variety of price ranges.
- **Alaska Airlines Vacations** (© 800/468-2248; www.alaskaair. com) sells packages to Ixtapa/Zihuatanejo, and others. The website offers unpublished discounts that are not available through the phone operators.
- **American Airlines Vacations** (© 800/321-2121; http://www. aavacations.com) has year-round deals to Acapulco, and others, and best deals are on the Web. You don't have to fly with American if you can get a better deal on another airline.
- **America West Vacations** (© 800/356-6611; www.americawest vacations.com) has deals to Acapulco, Ixtapa, and others.
- **Apple Vacations** (© 800/365-2775; www.applevacations.com) offers inclusive packages to all the beach resorts, and has the largest choice of hotels in Acapulco. Apple perks include baggage handling and the services of a company representative at major hotels.
- **Classic Custom Vacations** (© 800/635-1333; www.classic customvacations.com) specializes in package vacations to Mexico's finest luxury resorts. Not for bargain hunters.
- **Continental Vacations** (© 800/301-3800; www.covacations. com) has year-round packages to Acapulco, Ixtapa, and others, with best deals on the Web. You must fly Continental.
- **Delta Vacations** (© 800/221-6666; www.deltavacations.com) has year-round packages to Acapulco and others. Atlanta is the hub, so expect the best prices from there.

Finds Out-of-the-Ordinary Places to Stay

Mexico lends itself beautifully to the concept of small, private hotels in idyllic settings. **Mexico Boutique Hotels** (www.Mexico BoutiqueHotels.com) specializes in smaller places to stay with a high level of personal attention and service. Most options have less than 50 rooms, and the accommodations consist of entire villas, *casitas,* bungalows, or a combination.

- **Funjet Vacations** (book through any travel agent; www.funjet. com for general information) is one of the largest vacation packagers in the United States. Funjet has packages to Acapulco, Ixtapa, and others. You can choose a charter or fly on American, Continental, Delta, Aeromexico, US Airways, Alaska Air, or United.
- **GOGO Worldwide Vacations** (✆ 888/636-3942; www.gogo wwv.com) has trips to all the major beach destinations, including Acapulco. It offers several exclusive deals from higher-end hotels. Book through any travel agent.
- **Mexicana Vacations,** or MexSeaSun Vacations (✆ 800/531-9321; www.mexicana.com), offers getaways to all the resorts. Mexicana operates daily direct flights from Los Angeles to Los Cabos, Mazatlán, Cancún, Puerto Vallarta, Manzanillo, and Ixtapa/Zihuatanejo.
- **Online Vacation Mall** (✆ 800/839-9851; www.onlinevacation mall.com) allows you to search for and book packages offered by a number of tour operators and airlines to Acapulco, Ixtapa/ Zihuatanejo, and others.
- **Pleasant Mexico Holidays** (✆ 800/448-3333; www.pleasant holidays.com) is one of the largest vacation packagers in the United States, with hotels in Acapulco, Ixtapa/Zihuatanejo, and others.
- Several big **online travel agencies**—Expedia, Travelocity, Orbitz, Site59, and Lastminute.com—also do a brisk business in packages. If you're unsure about the pedigree of a smaller packager, check with the Better Business Bureau in the city where the company is based, or go online at www.bbb.org. If a packager won't tell you where they're based, don't fly with them.

10 Active Vacations in Pacific Coast Mexico

Golf, tennis, waterskiing, surfing, bicycling, and **horseback riding** are all sports visitors can enjoy in Pacific coast Mexico. **Scuba diving** is excellent, as is snorkeling, all along this coast. **Mountain climbing** is a rugged sport where you'll meet like-minded folks from around the world. A popular spot for this is in the mountainous areas surrounding Huatulco.

PARKS

Most of the national parks and nature reserves are understaffed or unstaffed. In addition to the reliable Mexican companies offering adventure trips (such as the AMTAVE members; see below), many

U.S.-based companies also offer this kind of travel, with trips led by specialists.

OUTDOORS ORGANIZATIONS & TOUR OPERATORS

AMTAVE (Asociación Mexicana de Turismo de Aventura y Ecoturismo, A.C.) is an active association of ecotour and adventure tour operators. It publishes an annual catalog of participating firms and their offerings, all of which must meet certain criteria for security, quality, and training of the guides, as well as for sustainability of natural and cultural environments. For more information, contact AMTAVE (℗ **800/509-7678;** www.turismoaventura.com).

The **Archaeological Conservancy,** 5301 Central Ave. NE, Suite 402, Albuquerque, NM 87108 (℗ **505/266-1540;** www.american archaeology.org), presents one trip per year led by an expert, usually an archaeologist. The trips change from year to year and space is limited; make reservations early.

Culinary Adventures, 6023 Reid Dr. NW, Gig Harbor, WA 98335 (℗ **253/851-7676;** fax 253/851-9532), specializes in a short but special list of cooking tours in Mexico, featuring well-known cooks and traveling to particular regions known for excellent cuisine. The owner, Marilyn Tausend, is the co-author of *Mexico the Beautiful Cookbook* and *Cocinas de la Familia* (Family Kitchens).

Mexico Art Tours (℗ **888/783-1331,** or 480/730-1764 in the U.S., fax: 480/730-1496; 1233 East Baker Drive, Tempe, AZ 85282; www.mexicanarttours.com). Led by Jean Grimm, a specialist in the arts and cultures of Mexico, these unique tours focusing on the authentic arts and cultures of Mexico are accompanied by compelling speakers who are themselves respected scholars and artists. Itineraries include visits to Oaxaca, Chiapas, Guadalajara and Puerto Vallarta, Mexico City, and other locales. Special tours include a Day of the Dead tour, and one on the Art of Mexican Masks.

Oaxaca Reservations/Zapotec Tours, 4955 North Claremont Ave., Suite B, Chicago, IL 60625 (℗ **800/44-OAXACA** outside Illinois, or 773/506-2444; fax 773/506-2445; www.oaxacainfo.com), offers a variety of tours to Oaxaca City and the Oaxaca coast (including Puerto Escondido and Huatulco). Its specialty trips include Day of the Dead in Oaxaca and the Food of the Gods Tour of Oaxaca. The coastal trips emphasize nature, while the Oaxaca City tours focus on the immediate area, with visits to weavers, potters, markets, and archaeological sites. This is also the U.S. contact for several hotels in Oaxaca City that offer a 10% discount for reserving online.

Trek America, P.O. Box 189, Rockaway, NJ 07866 (℗ **800/221-0596** or 973/983-1144; fax 973/983-8551; www.trekamerica.com), organizes lengthy, active trips that combine trekking, hiking, van transportation, and camping in the Yucatán, Chiapas, Oaxaca, the Copper Canyon, and Mexico's Pacific coast, and a trip that covers Mexico City, Teotihuacán, Taxco, Guadalajara, Puerto Vallarta, and Acapulco.

11 Getting Around

An important note: If your travel schedule depends on an important connection, say a plane trip between points or a ferry or bus connection, use the telephone numbers in this book or other information resources mentioned here to find out if the connection you are depending on is still available. Although we've done our best to provide accurate information, transportation schedules can and do change.

BY PLANE

To fly from point to point within Mexico, you'll rely on Mexican airlines. Mexico has two privately owned large national carriers: **Mexicana** (℗ **800/366-5400,** toll-free within Mexico) and **Aeromexico** (℗ **800/021-4000,** toll-free within Mexico). Mexicana and Aeromexico both offer extensive connections to the United States as well as within Mexico.

Several of the new regional carriers are operated by or can be booked through Mexicana or Aeromexico. Regional carriers are **Aerolitoral** (see Aeromexico, above) and **Aero Mar** (see Mexicana, above). For points inside the state of Oaxaca only—Oaxaca City, Puerto Escondido, and Huatulco—contact **Zapotec Tours** (℗ **800/44-OAXACA,** or 407/332-0707 in Illinois, www.oaxacainfo.com). The regional carriers are expensive, but they go to difficult-to-reach places. In each applicable section of this book, we've mentioned regional carriers with all pertinent telephone numbers.

Because major airlines can book some regional carriers, read your ticket carefully to see if your connecting flight is on one of these smaller carriers—they may leave from a different airport or check in at a different counter.

AIRPORT TAXES

Mexico charges an airport tax on all departures. Passengers leaving the country on an international departure pay $18—in dollars or the peso equivalent. It has become a common practice to include this departure tax in your ticket price, but double-check to make sure so you're not caught by surprise at the airport upon leaving. Taxes on each domestic departure you make within Mexico cost around $13, unless you're on a connecting flight and have already paid at the start of the flight, in which case you shouldn't be charged again.

Mexico also charges an additional $18 "tourism tax," the proceeds of which go into a tourism promotional fund. This may or may not be included in your ticket price, so be sure to set aside this amount in either dollars or pesos to pay at the airport upon departure.

RECONFIRMING FLIGHTS

Although Mexican airlines say it's not necessary to reconfirm a flight, it's still a good practice. To avoid getting bumped on popular, possibly overbooked flights, check in for an international flight the required hour and a half in advance of travel.

BY CAR

Most Mexican roads are not up to U.S. standards of smoothness, hardness, width of curve, grade of hill, or safety marking. Driving at night is dangerous—the roads aren't good and are rarely lit; trucks, carts, pedestrians, and bicycles usually have no lights; and you can hit potholes, animals, rocks, dead ends, or bridges out with no warning.

The spirited style of Mexican driving sometimes requires super vision and reflexes. Be prepared for new customs, as when a truck driver flips on his left turn signal when there's not a crossroad for miles. He's probably telling you the road's clear ahead for you to pass. Another custom that's very important to respect is turning left. Never turn left by stopping in the middle of a highway with your left signal on. Instead, pull onto the right shoulder, wait for traffic to clear, then proceed across the road.

GASOLINE

There's one government-owned brand of gas and one gasoline station name throughout the country—**Pemex** (Petroleras Mexicanas). There are two types of gas in Mexico: *magna,* 87-octane unleaded gas, and premium 93 octane. In Mexico, fuel and oil are sold by the liter, which is slightly more than a quart (40 liters equals about 10½ gal.). Many franchise Pemex stations have bathroom facilities and convenience stores—a great improvement over the old ones. *Important note:* No credit cards are accepted for gas purchases.

TOLL ROADS

Mexico charges some of the highest tolls in the world for its network of new toll roads; as a result, they are rarely used. Generally speaking though, using the toll roads will cut your travel time. Older toll-free roads are generally in good condition, but travel times tend to be longer.

BREAKDOWNS

If your car breaks down on the road, help might already be on the way. Radio-equipped green repair trucks operated by uniformed English-speaking officers patrol major highways during daylight hours to aid motorists in trouble. These **"Green Angels"** perform minor repairs and adjustments free, but you pay for parts and materials.

Your best guide to repair shops is the Yellow Pages. For repairs, look under "Automóviles y Camiones: Talleres de Reparación y Servicio"; auto-parts stores are under "Refacciones y Accesorios para Automoviles." To find a mechanic on the road, look for a sign that says TALLER MECANICO.

Places called *Vulcanizadora* or *Llantera* repair flat tires, and it is common to find them open 24 hours a day on the most traveled highways. Even if the place looks empty, chances are you will find someone who can help you fix a flat.

MINOR ACCIDENTS

When possible, many Mexicans drive away from minor accidents, or try to make an immediate settlement, to avoid involving the police. If the police arrive while the involved persons are still at the scene, everyone may be locked in jail until blame is assessed. In any case, you have to settle up immediately, which may take days. Foreigners who don't speak fluent Spanish are at a distinct disadvantage when trying to explain their version of the event. Three steps may help the foreigner who doesn't wish to do as the Mexicans do: If you were in your own car, notify your Mexican insurance company, whose job it is to intervene on your behalf. If you were in a rental car, notify the rental company immediately and ask how to contact the nearest adjuster. (You did buy insurance with the rental, right?) Finally, if all else fails, ask to contact the nearest Green Angel, who may be able to explain to officials that you are covered by insurance. See also "Mexican Auto Insurance" in "Getting There," earlier in this chapter.

CAR RENTALS

You'll get the best price if you reserve a car at least a week in advance in the United States. U.S. car-rental firms include **Advantage** (✆ 800/777-5500 in the U.S. and Canada), **Avis** (✆ 800/331-1212 in the U.S., or 800/TRY-AVIS in Canada), **Budget** (✆ 800/527-0700 in the U.S. and Canada), **Hertz** (✆ 800/654-3131 in the U.S. and Canada), **National** (✆ 800/CAR-RENT in the U.S. and Canada), and **Thrifty** (✆ 800/367-2277 in the U.S. and Canada; www.thrifty.com), which often offers discounts for rentals in Mexico. For European travelers, **Kemwel Holiday Auto** (✆ 800/678-0678) and **Auto Europe** (✆ 800/223-5555) can arrange Mexican rentals, sometimes through other agencies. These and some local firms have offices in Mexico City and most other large Mexican cities. You'll find rental desks at airports, all major hotels, and many travel agencies.

Cars are easy to rent if you have a major credit card, are 25 or over, and have a valid driver's license and passport with you. Without a credit card you must leave a cash deposit, usually a big one. Rent-here/leave-there arrangements are usually simple to make but more costly.

Car-rental costs are high in Mexico, because cars are more expensive here. The condition of rental cars has improved greatly over the years, however, and clean, comfortable, new cars are the norm. The basic cost of a 1-day rental of a Volkswagen Beetle, with unlimited mileage (but before 17% tax and $15 daily insurance), is about $48 in Puerto Escondido and $37 in Acapulco. Renting by the week gives you a lower daily rate. Prices may be considerably higher if you rent in these same cities around a major holiday. Also double-check charges for insurance—some companies will increase the insurance rate after several days. Always ask for detailed information about all charges you will be responsible for.

Deductibles Be careful—these vary greatly in Mexico; some are as high as $2,500, which comes out of your pocket immediately in case of car damage. Hertz's deductible is $1,000 on a VW Beetle; Avis's is $500 for the same car.

Insurance Insurance is offered in two parts: **Collision and damage** insurance covers your car and others if the accident is your fault, and **personal accident** insurance covers you and anyone in your car. Read the fine print on the back of your rental agreement and note that insurance may be invalid if you have an accident while driving on an unpaved road.

Damage   Always inspect your car carefully and note every damaged or missing item, no matter how minute, on your rental agreement, or you may be charged.

BY TAXI

Taxis are the preferred way to get around in almost all of the resort areas of Mexico, and also around Mexico City. Short trips within towns are generally charged by preset zones, and are quite reasonable compared with U.S. rates. For longer trips, or excursions to nearby cities, taxis can generally be hired for around $10 to $15 per hour, or for a negotiated daily rate. Even drops to different destinations, say between Huatulco and Puerto Escondido, can be arranged. A negotiated one-way price is usually much less than the cost of a rental car for a day, and service is much faster than traveling by bus. For anyone who is uncomfortable driving in Mexico, this is a convenient, comfortable alternative. An added bonus is that you have a Spanish-speaking person with you in case you run into any car or road trouble. Many taxi drivers speak at least some English. Your hotel can assist you with the arrangements.

BY BUS

Mexican buses are frequent, readily accessible, and can get you to almost anywhere you want to go. They're often the only way to get from large cities to other nearby cities and small villages. Don't hesitate to ask questions if you're confused about anything.

Dozens of Mexican companies operate large, air-conditioned, Greyhound-type buses between most cities. Travel class is generally labeled *segunda* (second), *primera* (first), and *ejecutiva* (deluxe), which is referred to by a variety of names. The deluxe buses often have fewer seats than regular buses, show video movies en route, are air-conditioned, and have few stops; some have complimentary refreshments. Many run express from origin to the final destination. They are well worth the few dollars more that you'll pay. In rural areas, buses are often of the school-bus variety, with lots of local color.

Whenever possible, it's best to buy your reserved-seat ticket, often via a computerized system, a day in advance on many long-distance routes and especially before holidays. Schedules are fairly dependable, so be at the terminal on time for departure. Current information may be obtained from local bus stations. See the appendix for a list of helpful bus terms in Spanish.

Bus Tip

Little English is spoken at bus stations, so come prepared with your destination written down, then double-check the departure.

FAST FACTS: Mexico

Abbreviations Dept. (apartments); Apdo. (post office box); Av. (*Avenida;* avenue); c/: (*calle;* street); Calz. (*Calzada;* boulevard). "C" on faucets stands for *caliente* (hot), and "F" stands for *fría* (cold). PB *(planta baja)* means ground floor, and most buildings count the next floor up as the first floor (1).

Business Hours In general, businesses in larger cities are open between 9am and 7pm; in smaller towns many close between 2 and 4pm. Most are closed on Sunday. In resort areas it is common to find more stores open on Sundays, as well as extended business hours for shops, often until 8pm or even 10pm. Bank hours are Monday through Friday from 9 or 9:30am to 5 or 6pm. Increasingly, banks are offering Saturday hours for at least a half-day.

Cameras & Film Film costs about the same as in the United States.

Doctors & Dentists Every embassy and consulate is prepared to recommend local doctors and dentists with good training and modern equipment; some of the doctors and dentists even speak English. See the list of embassies and consulates under "Embassies & Consulates," below. Hotels with a large foreign clientele are often prepared to recommend English-speaking doctors. Almost all first-class hotels in Mexico have a doctor on call.

Drug Laws To be blunt, don't use or possess illegal drugs in Mexico. Mexican officials have no tolerance for drug users, and jail is their solution, with very little hope of getting out until the sentence (usually a long one) is completed or heavy fines or bribes are paid. Remember, in Mexico the legal system assumes you are guilty until proven innocent. (*Important note:* It isn't uncommon to be befriended by a fellow user, only to be turned in by that "friend," who's collected a bounty.) Bring prescription drugs in their original containers. If possible, pack a copy of the original prescription with the generic name of the drug.

U.S. Customs officials are also on the lookout for diet drugs sold in Mexico but illegal in the United States, possession of which could also land you in a U.S. jail.

Drugstores *Farmacias* (pharmacies) will sell you just about anything, with or without a prescription. Most pharmacies are open Monday to Saturday from 8am to 8pm. The major resort areas generally have one or two 24-hour pharmacies. Pharmacies take turns staying open during off hours, so if you are in a smaller town and need to buy medicine during off hours, ask for the *farmacia de turno*.

Electricity The electrical system in Mexico is 110 volts AC (60 cycles), as in the United States and Canada. However, in reality it may cycle more slowly and overheat your appliances. To compensate, select a medium or low speed for hair dryers. Many older hotels still have electrical outlets for flat two-prong plugs; you'll need an adapter for any modern electrical apparatus that has an enlarged end on one prong or that has three prongs. Many first-class and deluxe hotels have the three-holed outlets (*trifásicos* in Spanish). Those that don't may have loan adapters, but to be sure, it's always better to carry your own.

Embassies & Consulates They provide valuable lists of doctors and lawyers, as well as regulations concerning marriages in Mexico. Contrary to popular belief, your embassy cannot get you out of a Mexican jail, provide postal or banking services, or fly you home when you run out of money. Consular officers can provide you with advice on most matters and problems, however.

The Embassy of the **United States** in Mexico City is at Paseo de la Reforma 305, next to the Hotel María Isabel Sheraton at the corner of Río Danubio (© 555/080-2000 or 555/511-9980). Visit www.usembassy-mexico.gov for addresses of the U.S. consulates inside Mexico. You'll find consular agencies in Acapulco (© 744/469-0556); Ixtapa/Zihuatanejo (© 755/553-2100); Oaxaca (© 951/514-3054); and other areas.

The Embassy of **Australia** in Mexico City is at Rubén Darío 55, Col. Polanco (© 55/1101-2200; fax 55/1101-2201).

The Embassy of **Canada** in Mexico City is at Schiller 529, Col. Polanco (© 555/724-7900). There are Canadian consulates in Acapulco (© 744/484-1305).

The Embassy of **New Zealand** in Mexico City is at José Luis Lagrange 103, 10th floor, Col. Los Morales Polanco (© 555/283-9460; kiwimexico@compuserve.com.mx).

The Embassy of the **United Kingdom** in Mexico City is at Río Lerma 71, Col. Cuauhtémoc (© 555/242-8500; www.embajada britanica.com.mx).

The Embassy of **Ireland** in Mexico City is at Cerrada Blvd. Avila Camacho 76, 3rd floor, Col. Lomas de Chapultepec (© 555/520-5803).

The **South African** Embassy in Mexico City is at Andres Bello 10, 9th floor, Col. Polanco (© 555/282-9260).

Emergencies In case of emergency, dial © 065 from any phone within Mexico. For police emergency numbers, turn to "Fast Facts" in the chapters that follow. The 24-hour **Tourist Help Line** in Mexico City is © 800/903-9200 or 555/250-0151. The operators don't always speak English, but they are always willing to help. The tourist legal assistance office (Procuraduría del Turista) in Mexico City (© 555/625-8153 or 555/625-8154) always has an English speaker available. Though the phones are frequently busy, they operate 24 hours.

Internet Access In large cities and resort areas, a growing number of five-star hotels offer business centers with Internet access. You'll also find cybercafes in destinations that are popular with expats and business travelers. Note that many ISPs will automatically cut off your Internet connection after a specified period of time (say, 10 min.), because telephone lines are at a premium.

Language Spanish is the official language in Mexico. English is spoken and understood to some degree in most tourist areas. Furthermore, you will find that Mexicans are very accommodating with foreigners who try to speak Spanish, even in broken sentences. For basic vocabulary, refer to the appendix.

Legal Aid **International Legal Defense Counsel,** 111 S. 15th St., 24th Floor, Packard Building, Philadelphia, PA 19102 (© 215/977-9982), is a law firm specializing in legal difficulties of Americans abroad. See also "Embassies & Consulates" and "Emergencies," above.

Liquor Laws The legal drinking age in Mexico is 18; however, it is extremely rare that anyone will be asked for ID or denied purchase (often, children are sent to the stores to buy beer for their parents). Grocery stores sell everything from beer and wine to national and imported liquors. You can buy liquor 24 hours a day; but during major elections, dry laws often are enacted for as much as 72 hours in advance of the election—and those laws apply to foreign tourists as well as local residents. Mexico also does not have any "open container" laws for transporting liquor in cars, but authorities are beginning to target drunk drivers more aggressively. It's a good idea to drive defensively.

It is not legal to drink in the street; however, many tourists do so. Use your better judgment—if you are getting too drunk you shouldn't drink in the street because you are more likely to get stopped by the police. As is the custom in Mexico, it is not so much what you do, it is how you do it.

Mail Postage for a postcard or letter is 1 peso; it may arrive anywhere from 1 to 6 weeks later. A registered letter costs $1.90. Sending a package can be quite expensive—the Mexican postal service charges $8 per kilo (2.20 lb.)—and unreliable; it takes 2 to 6 weeks, if it arrives at all. Packages are frequently lost within the Mexican postal system, although the situation has improved in recent years. The recommended way to send a package or important mail is through FedEx, DHL, UPS, or another reputable international mail service.

Passports **For Residents of the United States:** Whether you're applying in person or by mail, you can download passport applications from the U.S. State Department website at **http://travel.state.gov**. To find your regional passport office, either check the U.S. State Department website or call the **National Passport Information Center** toll-free number (© **877/487-2778**) for automated information.

For Residents of Canada: Passport applications are available at travel agencies throughout Canada or from the central **Passport Office,** Department of Foreign Affairs and International Trade, Ottawa, ON K1A 0G3 (© **800/567-6868**; www.ppt.gc.ca).

For Residents of the United Kingdom: To pick up an application for a standard 10-year passport (5-year passport for children under 16), visit your nearest passport office, major post office, or travel agency or contact the **United Kingdom Passport Service** at © **0870/521-0410** or search its website at www.ukpa.gov.uk.

For Residents of Ireland: You can apply for a 10-year passport at the **Passport Office,** Setanta Centre, Molesworth Street, Dublin 2 (© **01/671-1633**; www.irlgov.ie/iveagh). Those under age 18 and over 65 must apply for a €12 3-year passport. You can also apply at 1A South Mall, Cork (© **021/272-525**) or at most main post offices.

For Residents of Australia: You can pick up an application from your local post office or any branch of Passports Australia, but you must schedule an interview at the passport office to present your application materials. Call the **Australian Passport Information Service** at ℂ **131-232,** or visit the government website at www.passports.gov.au.

For Residents of New Zealand: You can pick up a passport application at any New Zealand Passports Office or download it from their website. Contact the **Passports Office** at ℂ **0800/ 225-050** in New Zealand or 04/474-8100, or log on to www. passports.govt.nz.

Pets Taking a pet into Mexico is easy but requires a little planning. Animals coming from the United States and Canada need to be checked for health within 30 days before arrival in Mexico and require paperwork from your vet. If your stay extends beyond the 30-day time frame of your U.S.-issued certificate, you'll need to get another Certificate of Health issued by a veterinarian in Mexico.

Police In Mexico City, police are to be suspected as frequently as they are to be trusted; however, you'll find many who are quite honest and helpful. In the rest of the country, especially in the tourist areas, the majority are very protective of international visitors. Several cities, including Acapulco, have gone as far as to set up a special corps of English-speaking Tourist Police to assist with directions, guidance, and more.

Smoking Smoking is permitted and generally accepted in most public places, including restaurants, bars, and hotel lobbies. Nonsmoking areas and hotel rooms for nonsmokers are becoming more common in higher-end establishments, but they tend to be the exception rather than the rule.

Taxes There's a 15% IVA (value-added) tax on goods and services in most of Mexico, and it's supposed to be included in the posted price. There is an exit tax of around $18 imposed on every foreigner leaving the country, usually included in the price of airline tickets.

Telephones Mexico's telephone system is slowly but surely catching up with modern times. All telephone numbers have 10 digits. Every city and town that has telephone access has a 2-digit (Mexico City, Monterrey, and Guadalajara) or 3-digit (everywhere else) area code. In Mexico City, Monterrey, and Guadalajara, local numbers have 8 digits; elsewhere, local numbers have 7 digits. To place a local call, you do not need to dial the area code. Many fax numbers are also regular telephone numbers; ask whoever answers for the fax tone *("me da tono de fax, por favor")*. Cellular phones are very popular for small businesses in resort areas and smaller communities. To call a cellular number inside the same area code, dial 044 and then the number. To dial the cellular phone from anywhere else in Mexico, first dial 01, and then the 3-digit area code and the 7-digit number. To dial it from the U.S., dial 011-52, plus the 3-digit area code and the 7-digit number.

The **country code** for Mexico is **52**.

To call Mexico: If you're calling Mexico from the United States:

1. Dial the international access code: 011
2. Dial the country code: 52
3. Dial the 2- or 3-digit area code, then the 8- or 7-digit number. For example, if you wanted to call the U.S. consulate in Acapulco, the whole number would be 011-52-744-469-0556. If you wanted to dial the U.S. embassy in Mexico City, the whole number would be 011-52-55-5209-9100.

To make international calls: To make international calls from Mexico, first dial 00, then the country code (U.S. or Canada 1, U.K. 44, Ireland 353, Australia 61, New Zealand 64). Next, dial the area code and number. For example, to call the British Embassy in Washington, you would dial 00-1-202-588-7800.

For directory assistance: Dial ℗ **040** if you're looking for a number inside Mexico. *Note:* Listings usually appear under the owner's name, not the name of the business, and your chances to find an English-speaking operator are slim to none.

For operator assistance: If you need operator assistance in making a call, dial 090 to make an international call, and 020 to call a number in Mexico.

Toll-free numbers: Numbers beginning with 800 within Mexico are toll-free, but calling a U.S. toll-free number from Mexico costs the same as an overseas call. To call an 800 number in the U.S., dial 001-880 and the last 7 digits of the toll-free number. To call an 888 number in the U.S., dial 001-881 and the last 7 digits of the toll-free number.

Time Zone Central standard time prevails throughout most of Mexico, and all of the areas covered in this book. Mexico observes **daylight saving time**.

Tipping Most service employees in Mexico count on tips for the majority of their income—this is especially true for bellboys and waiters. Bellboys should receive the equivalent of 50¢ to US$1 per bag; waiters generally receive 10% to 20%, depending on the level of service. It is not customary to tip taxi drivers, unless they are hired by the hour or provide touring or other special services.

Toilets Public toilets are not common in Mexico, but an increasing number are available, especially at fast-food restaurants and Pemex gas stations. These facilities and restaurant and club restrooms commonly have attendants, who expect a small tip (about 50¢).

Useful Phone Numbers **Tourist Help Line,** available 24 hours (© 800/903-9200 toll-free inside Mexico). **Mexico Hotline** (© 800/44-MEXICO). **U.S. Dept. of State Travel Advisory,** staffed 24 hours (© 202/647-5225). **U.S. Passport Agency** (© 202/647-0518). **U.S. Centers for Disease Control International Traveler's Hotline** (© 404/332-4559).

Water Most hotels have decanters or bottles of purified water in the rooms, and the better hotels have either purified water from regular taps or special taps marked *agua purificada*. Some hotels will charge for in-room bottled water. Virtually any hotel, restaurant, or bar will bring you purified water if you specifically request it, but you'll usually be charged for it. Bottled purified water is sold widely at drugstores and grocery stores. Some popular brands are Santa María, Ciel, and Bonafont. Evian and other imported brands are also widely available.

2

Acapulco

I like to think of Acapulco as a diva—maybe a little past her prime, perhaps overly made up, but still capable of captivating an audience. It's tempting to dismiss Acapulco as a passé resort, but the town's temptations are hard to resist. Where else do bronzed men dive from cliffs into the sea at sunset, and where else does the sun shine 360 days a year? Though most beach resorts are made for relaxing, Acapulco has nonstop, 24-hours-a-day energy. Its perfectly sculpted bay is an adult playground filled with water-skiers in *tanga* swimsuits and darkly tanned, mirror-shaded studs on jet skis. Visitors play golf and tennis with intensity, but the real sport is the nightlife, which has made this city famous for decades. Back in the days when there was a jet set, they came to Acapulco—filmed it, sang about it, wrote about it, and lived it.

It's not hard to understand why: The view of Acapulco Bay, framed by mountains and beaches, is breathtaking day or night. And I dare anyone to take in the lights of the city and not feel the pull to go out and get lively.

Though a few years ago tourism to Acapulco was in a state of decline, it's now attempting a renaissance, in a style reminiscent of Miami's South Beach. Classic hotels are slowly being renovated and areas gentrified. Clean-up efforts have put a whole new face on a place that was once aging less than gracefully.

International travelers began to reject Acapulco when it became clear that the cost of development was the pollution of the bay and surrounding areas. The city government responded, and invested over $1 billion in public and private infrastructure improvements. In addition, a program instituted in the early 1990s has cleaned up the water—whales have even been sighted offshore.

Acapulco tries hard to hold on to its image as the ultimate extravagant party town. It's still the top choice for those who want to have dinner at midnight, dance until dawn, and sleep all day on a sun-soaked beach.

1 Essentials

366km (229 miles) S of Mexico City; 272km (170 miles) SW of Taxco; 979km (612 miles) SE of Guadalajara; 253km (158 miles) SE of Ixtapa/Zihuatanejo; 752km (470 miles) NW of Huatulco

GETTING THERE & DEPARTING

BY PLANE   See chapter 1 for information on flying from the United States or Canada to Acapulco. Local numbers for major airlines with nonstop or direct service to Acapulco are **Aeromexico** (© **744/ 485-1625**), **American** (© **744/466-9232,** or 01-800/904-6000 inside Mexico for reservations), **Continental** (© **744/466-9063**), **Mexicana** (© **744/466-9121** or 744/486-7586), and **America West** (© **744/466-9257**).

Aeromexico flies from Guadalajara, Mexico City, and Tijuana; **Mexicana** flies from Mexico City. Check with a travel agent about **charter** flights.

The airport (airport code: ACA) is 22km (14 miles) southeast of town, over the hills east of the bay. Private **taxis** are the fastest way to get downtown; they cost $30 to $50. The major **rental-car** agencies all have booths at the airport. **Transportes Terrestres** has desks at the front of the airport where you can buy tickets for minivan *colectivo* transportation into town ($10). You must reserve return service to the airport through your hotel.

BY CAR   From Mexico City, take either the curvy toll-free Highway 95D south (6 hr.) or scenic Highway 95, the four- to six-lane toll highway (3½ hr.), which costs around $50 one-way. The free road from Taxco is in good condition; you'll save around $40 in tolls from there through Chilpancingo to Acapulco. From points north or south along the coast, the only choice is Highway 200, where you should (as on all Mexican highways) always try to travel by day.

BY BUS   The **Ejido/Central Camionera station,** Ejido 47, is on the far northern end of the bay and north of downtown (Old Acapulco). It's far from the hotels; however, it serves more bus lines and routes than any other Acapulco bus station. It also has a hotel-reservation service.

From this station, **Turistar, Estrella de Oro,** and **Estrella Blanca** have almost hourly service for the 5- to 7-hour trip to Mexico City ($42), and daily service to Zihuatanejo ($14). Buses also serve other points in Mexico, including Chilpancingo, Cuernavaca, Iguala, Manzanillo, Puerto Vallarta, and Taxco.

VISITOR INFORMATION

The **State of Guerrero Tourism Office** operates the **Procuraduría del Turista** (©/fax **744/484-4583** or 744/484-4416), on street level in front of the **International Center,** a convention center set back from the main Costera Alemán, down a lengthy walkway with fountains. The office offers maps and information about the city and state, as well as police assistance for tourists; it's open Monday to Saturday from 8am to 11pm, Sunday from 8am to 8pm.

CITY LAYOUT

Acapulco stretches more than 6km (4 miles) around the huge bay, so trying to take it all in by foot is impractical. The tourist areas are roughly divided into three sections: On the western end of the bay is **Old Acapulco (Acapulco Viejo),** the original town that attracted the jet-setters of the 1950s and 1960s—and today it looks as if it's still locked in that era, though a renaissance is slowly getting under way. The second section, in the center of the bay, is the **Hotel Zone (Zona Hotelera);** it follows the main boulevard, **Costera Miguel Alemán** (or just "the Costera"), as it runs east along the bay from downtown. Towering hotels, restaurants, shopping centers, and strips of open-air beach bars line the street. At the far eastern end of the Costera lie the golf course and the International Center (a convention center).

Avenida Cuauhtémoc is the major artery inland, running roughly parallel to the Costera. The third major area begins just beyond the Hyatt Regency Hotel, where the name of the Costera changes to **Carretera Escénica (Scenic Hwy.),** which continues all the way to the airport. The hotels along this section of the road are lavish, and extravagant private villas, gourmet restaurants, and flashy nightclubs built into the hillside offer dazzling views. The area fronting the beach here is **Acapulco Diamante,** Acapulco's most desirable address.

Street names and numbers in Acapulco can be confusing and hard to find—many streets are not well marked or change names unexpectedly. Street numbers on the Costera do not follow logic, so don't assume that similar numbers will be close together.

GETTING AROUND

BY TAXI Taxis are more plentiful than tacos in Acapulco—and practically as inexpensive, if you're traveling in the downtown area only. Just remember that you should always establish the price with the driver before starting out. Hotel taxis may charge three times the rate of a taxi hailed on the street, and nighttime taxi rides cost extra, too. Taxis are also more expensive if you're staying in the Diamante section or south. The minimum fare is $2 per ride for a roving VW Bug–style taxi in town; the fare from Puerto Marqués to the hotel zone is $8, or $10 into downtown. *Sitio* taxis are nicer cars, but more expensive, with a minimum fare of $4.

The fashion among Acapulco taxis is flashy, with Las Vegas–style lights—the more colorful and pulsating, the better.

BY BUS   Even though the city has a confusing street layout, using city buses is amazingly easy and inexpensive. Two kinds of buses run along the Costera: pastel color-coded buses and regular "school buses." The difference is the price: New air-conditioned tourist buses (Aca Tur Bus) are 50¢; old buses, 35¢. Covered bus stops are all along the Costera, with handy maps on the walls showing routes to major sights and hotels.

The best place near the *zócalo* to catch a bus is next to Sanborn's, 2 blocks east. CALETA DIRECTO or BASE-CALETA buses will take you to the Hornos, Caleta, and Caletilla beaches along the Costera. Some buses return along the same route; others go around the peninsula and return to the Costera.

For expeditions to more distant destinations, there are buses to **Puerto Marqués** to the east (marked PUERTO MARQUES–BASE) and **Pie de la Cuesta** to the west (marked ZOCALO–PIE DE LA CUESTA). Be sure to verify the time and place of the last bus back if you hop on one of these.

BY CAR   Rental cars are available at the airport and at hotel desks along the Costera. Unless you plan on exploring outlying areas, trust me, you're better off taking taxis or using the easy and inexpensive public buses.

Tips Car & Bus Travel Warning Eases

Car robberies and bus hijackings on Highway 200 south of Acapulco on the way to Puerto Escondido and Huatulco used to be common, and you may have heard warnings about the road. The trouble has all but disappeared, thanks to military patrols and greater police protection. However, as in most of Mexico, it's advisable to travel the highways during daylight hours only—not so much for personal safety, but because highways are unlit, and animals can wander on them.

Acapulco Bay Area

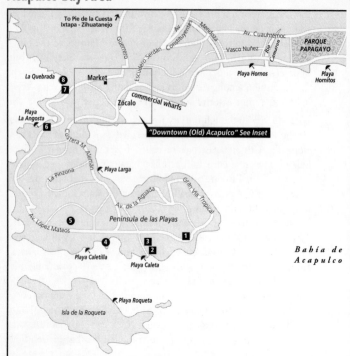

To Pie de la Cuesta
Ixtapa - Zihuatanejo

La Quebrada **8**
7

Market

Playa La Angosta

6

commercial wharfs

Zócalo

"Downtown (Old) Acapulco" See Inset

Av. Cuauhtémoc

PARQUE
PAPAGAYO

Vasco Nuñez

Playa Hornos

Playa Hornitos

Costera M. Alemán

La Pinzona

Playa Larga

Gran Vía Tropical

Av. de la Aguada

Av. López Mateos

5

Peninsula de las Playas

4

3
2

1

Playa Caletilla

Playa Caleta

Bahía de Acapulco

Playa Roqueta

Isla de la Roqueta

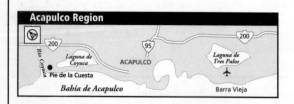

Acapulco Region

200

200

Río Coyuca

Laguna de Coyuca

ACAPULCO

95

Laguna de Tres Palos

Pie de la Cuesta

Bahía de Acapulco

Barra Vieja

ACCOMMODATIONS ■

Calinda Acapulco **12**
Camino Real Acapulco Diamante **31**
Fiesta Americana Condesa Hotel **11**
Hotel Coleta **2**
Hotel Costa Linda **3**
Hotel Elcano **15**
Hotel El Mirador **7**

Hotel Las Brisas **30**
Hotel Los Flamingos **1**
Hotel Misión **22**
Hotel Sands **10**
Hotel Villa Romana **6**
Hyatt Regency Acapulco **18**
Villa Vera Hotel & Racquet Club **14**

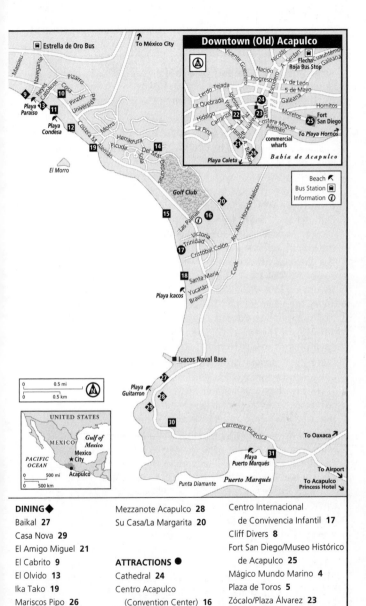

Downtown (Old) Acapulco

To México City

Estrella de Oro Bus

Vicente Guerrero
Nicolás
Flecha Roja Bus Stop
A. Serdán
Cuauhtémoc
Galeana
Nación
Progresoro
V. de León
5 de Mayo
Galeana
Lerdo Tejada
La Quebrada
Hidalgo
Carranza
La Paz
La Paz
La Piña
Morelos
Hornitos
Fort San Diego
To Playa Hornos

Massieu
Navegante
Reyes Católicos
Cosa
Pizarro
Pinzón
Universidad
Playa Paraíso
Playa Condesa
Costera M. Alemán
Morro
Herradura
Del Mar
Picuda
Scua
Golf Club
Las Palmas
El Morro
Victoria
Trinidad
Cristóbal Colón
Cook
Santa María
Yucatán
Bravo
Playa Icacos
Icacos Naval Base

commercial wharfs

Bahía de Acapulco

Beach
Bus Station
Information

Playa Caleta

Playa Guitarron
Playa Puerto Marqués

UNITED STATES
MEXICO
Gulf of Mexico
PACIFIC OCEAN
Mexico City
Acapulco

0   500 mi
0   500 km

Carretera Escénica
To Oaxaca
Punta Diamante
Puerto Marqués
To Airport
To Acapulco Princess Hotel

0   0.5 mi
0   0.5 km

DINING◆

Baikal **27**
Casa Nova **29**
El Amigo Miguel **21**
El Cabrito **9**
El Olvido **13**
Ika Tako **19**
Mariscos Pipo **26**

Mezzanote Acapulco **28**
Su Casa/La Margarita **20**

ATTRACTIONS ●

Cathedral **24**
Centro Acapulco
  (Convention Center) **16**

Centro Internacional
  de Convivencia Infantil **17**
Cliff Divers **8**
Fort San Diego/Museo Histórico
  de Acapulco **25**
Mágico Mundo Marino **4**
Plaza de Toros **5**
Zócalo/Plaza Álvarez **23**

FAST FACTS: Acapulco

American Express The main office is in the Gran Plaza shopping center, Costera Alemán 1628 (© **744/435-2200**). It's open Monday through Friday from 9am to 6pm and Saturday 9am to 1pm.

Area Code The telephone area code is **744**.

Climate Acapulco boasts sunshine 360 days a year, with average daytime temperatures of 80°F (27°C). Humidity varies, with approximately 59 inches of rain per year. June through October is the rainy season, though July and August are relatively dry. Tropical showers are brief and usually occur at night.

Consular Agents The **United States** has an agent at the Hotel Club del Sol, Costera Alemán at Reyes Católicos (© **744/481-1699** or 744/469-0556), across from the Hotel Acapulco Plaza; the office is open Monday through Friday from 10am to 2pm. The **Canadian** office is at the Centro Comercial Marbella, Local 23 (© **744/484-1305**). The toll-free emergency number inside Mexico is © **800/706-2900**. The office is open Monday through Friday from 9am to 5pm. The **United Kingdom** office is at the Las Brisas Hotel on Carretera Escénica near the airport (© **744/481-2533** or 744/484-1735). Most other countries in the European Union also have consulate offices in Acapulco.

Currency Exchange Numerous banks along the Costera are open Monday through Friday from 9am to 6pm, Saturday from 10am to 1:30pm. Banks and their ATMs generally have the best rates. *Casas de cambio* (currency-exchange booths) along the street may have better rates than hotels.

Hospital Try **Hospital Magallanes,** Av. Wilfrido Massieu 2, Fracc. Magallanes (© **744/485-6194** or 744/485-6197), which has an English-speaking staff and doctors, or **Hospital Pacífico,** Calle Fraile y Nao 4, Fracc. La Bocana (© **744/487-7180** or 744/487-7161). For local emergencies, call the **Red Cross,** Av. Ruiz Cortines s/n (© **065** or 744/445-5912).

Internet Access **@canet,** Costera Alemán 1632 Int., La Gran Plaza, Local D-1, lower floor (©/fax **744/486-9186** or 744/486-8182), is open daily from 10:30am to 9pm. Internet access costs $1.50 per hour. This is a computer shop that also offers Internet access and has a very helpful staff. Also along the Costera strip is the **Santa Clara Cafe,** Costera Alemán 136, serving coffee, pastries, and ice cream, along with Internet service for 90¢ for 20 minutes. It's open 9am to 11pm.

Parking It is illegal to park on the Costera at any time. Try parking along side streets, or in one of the few covered parking lots, such as in Plaza Bahía and in Plaza Mirabella.

Pharmacy One of the largest drugstores in town is **Farmacia Daisy,** Francia 49, across the traffic circle from the convention center (✆ **744/484-7664**). Sam's Club and Wal-Mart, both on the Costera, have pharmacy services and lower prices on medicine.

Post Office The *correo* is next door to Sears, close to the Fideicomiso office. It's open Monday through Friday from 9am to 5pm, Saturday from 9am to 1pm. Other branches are in the Estrella de Oro bus station on Cuauhtémoc, inland from the Acapulco Qualton Hotel, and on the Costera near Caleta Beach.

Safety Riptides claim a few lives every year, so pay close attention to warning flags posted on Acapulco beaches. Red or black flags mean stay out of the water, yellow flags signify caution, and white or green flags mean it's safe to swim.

As is the case anywhere, tourists are vulnerable to thieves. This is especially true when shopping in a market, lying on the beach, wearing jewelry, or visibly carrying a camera, purse, or bulging wallet.

Telephone Acapulco phone numbers seem to change frequently. The most reliable source for telephone numbers is the **Procuraduría del Turista,** on the Costera in front of the convention center (✆ **744/484-4583**), which has an exceptionally friendly staff.

Tourist Police Policemen in white-and-light-blue uniforms belong to the Tourist Police (✆ **065** for emergencies, or 744/485-0490), a special corps of English-speaking police established to assist tourists.

2 Where to Stay

The listings below begin with the very expensive resorts south of town (nearest the airport) and continue along Costera Alemán to the less expensive, more traditional hotels north of town, in the downtown or "Old Acapulco" part of the city. Especially in the "very expensive" and "expensive" categories, inquire about promotional rates or check with the airlines for air-hotel packages. During Christmas and Easter weeks, some hotels double their normal rates.

Private **villas** are available for rent all over the hills south of town; staying in one of these palatial homes is an unforgettable experience. **Se Renta** (www.acapulcoluxuryvillas.com) handles some of the most exclusive villas.

SOUTH OF TOWN

Acapulco's most exclusive and renowned hotels, restaurants, and villas nestle in the steep forested hillsides here, between the naval base and Puerto Marqués. This area is several kilometers from the heart of Acapulco; you'll pay the $12-to-$20 round-trip taxi fare every time you venture off the property into town.

VERY EXPENSIVE

Camino Real Acapulco Diamante ★★★ *Kids*   Tucked in a secluded location on 32 hectares (81 acres), this relaxing, self-contained resort is an ideal choice for families, or for those who already know Acapulco and don't care to explore much. I consider it one of Acapulco's finest places in terms of contemporary decor, services, and amenities. I like its location on the Playa Puerto Marqués, which is safe for swimming, but you do miss out on compelling views of Acapulco Bay. From Carretera Escénica, a handsome brick road winds down to the hotel, overlooking Puerto Marqués Bay. The lobby has an enormous terrace facing the water. The spacious rooms have balconies or terraces, small sitting areas, marble floors, ceiling fans (in addition to air-conditioning with remote control), and comfortable, classic furnishings.

Carretera Escénica Km 14, Baja Catita s/n, Pichilingue, 39867 Acapulco, Gro. ℰ **744/ 435-1010.** Fax 744/435-1020. www.caminoreal.com/acapulco. 157 units. High season $429 double; $611 master suite. Rates include American breakfast. Ask about low-season and midweek discounts. AE, MC, V. **Amenities:** 2 restaurants; lobby bar; 3 pools (1 for children); tennis court; health club w/aerobics, spa treatments, massage, and complete workout equipment (extra charge); watersports equipment rentals; children's activities; concierge; tour desk; car-rental desk; shopping arcade; salon; 24-hr. room service; babysitting; laundry service. *In room:* A/C, TV, dataport, minibar, hair dryer, iron, safe-deposit box.

Las Brisas ★★★ *Moments*   This is a local landmark, often considered Acapulco's signature hotel, and my personal favorite. Perched on a hillside overlooking the bay, Las Brisas is known for its tiered pink stucco facade, private pools, and 175 pink jeeps rented exclusively to guests. If you stay here, you ought to like pink, because the color scheme extends to practically everything. Las Brisas is also known for inspiring romance and is best enjoyed by couples indulging in time together—alone.

The hotel is a community unto itself: The simple, marble-floored rooms are like separate villas sculpted from a terraced hillside, with panoramic views of Acapulco Bay from a balcony or terrace. Each room has a private or semiprivate swimming pool. Las Brisas has a total of 250 pools. The spacious Regency Club rooms, at the apex of the property, offer the best views. You stay at Las Brisas more for the panache and setting than for luxury amenities, though rooms have been upgraded. Early each morning, continental breakfast arrives in a cubbyhole. If you tire of your own pool, Las Brisas has a beach club about a half-mile away, on Acapulco Bay; continuous shuttle service departs from the lobby. The club offers casual dining, a large swimming pool, and a natural saltwater pool—actually a rocky inlet. Mandatory service charges cover shuttle service from the hillside rooms to the lobby and from the lobby to the beach club, and all tips. The hotel is on the southern edge of the bay, overlooking the road to the airport and close to the hottest area nightclubs.

Apdo. Carretera Escénica 5255, Las Brisas, 39868 Acapulco, Gro. © **800/228-3000** in the U.S., or 744/469-6900. Fax 744/446-5332. 263 units. High season $330 shared pool, $435 private pool, $540 Royal Beach Club; low season $230 shared pool, $345 private pool, $432 Royal Beach Club. $20 per day service charge plus 17% tax. Rates include continental breakfast. AE, DC, MC, V. **Amenities:** 2 restaurants; deli; breakfast delivery; private beach club w/fresh- and saltwater pools; 5 tennis courts; access to nearby gym; concierge; guest-only tours and activity program; tour desk; car-rental desk; jeeps for rent; 24-hr. shuttle transportation around the resort; shopping arcade; salon; room service; in-room massage; babysitting; laundry service; dry cleaning. In room: A/C, TV, minibar, hair dryer, safe-deposit box.

COSTERA HOTEL ZONE

The following hotels are along the main boulevard, Costera Alemán, extending from the convention center (Centro Internacional) at the east to Papagayo Park, just outside Old Acapulco.

EXPENSIVE

Fiesta Americana Condesa Acapulco ⊛ Once the Condesa del Mar, the Fiesta Americana Condesa Acapulco is a long-standing favorite deluxe hotel located in the heart of the beach-bar action. The 18-story structure towers above Condesa Beach, just east and up the hill from the Glorieta Diana traffic circle. The unremarkable, but comfortable rooms have marble floors, and can be loud if you're overlooking the pool area. Each has a private terrace or balcony with ocean view. The more expensive rooms have the best bay views, and all have purified tap water. The hilltop swimming pool affords one of the city's finest views. The location is great for enjoying the numerous beach activities, shopping, and more casual nightlife of Acapulco.

Costera Alemán 97, 39690 Acapulco, Gro. ⓒ **800/FIESTA-1** in the U.S., or 744/484-2355. Fax 744/484-1828. www.fiestamericana.com. 500 units. High season $220 double, $315 suite; low season $90–$124 double, $253 suite. Ask about "Fiesta Break" packages, which include meals. AE, DC, MC, V. **Amenities:** 2 restaurants; coffee shop; lobby bar; theme nights w/buffet dinner; adults-only hilltop swimming pool; smaller children's pool; travel agency; shopping arcade; salon; room service; laundry service; pharmacy. *In room:* A/C, TV, minibar, safe-deposit box.

Hotel Elcano 𝒞𝒞𝒞 *(Finds)* An Acapulco classic, the Elcano is another personal favorite. It offers exceptional service and a prime location—on a broad stretch of beach in the heart of the hotel zone. The retro-style, turquoise-and-white lobby, and beachside pool area are the closest you can get to a South Beach Miami atmosphere in Acapulco, and its popular open-air restaurant adds to the lively waterfront scene. On the whole, the Elcano reminds me of a set from a classic Elvis-in-Acapulco movie. Rooms are continually upgraded, bright, and very comfortable. They feature classic navy-and-white tile accents, ample oceanfront balconies, and tub/shower combinations. The very large junior suites, all on corners, have two queen-size beds and huge closets. Studios are small but adequate, with king-size beds and small sinks outside the bathroom area. In the studios, a small portion of the TV armoire serves as a closet, and there are no balconies, only large sliding windows. All rooms have purified tap water. This is an ideal place if you're attending a convention or simply want the best of all possible locations, between hillside nightlife and the Costera beach zone. It's an excellent value.

Costera Alemán 75, 39690 Acapulco, Gro. ⓒ **800/972-2162** in the U.S., or 744/435-1500. Fax 744/484-2230. http://hotel-elcano.com. 182 units. $176 studio; $208 standard double; $240 junior suite; $299 master suite. Ask about promotional discounts. AE, DC, MC, V. **Amenities:** 3 restaurants; beachside pool; small workout room; video-game room; travel agency; shopping arcade; salon; 24-hr. room service; massage; babysitting; laundry service. *In room:* A/C, TV, minibar, hair dryer, safe-deposit box.

Hyatt Regency Acapulco 𝒞𝒞 A sophisticated oasis, the Hyatt is one of the largest and most modern of Acapulco's hotels—which still isn't as modern as other resorts. A free-form pool fronts a broad stretch of beautiful beach, one of the most inviting in Acapulco. The sleek lobby encloses a sitting area and bar where there's live music every evening. The stylishly decorated rooms are large, with sizable balconies overlooking the pool and ocean. Some contain kitchenettes. Regency Club guests receive continental breakfast, afternoon canapés, and other upgraded amenities. Children are not allowed in Regency Club rooms. This hotel caters to a large Jewish clientele and has a full-service kosher restaurant, synagogue, and Sabbath elevator.

Costera Alemán 1, 39869 Acapulco, Gro. ℂ **800/233-1234** in the U.S. and Canada, 01-800/005-0000 in Mexico, or 744/469-1234. Fax 744/484-3087. www.hyatt acapulco.com.mx. 646 units. High season $234 double, $260 Regency Club, $338 suite; low season $208 double, $234 Regency Club, $312 suite. AE, DC, MC, V. **Amenities:** 3 restaurants; cantina; lobby bar; 2 large, shaded free-form pools; 3 lighted tennis courts; access to a nearby gym; children's programs; concierge; tour desk; car-rental desk; business center; shopping arcade; salon; room service; in-room massage; babysitting; laundry service; dry cleaning; safe-deposit box in lobby. *In room:* A/C, TV, minibar, hair dryer, iron, safe-deposit box, bathrobes.

Villa Vera Hotel & Racquet Club 🏆🏆🏆 *Finds*   The legendary Villa Vera started off as a private home with adjacent villas for houseguests. It continues to offer the closest experience to Acapulco villa life that you'll find in a public property. After a while, it became a popular hangout for stars such as Liz Taylor, who married Mike Todd here. This hotel is also where Richard and Pat Nixon celebrated their 25th wedding anniversary and where Elvis's film *Fun in Acapulco* was shot. Lana Turner even made it her home for 3 years.

Villa Vera has undergone significant renovations and upgrades in facilities in recent years that have transformed it into an exclusive boutique-style hotel. The spa offers world-class services 7 days a week. Rooms are tastefully decorated in sophisticated light tones. The complex has 14 pools, including 8 private pools for the six villas and two houses. Most other rooms share pools; guests in standard rooms have the use of the large public pool across from the restaurant. The hotel is several blocks from the Condesa beach, up a hill.

Lomas del Mar 35, Fracc. Club Deportivo, 39693 Acapulco, Gro. ℂ **800/710-9300** in Mexico, 744/484-0334, or -0335. Fax 744/484-7479. www.clubregina.com, hotel_ villavera_aca@clubregina.com. 69 units, 2 houses. High season $246 studio, $246 double, $340–$405 suite, $481 villa, $1,222 Casa Teddy (4 people), $1,261 Casa Julio (6 people). Ask about low-season rates. AE, MC, V. **Amenities:** Restaurant; pool bar; pool; 2 clay tennis courts; gym; complete European spa; travel agency; car rental; 2 lighted racquetball courts. *In room:* A/C, TV, minibar, safe-deposit box.

MODERATE

Calinda Acapulco   You'll see this tall cylindrical tower rising at the eastern edge of Condesa Beach. Each room has a view, usually of the bay. Though not exceptionally well furnished, guest rooms are large and comfortable; most have two double beds. It's the most modern of the reasonably priced lodgings along the strip of hotels facing popular Condesa Beach. Package prices are available, and the hotel frequently offers promotions, such as rates that include breakfast; otherwise it is expensive for what it provides.

Costera Alemán 1260, 39300 Acapulco, Gro. ℂ **800/228-5151** in the U.S., or 744/ 484-0410. Fax 744/484-4676. www.hotelescalinda.com.mx. 357 units. $169 double.

Ask about promotional specials. AE, DC, MC, V. Limited free parking. **Amenities:** 3 restaurants; poolside snacks; lobby bar w/live music; swimming pool; concierge; travel agency; shopping arcade; salon; room service; babysitting; laundry service; pharmacy. *In room:* A/C, TV, safe-deposit boxes.

Hotel Sands ⟨*Kids*⟩ ⟨*Value*⟩   A great option for budget-minded families, this unpretentious, comfortable hotel nestles on the inland side, opposite the giant resort hotels and away from the din of Costera traffic. A stand of umbrella palms and a pretty garden restaurant—with terrific, authentic Mexican food at reasonable prices—lead into the lobby. The rooms are light and airy in the style of a good modern motel, with basic furnishings and wall-to-wall carpeting. Some units have kitchenettes, and all have a terrace or balcony. The rates are reasonable, the accommodations satisfactory, and the location excellent.

Costera Alemán 178, 39670 Acapulco, Gro. ℭ **744/484-2260.** Fax 744/484-1053. www.sands.com.mx. 93 units. $62 standard double; $50 bungalow. Rates include coffee in the lobby and are higher during Christmas, Easter, and other major holidays. AE, MC, V. Limited free parking. **Amenities:** Restaurant; 2 swimming pools (1 for children); children's playground; concierge; babysitting; laundry service; dry cleaning; squash court; volleyball; Ping-Pong area. *In room:* A/C, TV, minibar.

DOWNTOWN (ON LA QUEBRADA) & OLD ACAPULCO BEACHES

Numerous budget hotels dot the streets fanning out from the *zócalo.* They're among the best values in town, but be sure to check your room first to see that it meets your needs. Several hotels in this area are close to Caleta and Caletilla beaches, or on the back of the hilly peninsula, at Playa la Angosta. Many have gorgeous views of the city and bay.

MODERATE

El Mirador Acapulco ⟨*⟩   One of the landmarks of Old Acapulco, the El Mirador Hotel overlooks the famous cove where the cliff divers perform. Renovated with tropical landscaping and lots of Mexican tile, this hotel offers attractively furnished rooms. Each holds double or queen-size beds, a small kitchenette area with minifridge and coffeemaker, and a large bathroom with marble counters. Most have a separate living room, some have a whirlpool tub, and all are accented with colorful Saltillo tile and other Mexican decorative touches. Ask for a room with a balcony or ocean view.

A set-price dinner ($29) offers great views of the cliff-diving show. The large, breezy lobby bar is a favorite spot to relax as day fades into night on the beautiful cove and bay. Nearby is a protected cove with good snorkeling.

Quebrada 74, 39300 Acapulco, Gro. © **744/483-1221** or 744/484-0909 for reservations. Fax 744/482-4564. www.hotelmiradoracapulco.com.mx. 132 units. High season $185 double, $231 suite with whirlpool; low season $108 double, $135 suite with whirlpool. Add $13 for kitchenette. AE, MC, V. Street parking. **Amenities:** Restaurant; coffee shop; lobby bar; 3 pools, including 1 rather rundown saltwater pool; travel agency; room service; laundry service. *In room:* A/C, TV.

Hotel Caleta ℛ   The all-inclusive Hotel Caleta (formerly the Grand Meigas) is more familiar to Mexican travelers than to their U.S. counterparts. This high-quality, nine-floor resort, adjacent to one of the liveliest beaches in Old Acapulco, offers excellent value. Stay here if you seek the authentic feel of a Mexican holiday, with all its boisterous, family-friendly charms. The hotel is built into a cliff on the Caleta peninsula, overlooking the beach. Rooms surround a plant-filled courtyard, topped by a glass ceiling. All have large terraces with ocean views, although some connect to the neighboring terrace. The simply decorated rooms are very clean and comfortable, with a large closet and desk. Each room has two queen-size beds with firm mattresses, and cable TV.

A succession of terraces holds tropical gardens, restaurants, and pools. A private beach and boat dock are down a brief flight of stairs. The resort has a changing agenda of theme nights and evening entertainment.

Cerro San Martín 325, Fracc. Las Playas, 39390 Acapulco, Gro. © **744/483-9940** or 744/483-9140. Fax 744/483-9125. meigaca@prodigy.net.mx. 255 units. High season $188 double; low season $90 double. Rates are all-inclusive. Room-only prices sometimes available. AE, DC, MC, V. Free private parking. **Amenities:** 3 restaurants; snack bar; bars; large fresh- and saltwater pools; tour desk; car-rental desk; shopping arcade. *In room:* A/C, TV, fan.

INEXPENSIVE

Hotel Costa Linda   Budget-minded American and Mexican couples are drawn to the sunny, well-kept rooms of the Costa Linda, one of the best values in the area. All rooms have individually controlled air-conditioning and a minifridge, and some have a small kitchenette (during low season there is a $5 charge for using the kitchenette). Closets and bathrooms are ample in size, and mattresses are firm. Cozy as the Costa Linda is, it is adjacent to one of the busier streets in Old Acapulco, so traffic noise can be bothersome. It's just a 1-block walk down to lively Caleta beach.

Costera Alemán 1008, 39390 Acapulco, Gro. © **744/482-5277** or 744/482-2549. Fax 744/483-4017. 44 units. High season $89 double; low season $35 double. 2 children under 8 stay free in parent's room. MC, V. Free parking. **Amenities:** Restaurant; bar; small pool; tennis court; tour desk. *In room:* A/C, TV, minibar.

Hotel Los Flamingos ★★★ *Finds* An Acapulco landmark, this hotel, perched on a cliff 152m (500 ft.) above Acapulco Bay, once entertained John Wayne, Cary Grant, Johnny Weissmuller, Fred McMurray, Errol Flynn, Red Skelton, Roy Rogers, and others. In fact, the stars liked it so much that at one point they bought it and converted it into a private club. The place is a real find—it's in excellent shape and exceptionally clean, offering visitors a totally different perspective of Acapulco as it maintains all the charm of a grand era. All rooms have dramatic ocean views and a large balcony or terrace, but most of them are not air-conditioned (those that are also have TVs). Still, the constant sea breeze is cooling enough. Rooms are colorful, with mosaic-tile tables and mirrors. Thursdays at Los Flamingos are especially popular, with a *pozole* party and live music by a Mexican band that was probably around in the era of Wayne and Weissmuller—note the seashell-pink bass. Even if you don't stay here, plan to at least come for a margarita at sunset and a walk along the dramatic lookout point.

López Mateos s/n, Fracc. Las Playas, 39300 Acapulco, Gro. © 744/482-0690. Fax 744/483-9806. 40 rooms. High season $85 double, $91 double with A/C, $130 junior suite; low season $65 double, $78 double with A/C, $91 junior suite. AE, MC, V. **Amenities:** Restaurant; bar; pool; tour desk; car rental; room service; laundry service.

Hotel Misión Enter this hotel's plant-filled brick courtyard, shaded by two enormous mango trees, and you'll retreat into an earlier, more peaceful Acapulco. This tranquil 19th-century hotel lies 2 blocks inland from the Costera and the *zócalo*. The original L-shaped building is at least a century old. The rooms have colonial touches, such as colorful tile and wrought iron, and come simply furnished, with a fan and one or two beds with good mattresses. Unfortunately, the promised hot water is not reliable—request a cold-water-only room and receive a small discount. Breakfast is served on the patio. The hotel is 2 blocks inland from the fishermen's wharf, main square, and La Quebrada.

Felipe Valle 12, 39300 Acapulco, Gro. © 744/482-3643. Fax 744/482-2076. 27 units. $56 double. No credit cards. **Amenities:** Restaurant.

Hotel Villa Romana This is one of the most comfortable inns in the area for a long stay. Some rooms are tiled and others carpeted; nine have small kitchens with refrigerators. Terraces face Playa la Angosta. The small, plant-filled terrace on the second floor holds tables and chairs; the fourth-floor pool offers a great view of the bay.

Av. López Mateos 185, Fracc. Las Playas, 39300 Acapulco, Gro. © 744/482-3995. www.aca-novenet.com.mx/villaromana. 9 units. High season $55 double; low season $45 double. MC, V. Street parking. *In room:* A/C, TV.

3 Where to Dine

Diners in Acapulco enjoy stunning views and fresh seafood. The quintessential setting is a candlelit table with the glittering bay spread out before you. If you're looking for a romantic spot, Acapulco brims with such inviting places; most sit along the southern coast, with views of the bay. If you're looking for simple food or an authentic local dining experience, you're best off in Old Acapulco.

A deluxe establishment in Acapulco may not be much more expensive than a mass-market restaurant. The proliferation of U.S. franchise restaurants has increased competition, and even the more expensive places have reduced prices. Trust me—the locally owned restaurants offer the best food and the best value.

SOUTH OF TOWN: LAS BRISAS AREA
VERY EXPENSIVE

Baikal ✺✺✺ FUSION/FRENCH/ASIAN   The exquisite and ultrahot Baikal is the best place in Acapulco for an over-the-top dining experience. You enter from the street then descend a spiral staircase into the stunning bar and restaurant, awash in muted tan and cream colors of luxurious fabrics and natural accents of stone, wood, and water. The restaurant itself is constructed into the cliff, providing sweeping views of Acapulco Bay's glittering lights. The large dining room, with a two-story ceiling, has comfortable seating, including sofas that border the room. The creative menu combines fusion fare, then adds a dash of Mexican flare. Start with the scallops in a chipotle vinaigrette, or the black-bean soup with duck fois gras. Notable entrees include steamed red snapper with lobster butter sauce, chicken breast rolled and stuffed with asparagus in a white-whine reduction, or medallions of New Zealand lamb in a sweet garlic sauce. The service is as impeccable as the presentation. There's also an extensive selection of wines, as well as live piano music nightly. Periodically during the evening, large projector screens descend over the floor-to-ceiling glass windows, and show short films of Old Acapulco or cavorting whales and dolphins, providing a brief reprise from conversation and dining. A fashionably late dining spot (expect a crowd at midnight), the attire is chic resort wear, as most patrons are headed to the clubs following dinner. Baikal also has wheelchair access, a private VIP dining room, a wine cellar, and an ample bar, ideal for enjoying a sunset cocktail or after-dinner drink. It's located east of town on the scenic highway just before the entrance to the Las Brisas hotel.

Carretera Escénica 16 and 22. ⒸⒻ **744/446-6845** or 744/446-6867. www.baikal.com. mx. Reservations required. Main courses $20–$60. AE, MC, V. Daily 7pm–2am. Closed Mon during the summer.

Casa Nova ⒻⒻ GOURMET ITALIAN   Enjoy an elegant meal and a fabulous view of glittering Acapulco Bay at this spot east of town. The cliff-side restaurant offers several elegantly appointed dining rooms awash in marble and stone accents, and outdoor terrace dining with a stunning view. If you arrive before your table is ready, have a drink in the comfortable lounge. This is a long-standing favorite of Mexico City's elite; dress tends toward fashionable, tropical attire. The best dishes include veal scaloppine and homemade pastas, such as linguine with fresh clams. A changing tourist menu offers a sampling of the best selections for a fixed price. There's also an ample selection of reasonably priced national and imported wines. And there's live piano music nightly.

Carretera Escénica 5256. ⒸⒻ **744/446-6237.** Reservations required. Main courses $28–$50; fixed-price 4-course meal $39. AE, MC, V. Daily 7–11:30pm.

Mezzanotte Acapulco Ⓕ ITALIAN/FRENCH/MEXICAN Mezzanotte offers a contemporary blending of classic cuisines, but its strongest asset is the view of the bay. This location has changed hands several times; it currently offers a mix of trendy international dishes served in an atmosphere that tries a bit too hard to be upscale and fashionable. Music is loud and hip, so if you're looking for a romantic evening, this is probably not the place. It's a better choice if you want a taste of Mexican urban chic. The view of the bay remains outstanding, though the food still strives for consistency. Dress up a bit for dining here. Mezzanotte is in the La Vista complex near the Las Brisas hotel.

Plaza La Vista, Carretera Escénica a Puerto Márquez 28-2. ⒸⒻ **744/446-5727** or 744/446-5728. Reservations required. Main courses $20–$35. AE, MC, V. Daily 6:30pm–midnight. Closed Mon during low season.

COSTERA HOTEL ZONE
VERY EXPENSIVE

El Olvido ⒻⒻ NUEVA COCINA   Once you make it past the entrance of this handsome terrace restaurant, you'll almost forget that it's in a shopping mall. It gives you all the glittering bay-view ambience of the posh Las Brisas restaurants, without the taxi ride. The menu is one of the most sophisticated in the city. It's expensive, but each dish is delightful in both presentation and taste. Start with 1 of the 12 house specialty drinks, such as Olvido, made with tequila,

---

Moments Dining with a View

Restaurants with unparalleled views of Acapulco include **Baikal, Madeiras, Spicey, Mezzanotte,** and **Casa Nova** in the Las Brisas area, **El Olvido** along the Costera, **Su Casa** on a hill above the convention center, and the **Bella Vista Restaurant** at the Las Brisas hotel.

---

rum, Cointreau, tomato juice, and lime juice. Soups include delicious cold melon, and thick black bean and sausage. Among the innovative entrees are quail with honey and *pasilla* chiles, and thick sea bass with a mild sauce of cilantro and avocado. For dessert, try chocolate fondue or *guanábana* (a tropical fruit) mousse in a rich *zapote negro* (black tropical fruit) sauce. El Olvido is in the Plaza Mirabella shopping center fronting Diana Circle. Walk into the passage to the right of Aca Joe and bear left; it's at the back.

Glorieta Diana traffic circle, Plaza Marbella. ℂ **744/481-0203,** 744/481-0256, 744/481-0214, or 744/481-0240. Reservations recommended. Main courses $14–$33. AE, MC, V. Daily 6pm–midnight.

Su Casa/La Margarita ℛ INTERNATIONAL Relaxed elegance and terrific food at reasonable prices are what you get at Su Casa. Owners Shelly and Angel Herrera created this pleasant, breezy, open-air restaurant on the patio of their hillside home overlooking the city. Both are experts in the kitchen and are on hand nightly to greet guests on the patio. The menu changes often. Some items are standard, such as shrimp *a la patrona* in garlic; grilled fish, steak, and chicken; and flaming *filet al Madrazo,* a delightful brochette marinated in tropical juices. Most entrees come with garnishes of cooked banana or pineapple. The margaritas are big and delicious. Su Casa is the hot-pink building on the hillside above the convention center.

V. Anahuac 110. ℂ **744/484-4350** or 744/484-1261. Fax 744/484-0803. Reservations recommended. Main courses $14–$50. MC, V. Daily 6pm–midnight.

MODERATE

El Cabrito NORTHERN MEXICAN With its hacienda-inspired entrance, waitresses in white dresses and *charro*-style neckties, and location in the heart of the Costera, this restaurant targets tourists. But its authentic, well-prepared specialties attract Mexicans in the know—a comforting stamp of approval. Among its specialties are *cabrito al pastor* (roasted goat), *charro* beans, Oaxaca-style *mole,* and *burritos de machaca.* It's on the ocean side of the Costera, south of the convention center.

Costera Alemán 1480. © 744/484-7711. Main courses $5–$15. AE, MC, V. Mon–Sat 2pm–1am; Sun 2–11pm.

INEXPENSIVE

Ika Tako 🐟🐟🐟 *Finds* SEAFOOD/TACOS   This is my favorite place to eat in Acapulco, and I never miss it. Perhaps I have simple tastes, but these fresh fish, shrimp, and seafood tacos (served in combinations that include grilled pineapple, fresh spinach, grated cheese, garlic, and bacon) are so tasty that they're addicting. Unlike most inexpensive places to eat, the setting is also lovely, with a handful of tables overlooking tropical trees and the bay below. The lighting may be bright, the atmosphere occasionally hectic, and the service dependably slow, but the tacos are delectable. You can also order beer, wine, soft drinks, and dessert. This restaurant is along the Costera, next to Beto's lobster restaurant. A branch across from the Hyatt Regency hotel lacks the atmosphere of this one.

Costera Alemán 99. No phone. Main courses $2.50–$5. No credit cards. Daily 6pm–5am.

DOWNTOWN: THE ZOCALO AREA

The old downtown area abounds with simple, inexpensive restaurants serving tasty eats. It's easy to pay more elsewhere and not get food as consistently good as you'll find in this part of town. To explore this area, start at the *zócalo* and stroll west along Juárez. After about 3 blocks, you'll come to Azueta, lined with small seafood cafes and street-side stands.

Moments If There's *Pozole*, It Must Be Thursday

If you're visiting Acapulco on a Thursday, indulge in the local custom of eating *pozole*, a bowl of white hominy and meat in broth, garnished with sliced radishes, shredded lettuce, onions, oregano, and lime. The traditional version includes pork, but a newer chicken version has also become a standard. You can also find green *pozole*, which is made by adding a paste of roasted pumpkin seeds to the traditional *pozole* base. Green *pozole* is also traditionally served with a side of sardines. For a singular Acapulco experience, enjoy your Thursday *pozole* at the cliff-side restaurant of the **Hotel Los Flamingos** (see earlier in this chapter).

MODERATE

El Amigo Miguel ★★ *Finds* MEXICAN/SEAFOOD   Locals know that El Amigo Miguel is a standout among downtown seafood restaurants—you can easily pay more elsewhere but not eat better. Impeccably fresh seafood reigns; the large, open-air dining room, 3 blocks west of the *zócalo,* is usually brimming with seafood lovers. When it overflows, head to a branch across the street, with the same menu. Try delicious *camarones borrachos* (drunken shrimp), in a sauce made with beer, applesauce, ketchup, mustard, and bits of fresh bacon—it tastes nothing like the individual ingredients. *Filete Miguel* is red snapper filet stuffed with seafood and covered in a wonderful chipotle pepper sauce. Grilled shrimp with garlic and whole red snapper *(mojo de ajo)* are served at their classic best.

Juárez 31, at Azueta. © 744/483-6981. Main courses $2.20–$23. AE, MC, V. Daily 10am–11pm.

Mariscos Pipo ★ SEAFOOD   Check out the photographs of Old Acapulco on the walls while relaxing in this airy dining room decorated with hanging nets, fish, glass buoys, and shell lanterns. The English-language menu lists a wide array of seafood, including *ceviche,* lobster, octopus, crayfish, and baby-shark quesadillas. This local favorite is 2 blocks west of the *zócalo* on Breton, just off the Costera. Another bustling branch, open daily from 1 to 9:30pm, is at Costera Alemán and Canadá (© **744/484-0165**).

Almirante Breton 3. © 744/482-2237. Main courses $5.60–$33. AE, MC, V. Daily noon–8pm.

4 Activities On & Off the Beach

Acapulco is known for its great beaches and watersports, and few visitors bother to explore its traditional downtown area. But the shaded *zócalo* (also called Plaza Alvarez) is worth a trip, to experience a glimpse of local life and color. Inexpensive cafes and shops border the plaza. At its far north end is the **cathedral Nuestra Señora de la Soledad,** with blue, onion-shaped domes and Byzantine towers. Though reminiscent of a Russian Orthodox church, it was originally (and perhaps appropriately) built as a movie set, then later adapted into a house of worship. From the church, turn east along the side street going off at a right angle (Calle Carranza, which doesn't have a marker) to find an arcade with newsstands and more shops. The hill behind the cathedral provides an unparalleled view of Acapulco. Take a taxi to the top of the hill from the main plaza, and follow signs to **El Mirador (lookout point).**

Tips To Swim or Not to Swim in the Bay?

In the past decade, the city has gone to great lengths (and great expense) to clean up the waters off Acapulco. Nevertheless, this is an industrial port that was once heavily polluted, so many choose to stick to the hotel pool. You may notice the fleet of power-sweeper boats that skim the top of the bay each morning to remove debris and oil.

Among the bay beaches that remain popular with visitors and locals are **Caleta** and **Caletilla beaches,** as well as **Playa Puerto Marqués.**

Local travel agencies book city tours, day trips to Taxco, cruises, and other excursions and activities. Taxco is about a 3-hour drive inland from Acapulco (see chapter 5 for more information).

THE BEACHES

Here's a rundown on the beaches, going from west to east around the bay. **Playa la Angosta** is a small, sheltered, often-deserted cove just around the bend from **La Quebrada** (where the cliff divers perform).

South of downtown on the Peninsula de las Playas lie the beaches **Caleta** and **Caletilla.** Separating them is a small outcropping of land that contains the aquarium and water park **Mágico Mundo Marino** (daily 9am–7pm). You'll find thatched-roofed restaurants, watersports equipment for rent, and brightly painted boats that ferry passengers to **Roqueta Island.** You can rent beach chairs and umbrellas for the day. Mexican families favor these beaches because they're close to several inexpensive hotels. In the late afternoon, fishermen pull their colorful boats up on the sand; you can buy the fresh catch of the day and, occasionally, oysters on the half shell.

Pleasure boats dock at **Playa Manzanillo,** south of the *zócalo.* Charter fishing trips sail from here. In the old days, the downtown beaches—Manzanillo, Honda, Caleta, and Caletilla—were the focal point of Acapulco. Today, beaches and resort developments stretch along the 6.4km (4-mile) length of the shore.

East of the *zócalo,* the major beaches are **Hornos** (near Papagayo Park), **Hornitos, Paraíso, Condesa,** and **Icacos,** followed by the naval base (La Base) and **Punta del Guitarrón.** After Punta del Guitarrón, the road climbs to the legendary Las Brisas hotel. Past Las Brisas, the road continues to the small, clean bay of **Puerto Marqués,** followed by **Punta Diamante,** about 19km (12 miles) from the *zócalo.*

The fabulous Acapulco Princess, the Quinta Real, and the Pierre Marqués hotels dominate the landscape, which fronts the open Pacific.

Playa Puerto Marqués, in the bay of Puerto Marqués, is an attractive area for swimming. The water is calm and the bay sheltered. Water-skiing can also be arranged. Past the bay lies **Revolcadero Beach,** a magnificent wide stretch of beach on the open ocean, where many of Acapulco's grandest resorts are found.

Other beaches are farther north and best reached by car, though buses also make the trip. **Pie de la Cuesta** is 13km (8 miles) west of town. Buses along the Costera leave every 5 or 10 minutes; a taxi costs about $22. The water is too rough for swimming, but it's a great spot for checking out big waves and the spectacular sunset, especially over *coco locos* (drinks served in fresh coconuts with the tops whacked off) at a rustic beachside restaurant. The area is known for excellent birding and surrounding coconut plantations.

If you're driving, continue west along the peninsula, passing **Coyuca Lagoon** on your right, until almost to the small air base at the tip. Along the way, various private entrepreneurs, mostly young boys, will invite you to park near different sections of beach. You'll also find *colectivo* boat tours of the lagoon offered for about $10.

BAY CRUISES & ROQUETA ISLAND

Acapulco has virtually every kind of boat to choose from—yachts, catamarans, and trimarans (single- and double-deckers). Cruises run morning, afternoon, and evening. Some offer buffets, open bars, and live music; others just snacks, drinks, and taped music. Prices range from $24 to $60. Cruise operators come and go, and their phone numbers change so frequently from year to year that it's pointless to list them here; to find out what cruises are currently operating, contact any Acapulco travel agency or your hotel's tour desk, and ask for brochures or recommendations.

Tips Tide Warning

Each year, at least one or two unwary swimmers drown in Acapulco because of **deadly riptides and undertow** (see "Safety" in "Fast Facts: Acapulco," earlier in this chapter). Swim only in Acapulco Bay or Puerto Marqués Bay—and be careful of the undertow no matter where you go. If you find yourself caught in the undertow, head back to shore at an angle instead of trying to swim straight back.

Boats from Caletilla Beach to **Roqueta Island**—a good place to snorkel, sunbathe, hike to a lighthouse, visit a small zoo, or have lunch—leave every 15 minutes from 7am until the last one returns at 7pm. There are also primitive-style glass-bottom boats that circle the bay as you look down at a few fish and watch a diver swim down to the underwater sanctuary of the Virgin of Guadalupe, patron saint of Mexico. The statue of the Virgin—created by sculptor Armando Quesado—was placed there in 1958, in memory of a group of divers who lost their lives at the spot. You can purchase tickets ($5) directly from any boat that's loading.

WATERSPORTS & BOAT RENTALS

An hour of **water-skiing** can cost as little as $35 or as much as $65. Caletilla Beach, Puerto Marqués Bay, and Coyuca Lagoon have facilities. The **Club de Esquís,** Costera Alemán 100 (✆ 744/482-2034), charges $50 per hour.

Scuba diving costs $40 for 1½ hours of instruction if you book directly with the instructor on Caleta Beach. It costs $45 to $55 if you book through a hotel or travel agency. Dive trips start at around $40 per person for one dive. One reputable shop, near Club de Esquís, is **Divers de México** (✆ 744/482-1398). Another recommended company, both PADI and NAUI-certified, is the **Acapulco Scuba Center,** Tlacopanocha 13–14, Paseo del Pescador, downtown Acapulco (✆ 744/480-1962). They offer a variety of dives from half-day (9am–2pm) shallow dives for beginners to instructor training. Prices for two-tank dives are $70, and include transportation from your hotel, onboard lunch, boat, and gear. **Boat rentals** are cheapest on Caletilla Beach, where an information booth rents inner tubes, small boats, canoes, paddleboats, and chairs. It also arranges water-skiing and scuba diving (see "Bay Cruises & Roqueta Island," above).

For **deep-sea fishing** excursions, go to the boat cooperative's pink building opposite the *zócalo,* or book a day in advance (✆ 744/482-1099). Charter trips run $200 to $300 for 6 hours, tackle and bait included, with an extra charge for ice, drinks, and lunch. Credit cards are accepted, but you're likely to get a better deal by paying cash. Boats leave at 7am and return at 2pm. If you book through a travel agent or hotel, prices start at around $200 for four people. Also recommendable is Fish-R-Us, Costera Alemán 100 (✆ 877/347-4787 toll-free in the U.S., or 744/482-8282). In addition to traditional fishing charters, they also offer private yacht charters, scuba diving, and a 3-hour Night of Delight cruise, complete with dinner served on board. Prices vary with the service requested, and number of people, so call for details.

Parasailing, though not free from risk (the occasional thrill-seeker has collided with a palm tree or even a building), can be brilliant. Floating high over the bay hanging from a parachute towed by a motorboat costs about $25. Most of these rides operate on Condesa Beach, but they also can be found independently operating on the beach in front of most hotels along the Costera.

Skydiving over Acapulco Bay is now possible. Following a 20-minute orientation, take a thrilling leap, attached to a tandem instructor from an altitude of 3,000m (10,000 ft.). The cost is $220 for the 45-second freefall and 5-minute dive, and a video of the experience is an extra $90. For experienced divers, the price drops to $27, with packages available. Contact **Skydive Acapulco,** Costera Alemán 130, Local 4, Hotel Romano Palace (℃/fax **744/484-6672;** www.skydiveacapulco.com). They're open from 8am to sunset.

GOLF, TENNIS, RIDING & BULLFIGHTS

Both the **Acapulco Princess** (℃ **744/469-1000**) and **Pierre Marques** (℃ **744/466-1000**) hotels have top-notch courses. The Princess's course is a rather narrow, level, Ted Robinson design. The Marques course, redesigned by Robert Trent Jones, Sr., in 1972 for the World Cup Golf Tournament, is longer and more challenging. A round of 18 holes at either course costs $125 for guests and $145 for nonguests; American Express, Visa, and MasterCard are accepted. Tee times begin at 7:35am, and reservations should be made a day in advance. Club rental is available and costs an extra $21. The **Mayan Palace Golf Club,** Geranios 22 (℃ **744/469-6043** or 744/469-0221), designed by Latin American golf great Pedro Guericia, lies farther east. Greens fees are $115, and caddies are available for an additional $15. At the **Club de Golf Acapulco,** off the Costera next to the convention center (℃ **744/484-0781**), you can play 9 holes for $40 and 18 holes for $60, with equipment renting for $16.

The newest addition to Acapulco's golf scene is the spectacular Robert von Hagge–designed course at the exclusive **Tres Vidas Golf Club,** Carretera a Barra Vieja Km 7 (℃ **744/444-5138** or 744/444-5135). The par-72, 18-hole course, right on the edge of the ocean, is landscaped with nine lakes, dotted with palms, and home to a flock of ducks and other birds. The club is open only to members, guests of members, and guests at Tres Vidas. Greens fees are $144, including cart; a caddy costs $20. Also here is a clubhouse with a restaurant (daily 7:30am–7:30pm), as well as a pool and beach club. American Express, Visa, and MasterCard are accepted.

The **Club de Tenis Hyatt,** Costera Alemán 1 (© **744/484-1225**), is open daily from 7am to 11pm. Outdoor courts cost $8 during the day, $15 per hour at night. Rackets rent for $3.50 and a set of balls for $3.50. Many of the hotels along the Costera have tennis facilities for guests; the best are at the Acapulco Princess, Pierre Marqués, Mayan Palace, and Las Brisas hotels. Tennis is also available at both the Club de Golf Acapulco and Tres Vidas golf clubs (above).

You can go **horseback riding** along the beach. Independent operators stroll the Hotel Zone beachfront offering rides for about $20 to $40 for 1 to 2 hours. Horses are also commonly found on the beach in front of the Acapulco Princess Hotel. There is no phone; you go directly to the beach to make arrangements.

Traditionally called Fiesta Brava, **bullfights** are held during Acapulco's winter season at a ring up the hill from Caletilla Beach. Tickets purchased through travel agencies cost around $17 to $40 and usually include transportation to and from your hotel. You can also buy a general admission ticket at the stadium for $4.50. Be forewarned that this is a true bullfight—meaning things generally do not fare well for the bull. The festivities begin at 5:30pm each Sunday from December to March.

A MUSEUM & A WATER PARK

The original **Fuerte de San Diego,** Costera Alemán, east of the *zócalo* (© **744/482-3828**), was built in 1616 to protect the town from pirate attacks. At that time, the port reaped considerable income from trade with the Philippine Islands (which, like Mexico, were part of the Spanish Empire). The fort you see today was rebuilt after considerable earthquake damage in 1776, and most recently underwent renovation in 2000. The structure houses the **Museo Histórico de Acapulco (Acapulco Historical Museum)** ☆☆, with exhibits that tell the story of Acapulco from its role as a port in the conquest of the Americas to a center for local Catholic conversion campaigns and for exotic trade with the Orient. Other exhibits chronicle Acapulco's pre-Hispanic past, the coming of the conquistadors (complete with Spanish armor), and Spanish imperial activity. Temporary exhibits are also on display. Admission to the museum is $3, free on Sunday. It's open Tuesday through Sunday from 9:30am to 6:30pm. The new **Foro Cultural Multimedia,** a spectacular light-and-sound show, starts at 8pm in Spanish, with special accommodations and shows available for groups in English afterward. Enter at 7pm to have enough time to tour the museum before the show; the $10 charge includes museum admission. Call in advance to make group reservations for English shows.

> ## (Moments) Death-Defying Divers
>
> High divers perform at La Quebrada each day at 12:30, 7:15, 8:15, 9:15, and 10:15pm. Admission is $2.50. From a spotlit ledge on the cliffs, divers (holding torches for the final performance) plunge into the roaring surf of an inlet that's just 7m (20 ft.) wide, 4m (12 ft.) deep, and 40m (130 ft.) below—after wisely praying at a small shrine nearby. To the applause of the crowd, divers climb up the rocks and accept congratulations and gifts of money from onlookers. This is the quintessential Acapulco experience. No visit is complete without watching the cliff divers—and that goes for jaded travelers as well. To get there from downtown, take the street called La Quebrada from behind the cathedral for 4 blocks.
>
> The public areas have great views, but arrive early, because performances quickly fill up. Another option is to watch from the lobby bar and restaurant terraces of the **Hotel Plaza Las Glorias/El Mirador**. The bar imposes a $9.50 cover charge, which includes two drinks. You can get around the cover by having dinner at the hotel's **La Perla restaurant**. Reservations (© **744/483-1155**, ext. 802) are recommended during high season.

To reach the fort, follow Costera Alemán past Old Acapulco and the *zócalo;* the fort is on a hill on the right.

The **Centro Internacional de Convivencia Infantil (CICI)** *(★*, Costera Alemán at Colón (© **744/484-8033**), is a sea-life and water park east of the convention center. It offers guests swimming pools with waves, water slides, and water toboggans, and has a cafeteria and restrooms. The park, which recently underwent a $3-million renovation, is open daily from 10am to 6pm. General admission is $10 and free for children under 2. There are **dolphin shows** (in Spanish) weekdays at 2pm, and weekends at 2 and 4pm. There's also a dolphin swim program, which includes 30 minutes of introduction and 30 minutes of swim time. The cost for this option is $95 for a half-hour swim, $120 for an hour, and they are by prior reservation only. Shows are at 10am, 12:30, and 4pm. Reservations are required; there is a 10-person maximum per show for the dolphin swim option. The minimum age is 4 years.

5 Shopping

Acapulco is not among the best places to buy Mexican crafts, but it does have a few interesting shops, and the Costera is lined with places to buy tourist souvenirs, including silver jewelry, Mexico knickknacks, and the ubiquitous T-shirt.

The shopkeepers aren't pushy, but they'll test your bargaining mettle. The starting price will be steep, and dragging it down may take some time. Before buying silver, examine it carefully and look for ".925" stamped on the back. This supposedly signifies that the silver is 92.5% pure, but the less expensive silver metal called "alpaca" may also bear this stamp. (Alpaca is generally stamped MEXICO or MEX, often in letters so tiny that they look similar to the three-digit ".925") and are nearly impossible to read. The market is open daily from 9am to 6pm.

Sanborn's, a good department store and drugstore chain, offers an array of staples, including cosmetics, music, clothing, books, and magazines. It has a number of locations in Acapulco including downtown at Costera Miguel Alemán 209, across from the boat docks (© **744/484-4413**); Costera Miguel Alemán 1226 at the Condo Estrella Tower, close to the convention center (© **744/484-2025**); and also on Costera Miguel Alemán 163, at the Hotel Calinda (© **744/481-2426** or 744/484-4465).

Acapulco also has a Sam's Club and a Wal-Mart located on the inland side of the main highway just prior to its ascent to Las Brisas.

Boutiques selling resort wear crowd the Costera Alemán. These stores carry attractive summer clothing at prices lower than you generally pay in the United States. If there's a sale, you can find incredible bargains. One of the nicest air-conditioned shopping centers on the Costera is **Plaza Bahía,** Costera Alemán 125 (© **744/485-6939** or 744/485-6992), which has four stories of shops, movie theaters, a bowling alley, and small fast-food restaurants. The center is just west of the Costa Club Hotel. The bowling alley, **Aca Bol in Plaza Bahía** (© **744/485-0970** or 744/485-7464), is open Monday through Sunday from noon to 1:30am. Another popular shopping strip is the **Plaza Condesa,** adjacent to the Fiesta Americana Condesa, with shops that include Guess, Izod, and Bronce Swimwear. **Olvida Plaza,** near the restaurant of the same name, has Tommy Hilfiger and Aca Joe.

Acapulco has a few notable fine-art galleries. My favorite, **Galería Espacio Pal Kepenyes** ⟨⟨, Costera Guitarrón 140, on the road to the Radisson (© **744/484-3738**), carries the work of Pal Kepenyes, whose stunning bronzes are among Acapulco's most notable public sculptures. The gallery shows smaller versions, as well as signature pieces of jewelry in brass, copper, and silver, by appointment only.

6 Acapulco After Dark

SPECIAL ATTRACTIONS

The "Gran Noche Mexicana" combines a performance by the Acapulco Ballet Folklórico with one by Los Voladores (flying pole dancers) from Papantla. It takes place in the plaza of the convention center Monday, Wednesday, and Friday at 7pm. With dinner and open bar, the show costs $62; general admission (including three drinks) is $42. Call for reservations (© 744/484-7046) or consult a local travel agency. Many major hotels also schedule Mexican fiestas and other theme nights that include dinner and entertainment. Local travel agencies will have information.

NIGHTCLUBS & DANCE CLUBS

Acapulco is even more famous for its nightclubs than for its beaches. Because clubs frequently change ownership—and, often names—it's difficult to give specific and accurate recommendations. But some general tips will help. Every club seems to have a cover charge of around $20 in high season and $10 in low season; drinks can cost anywhere from $3 to $10. Women can count on paying less or entering free. Don't even think about going out to one of the hillside dance clubs before 11pm, and don't expect much action until after midnight. But it will keep going until 4 or 5am.

Many dance clubs periodically waive their cover charge or offer some other promotion to attract customers. Look for promotional materials in hotel reception areas, at travel desks or concierge booths, in local publications, and on the beach.

The high-rise hotels have their own bars and sometimes dance clubs. Informal lobby or poolside cocktail bars often offer free live entertainment.

THE BEACH BAR ZONE

Prefer a little fresh air with your nightlife? The young, hip crowd favors the growing number of open-air oceanfront dance clubs along Costera Alemán, most of which feature techno or alternative rock. There's a concentration of them between the Fiesta Americana and Continental Plaza hotels. An earlier and more casual option to the glitzy dance clubs, these clubs include the jamming **Disco Beach** (© 744/484-8230), **El Sombrero** (you'll know it when you see it), **Tabú,** and the pirate-themed **Barbaroja.** These mainly charge a cover (around $10) and offer an open bar. Women frequently drink free with a lesser charge (men may pay more, but then, this is where the beach babes are). Disco Beach is the most popular of the bunch, and occasionally—such as during spring break—has live bands on the beachfront stage. Their Friday night foam parties are especially popular. Most of the smaller establishments do not accept credit cards; when they do, MasterCard and Visa are more widely accepted than American Express.

If you are brave enough—or inebriated enough—there's a **bungee jump** in the midst of the beach bar zone at Costera Alemán 101 (© **744/484-7529**). For $62 you get one jump, plus a T-shirt, diploma, and membership. Additional jumps are $28, and your fourth jump is free. For $67, you can jump as many times as you like from 4 to 11pm.

Alebrijes   This high-tech club boasts an exterior of reflection pools, gardens, and flaming torches. Inside, stadium seating, booths and round tables surround the vast dance floor—the dance club (capacity 1,200) doubles as a venue for concerts and live performances by some of Mexico's most notable singers. The dress code forbids shorts, T-shirts, tennis shoes, sandals, and jeans. Average age here is late teens to early 20s. Open daily from 11pm to 5am. Costera Alemán 3308, across from the Hyatt Regency Acapulco. © **744/484-5902**. Cover (including open bar with national drinks) $5–$25 for women, $8–$35 for men.

Baby-O 🐝🐝   This longtime Acapulco favorite is a throwback to the town's heady disco days, although the music is exceptionally contemporary. The mid-to-late-20s crowd dances to everything from house to hip-hop, techno to dance. Located across from the Romano Days Inn, Baby-O has a dance floor surrounded by several tiers of tables and sculpted, cavelike walls, serviced by five bars. Drinks cost $4 to $5. Three-dimensional laser shows and H_2O cooling effects keep the dancing going strong. Service is excellent. This is a great choice for those who shun mammoth clubs in favor of a more intimate setting—although there's generally a good crowd. It opens at 10:30pm. Costera Alemán 22. © **744/484-7474** or 744/481-1035. www.babyo.com.mx. Cover $5–$17 for women, $10–$35 for men.

Carlos 'n' Charlie's   For fun, danceable music and good food, you can't go wrong with this branch of the Carlos Anderson chain. It's always packed. Come early and get a seat on the terrace overlooking the Costera. This is a great place to go for late dinner and a few drinks before moving on to a club. It's east of the Glorieta Diana traffic circle, across the street from the Fiesta Americana Condesa.

It's open daily from 1pm to 1am. Costera Alemán 999. © **744/484-1285** or 744/484-0039.

Hard Rock Cafe   If you like your music loud, your food trendy, and your entertainment international, you'll feel at home in Acapulco's branch of this chain bent on world domination. Elvis memorabilia greets you in the entry area, and among other numerous mementos is the Beatles' gold record for "Can't Buy Me Love." There's a bandstand for live music—played every night between 10pm and 2am—and a small dance floor. It's on the seaward side toward the southern end of the Costera, south of the convention center and opposite El Cabrito. Open daily from noon to 2am. Costera Alemán 37. © **744/484-0047.**

Mandara 🎭🎭 *(Moments)*   Venture into this stylish chrome-and-neon extravaganza (formerly Enigma) perched on the side of the mountain for a true Acapulco nightlife experience. The plush, dim club has a sunken dance floor and panoramic view of the lights of Acapulco Bay. The club also has an intimate piano bar upstairs overlooking the dance club, called Siboney, with a special champagne menu, which draws a more mature and moneyed crowd. The after-hours lounge Privado, also in the same building, opens its doors at 3am. Downstairs, there's pumped-in mood smoke, alternating with fresh oxygen to keep you dancing. Tight and slinky is the norm for women; no shorts for men. The club opens nightly at 10:30pm; fireworks rock the usually full house at 3am, which is when a stylized dance performance takes place on weekends in the style of Euro clubs. Call to find out if you need reservations; this club tends to be busiest on Friday nights. Carretera Escénica, between Los Rancheros Restaurant and La Vista Shopping Center. © **744/446-5711** or -5712. Fax 744/446-5726. Cover $26 for women, $32 for men, includes open bar; or pay $10 for entrance to Siboney, and pay for drinks separately.

Palladium 🎭🎭   This cliff-side club currently reins as the top spot in town, and is found just down the road from Mandara. Generally, it welcomes a younger, rowdier crowd that enjoys the equally fabulous views and the dancing platforms set in the 48m-wide (160-ft.) glass windows overlooking the bay. Around 3am, Silver Man, complete with an Aztec headdress, performs, followed by a spray of fireworks outside the windows. Palladium has welcomed the world's finest DJs as special guests. The layout of the club is more open, which makes meeting people most accessible. Carretera Escénica. © **744/481-0330** or 744/446-5483; www.palladium.com.mx. Cover $26 for women, $36 for men, includes open bar.

Pepe's Piano Bar   Pepe's has surely been one of the most famous piano bars in the hemisphere, although it appears those days may be numbered. It has inspired patrons of all ages to sing their hearts out for more than 40 years, and it still draws a crowd, though it now caters to karaoke instead of piano—a big mistake, in my opinion. I keep hoping the owners will come to their senses and return to their roots. It's open Wednesday to Sunday from 10pm to 4am. Carretera Escénica, Comercial La Vista, Local 5. ℂ 744/446-5736.

Salon Q   This place bills itself as "the cathedral of salsa," and it's a fairly accurate claim—Salon Q is *the* place to get down and enjoy the Latin rhythms. Frequently, management raises the cover and features impersonators of top Latin American musical acts. Open daily from 10pm to 4am. Costera Alemán 3117. ℂ 744/481-0114. Cover $13–$25.

ZUCCA   This club offers a fantastic bay view. It caters to a more mature crowd—it allegedly admits only those over 25, though the attendants seem to bend the rules for women—and is particularly popular with the moneyed Mexico City set. The club periodically projects a laser show across the bay. The dress code prohibits shorts, jeans, T-shirts, or sandals. Reservations are recommended. It's open nightly from 10:30pm to 2:30am, until 4am on weekends and when the crowd demands it. In the La Vista Shopping Center, Carretera Escénica 28. ℂ 744/446-5690 or -5691. Cover $5–$10.

Northward to Zihuatanejo & Ixtapa

Side-by-side beach resorts, Ixtapa and Zihuatanejo share geography, but they couldn't be more different in character. Ixtapa is a model of modern infrastructure, services, and luxury hotels, while Zihuatanejo—"Zihua" to the locals—is the quintessential Mexican beach village. For travelers, this offers the intriguing possibility of visiting two distinct destinations in one vacation. Those looking for luxury should opt for Ixtapa (eex-*tah*-pah). You can easily and quickly make the 6.5km (4-mile) trip into Zihuatanejo for a sampling of the simple life in a *pueblo* by the sea. Those who prefer a more rustic retreat with real personality should settle in Zihuatanejo (see-wah-tah-*neh*-hoh). It's known for its long-standing community of Swiss and Italian immigrants, and its legendary beach playboys.

The area, with a backdrop of the Sierra Madre and a foreground of Pacific Ocean waters, provides a full range of activities and diversions. Scuba diving, deep-sea fishing, bay cruises to remote beaches, and golf are among the favorites. Nightlife in both towns borders on subdued; Ixtapa is the livelier.

This dual destination is the choice for the traveler looking for a little of everything, from resort-style indulgence to unpretentious simplicity. These two resorts are more welcoming to couples and adults than families, with a number of places that are off-limits to children under 16—something of a rarity in Mexico.

1 Essentials

576km (360 miles) SW of Mexico City; 565km (353 miles) SE of Manzanillo; 253km (158 miles) NW of Acapulco

GETTING THERE & DEPARTING

BY PLANE   These destinations tend to be even more seasonal than most resorts in Mexico. Flights are available year-round from U.S. gateways, but they operate less frequently in the summer. See chapter 1, "Planning Your Trip to Southern Pacific Mexico," for information on flying to Ixtapa/Zihuatanejo from the United States and Canada. Both **Aeromexico** and **Mexicana** fly daily from Mexico City and Guadalajara, and less often from Acapulco. Here are the local numbers of some international carriers: **Aeromexico** (© 755/554-2018 or -2019), **Alaska Airlines** (© 755/554-8457), **America West** (© 755/554-8634), **Continental** (© 755/554-4219), and **Mexicana** (© 755/554-2208 or -2209). Ask your travel agent about **charter** flights and packages.

Arriving: The **Ixtapa-Zihuatanejo airport** (© 755/554-2070) is about 11km (7 miles) and 15 minutes south of Zihuatanejo. Taxi fares are $12 to $19. **Transportes Terrestres** *colectivo* minivans transport travelers to hotels in Zihuatanejo and Ixtapa and to Club Med; buy tickets ($3–$6) just outside the baggage-claim area. Car-rental agencies with booths in the airport include **Hertz** (© 800/654-3131 in the U.S., or 755/554-2952), and **Budget** (© 800/527-0700 in the U.S., or 755/553-0397).

BY CAR   From Mexico City (about 7 hr.), the shortest route is Highway 15 to Toluca, then Highway 130/134 the rest of the way. On the latter road, highway gas stations are few. The other route is the four-lane Highway 95D to Iguala, then Highway 51 west to Highway 134. A new toll road, Highway 37 from Morelia to Ixtapa, was almost completed at press time, and should make the trip between these two cities about 4 hours.

From Acapulco (2½–3 hr.) or Manzanillo (11 hr.), the only choice is the coastal Highway 200. The ocean views along the winding, mountain-edged drive from Manzanillo can be spectacular.

Tips Motorist Advisory

Motorists planning to follow Highway 200 northwest up the coast from Ixtapa or Zihuatanejo toward Lázaro Cárdenas and Manzanillo should be aware of reports of car and bus hijackings on that route, especially around Playa Azul, with bus holdups more common than car holdups. Before heading in that direction, ask locals and the tourism office about the status of the route. Don't drive at night. According to tourism officials, police and military patrols of the highway have recently been increased, and the number of incidents has dropped dramatically.

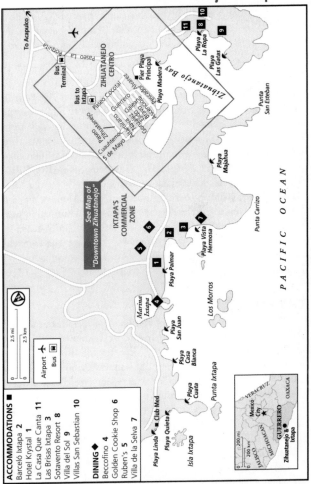

Zihuatanejo & Ixtapa Area

ACCOMMODATIONS ■
Barceló Ixtapa **2**
Hotel Krystal **1**
La Casa Que Canta **11**
Las Brisas Ixtapa **3**
Sotavento Resort **8**
Villa del Sol **9**
Villas San Sebastian **10**

DINING ◆
Beccofino **4**
Golden Cookie Shop **6**
Ruben's **5**
Villa de la Selva **7**

BY BUS Zihuatanejo has two bus terminals: the **Central de Autobuses,** Paseo Zihuatanejo at Paseo la Boquita, opposite the Pemex station and IMSS Hospital (© 755/554-3477), from which most lines operate, and the **Estrella de Oro** station (© 755/554-2175), a block away. At the Central de Autobuses, several companies offer daily service to and from Acapulco, Puerto Escondido, Huatulco, Manzanillo, Puerto Vallarta, and other cities. At the other station, first-class Estrella de Oro buses run daily to Acapulco.

The trip from Mexico City to Zihuatanejo (bypassing Acapulco) takes 9 hours; from Acapulco, 4 to 5 hours. From Zihuatanejo, it's 6 or 7 hours to Manzanillo, and an additional 6 hours to Puerto Vallarta.

VISITOR INFORMATION

The **State Tourism Office** (©/fax **755/553-1967** or -1968) is in the La Puerta shopping center in Ixtapa, across from the Presidente Inter-Continental Hotel; it's open Monday through Friday from 8am to 8:30pm and Saturday from 8am to 2pm. This is mainly a self-service office to collect brochures; the staff is less helpful than that at other offices in Mexico. The **Zihuatanejo Tourism Office Module** (no phone; www.ixtapa-zihuatanejo.com) is on the main square by the basketball court at Alvarez; it's open Monday through Friday from 9am to 3pm and serves basic tourist-information purposes. The administrative office, in City Hall (© **755/554-2355**), is open Monday through Friday from 8am to 4pm. The **Convention and Visitor's Bureau** is another source of information, it's located in Ixtapa at Paseo de Las Gaviotas 12 (© **755/553-1270;** www.ixtapa-zihuatanejo.org).

CITY LAYOUT

The fishing village and resort of **Zihuatanejo** spreads out around the beautiful Bay of Zihuatanejo, framed by downtown to the north and a beautiful long beach and the Sierra foothills to the east. The heart of Zihuatanejo is the waterfront walkway **Paseo del Pescador** (also called the *malecón*), bordering the Municipal Beach. Rather than a plaza as in most Mexican villages, the town centerpiece is a **basketball court,** which fronts the beach. It's a point of reference for directions. The main thoroughfare for cars is **Juan Alvarez,** a block behind the *malecón.* Sections of several of the main streets are designated *zona peatonal* (pedestrian zone).

A cement-and-sand walkway runs from the *malecón* in downtown Zihuatanejo along the water to **Playa Madera.** The walkway is lit at night. Access to Playa La Ropa (Clothing Beach) is by the main road, **Camino a Playa La Ropa.** Playa La Ropa and Playa Las Gatas (Cats Beach) are connected only by boat.

A good highway connects Zihua to **Ixtapa,** 6km (4 miles) northwest. The 18-hole **Ixtapa Golf Club** marks the beginning of the inland side of Ixtapa. Tall hotels line Ixtapa's wide beach, **Playa Palmar,** against a backdrop of lush palm groves and mountains. Access is by the main street, **Bulevar Ixtapa.** On the opposite side of the main boulevard lies a large expanse of small shopping plazas (many with air-conditioned shops) and restaurants. At the far end of Bulevar Ixtapa, **Marina Ixtapa** has excellent restaurants, private yacht slips, and an 18-hole golf course. Condominiums and private homes surround the marina and golf course, and more developments of exclusive residential areas are rising in the hillsides past the marina on the road to Playa Quieta and Playa Linda. Ixtapa also has a paved bicycle track that begins at the marina and continues around the golf course and on toward Playa Linda.

GETTING AROUND

BY TAXI   Fares are reasonable, but from midnight to 5am, rates increase by 50%. The average fare between Ixtapa and Zihuatanejo is $4.50. Within Zihua, the fare runs about $2.50; within Ixtapa it averages $2.50 to $5. Radio cabs are available by calling ✆ 755/554-3680 or 755/554-3311; however, taxis are available from most hotels. A **shuttle bus** (35¢) runs between Zihuatanejo and Ixtapa every 15 or 20 minutes from 5am to 11pm daily, but is almost always very crowded with commuting workers. In Zihuatanejo, it stops near the corner of Morelos/Paseo Zihuatanejo and Juárez, about 3 blocks north of the market. In Ixtapa, it makes numerous stops along Bulevar Ixtapa.

Note: The road from Zihuatanejo to Ixtapa is a broad, four-lane highway, which makes driving between the towns easier and faster than ever. Street signs are becoming more common in Zihuatanejo, and good signs lead in and out of both towns. However, both locations have an area called the "Zona Hotelera" (Hotel Zone), so if you're trying to reach Ixtapa's Hotel Zone, signs in Zihuatanejo pointing to that village's Hotel Zone may be confusing.

FAST FACTS: Zihuatanejo & Ixtapa

American Express   The main office is in Av. Colegio Heróico Militar 38 in Plaza San Rafael, Local 7, Centro (✆ 755/544-6242; fax 755/544-6242). It's open Monday through Friday from 9am to 6pm.

Area Code   The telephone area code is **755**.

Banks   Ixtapa's banks include **Bancomer,** in the La Puerta Centro shopping center. The most centrally located of Zihuatanejo's banks is **Banamex,** Cuauhtémoc 4. Banks change money during normal business hours, which are generally Monday through

Friday from 9am to 3 or 5pm, Saturday from 10am to 1pm. Automatic tellers and currency exchange are available during these and other hours.

Climate Summer is hot and humid, though tempered by sea breezes and brief showers; September is the peak of the tropical rainy season, with showers concentrated in the late afternoons.

Hospital **Hospital de la Marina Ixtapa** is at Bulevar Ixtapa s/n, in front of the Hotel Aristos (© **755/553-0499**). In Zihuatanejo, there's the **Clinica Maciel** (© **755/554-2380**; La Palmas 12), or **Hospital Hernández Montejano,** Juan Alvarez s/n (© **755/554-5404**). Dial © **065** from any phone for emergencies.

Internet Access Ixtapa has many Internet cafes. **Dolfy's Internet Café** (© **755/553-1177**) is in the Los Patios Shopping Center in Ixtapa, on the second floor, next to the Golden Cookie Shop. The cost of Internet access is $3 for 20 minutes, and $1 for each additional minute. It's open daily from 8am to 9pm. Access is cheaper in Zihuatanejo; the most popular is **Zihuatanejo Bar Net,** Agustín Ramírez 9, on the ground floor of the Hotel Zihuatanejo Centro (© **755/554-3661**). Offering high-speed access for $1 per 30 minutes, it's open from 9am to 11pm daily.

Pharmacy There's a branch of **Farmacias Coyuca** in each town. They are open 24 hours a day, and will deliver. The Ixtapa branch doesn't have a phone number; in Zihuatanejo, call © **755/554-5390**.

Post Office The *correo* is in the SCT building, Edificio SCT, behind El Cacahuate in Zihuatanejo (© **755/554-2192**). It's open Monday through Friday from 8am to 6pm, Saturday from 9am to 1pm.

2 Where to Stay

Larger, more expensive hotels, including many well-known chains, dominate accommodations in Ixtapa and on Playa Madera. There are only a few choices in the budget and moderate price ranges. If you're looking for lower-priced rooms, Zihuatanejo offers a better selection and better values. Many long-term guests in Ixtapa and Zihuatanejo rent apartments and condos. **Lilia Valle** (© **755/554-2084** or 755/554-4649) is an excellent source for apartment and villa rentals. All lodgings in both towns offer free parking.

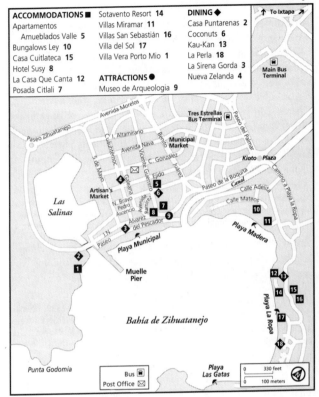

Downtown Zihuatanejo

ACCOMMODATIONS ■
Apartamentos
  Amueblados Valle **5**
Bungalows Ley **10**
Casa Cuitlateca **15**
Hotel Susy **8**
La Casa Que Canta **12**
Posada Citlali **7**

Sotavento Resort **14**
Villas Miramar **11**
Villas San Sebastián **16**
Villa del Sol **17**
Villa Vera Porto Mio **1**

ATTRACTIONS ●
Museo de Arqueologia **9**

DINING ◆
Casa Puntarenas **2**
Coconuts **6**
Kau-Kan **13**
La Perla **18**
La Sirena Gorda **3**
Nueva Zelanda **4**

↑ To Ixtapa ↗

Main Bus Terminal

Avenida Morelos

Tres Estrellas Bus Terminal

Paseo Zihuatanejo

Paseo del Palmar

I. Altamirano

Avenida Nava

Cuauhtémoc

5 de Mayo

Vicente Guerrero

Benito Juárez

C. González

Municipal Market

Kioto Plaza

Galeana

Ejido

Paseo de la Boquita

Canal

Camino a playa la Ropa

Artisan's Market

N. Bravo
Pedro
Ascencio

Calle Adelita

Calle Mateos

10

11

Álvarez
del Pescador

J.N.
Paseo

3

8 **7**

5

6

9

Playa Madera

Las Salinas

Playa Municipal

2

1

Muelle Pier

12 **13**

14 **15**

16

17

Playa La Ropa

18

Bahía de Zihuatanejo

Punta Godomia

Bus ■
Post Office ✉

Playa
Las Gatas

0   330 feet
0   100 meters

ZIHUATANEJO

Hotels in Zihuatanejo and its nearby beach communities are more economical than those in Ixtapa. The term "bungalow" is used loosely—it may mean an individual unit with a kitchen and bedroom, or just a bedroom. It may also be like a hotel, in a two-story building with multiple units, some of which have kitchens. It may be cozy or rustic, with or without a patio or balcony. Accommodations in town are generally very basic, though clean and comfortable.

Playa Madera and Playa La Ropa, separated by a craggy shoreline, are both accessible by road. Prices tend to be higher here than in town, but the value is much better, and people tend to find that the beautiful, tranquil setting is worth the extra cost. The town is 5 (by taxi) to 20 (on foot) minutes away.

IN TOWN

Apartamentos Amueblados Valle 🐟🐟　These well-furnished apartments cost only as much as an inexpensive hotel room. Five one-bedroom units accommodate up to three people; the three two-bedroom apartments fit four comfortably. Units that do not face the street are less noisy than those that do. Each airy apartment is different; all have ceiling fans, private balconies, and kitchenettes. There's daily maid service, and a paperback-book exchange in the office. Owner Guadalupe Rodríguez and her son Luis Valle are good sources of information about cheaper apartments elsewhere, for long-term visitors. Reserve well in advance during high season. It's about 2 blocks from the waterfront.

Vicente Guerrero 33 (between Ejido and N. Bravo), 40880 Zihuatanejo, Gro. 🄯 755/554-2084. Fax 755/554-3220. 8 units. High season $60 1-bedroom apt, $90 2-bedroom apt; low season $40 1-bedroom apt, $60 2-bedroom apt. Ask about low-season and long-term discounts. No credit cards. *In room:* Fan, kitchenette.

Hotel Susy　This two-story hotel, with lots of plants along a shaded walkway set back from the street, offers small rooms with fans and screened louvered-glass windows. Upper-floor rooms have balconies overlooking the street.

Juan Alvarez 3 (at Guerrero), 40880 Zihuatanejo, Gro. 🄯 755/554-2339. 18 units. High season $78 double; low season $34 double. MC, V. Facing away from the water at the basketball court on the *malecón,* turn right and walk 2 blocks; the hotel is on your left. *In room:* TV.

Posada Citlali　In this pleasant, three-story hotel, small rooms with fans surround a shaded, plant-filled courtyard that holds comfortable rockers and chairs. It's a good value for the price. Bottled water is in help-yourself containers on the patio. The stairway to the top two floors is narrow and steep.

Vicente Guerrero 3 (near Alvarez), 40880 Zihuatanejo, Guerrero. 🄯 755/554-2043. citlali@zihuatanejo.com.mx. 19 units. $39 double. No credit cards.

PLAYA MADERA

Madera Beach is a 15-minute walk along the street, a 10-minute walk along the beach pathway, or a cheap taxi ride from Zihuatanejo. Most of the accommodations are on Calle Eva S. de López Mateos, the road overlooking the beach. Most hotels are set against the hill and have steep stairways.

Bungalows Ley 🐟　No two suites are the same at this small complex, one of the nicest on Playa Madera. If you're traveling with a group, you may want to book the most expensive suite (Club

⟮*Value*⟯ Authentic Zihua: Playa Madera Bungalows

If you want an inexpensive, authentic stay in Zihuatanejo, try the hillside bungalows on Calle Eva S. de López Mateos, overlooking Playa Madera. This is the anti-Ixtapa. Small hotels, each with the rugged charm of an old house, are run by lively locals full of stories. Try **Bungalows Ley** and **Villas Miramar** (see below), or go to **Bungalows Pacifico**, Cerro de la Madera (✆ **755/554-2112**), run by the affable Anita Hafner. Two-bedroom suites with simple kitchens, a bathroom, and fan (no A/C) start at just $82 per night.

Madera); it has a rooftop terrace with a tiled hot tub, outdoor bar and grill, and spectacular view. All the units are immaculate; the simplest are studios with one bed and a kitchen in the same room. All rooms have terraces or balconies just above the beach, and all are decorated in Miami Beach colors. Bathrooms, however, tend to be small and dark. Guests praise the management and the service.

Calle Eva S. de López Mateos s/n, Playa Madera (Apdo. Postal 466), 40880 Zihuatanejo, Gro. ✆ **755/554-4087**. Fax 755/554-4563. 8 units. $103 double with A/C; $162 2-bedroom suite with kitchen (up to 4 persons) or $212 (up to 6 persons). AE, MC, V. Follow Mateos to the right up a slight hill; it's on your left. *In room:* TV.

Villas Miramar ⟨⟨ This lovely hotel with beautiful gardens offers a welcoming atmosphere, attention to detail, and superb cleanliness. Some of the elegant suites are around a shady patio that doubles as a restaurant. Those across the street center on a lovely pool and have private balconies and sea views. A terrace with a bay view has a bar that features a daily happy hour (5–7pm). TVs get cable channels, and the restaurant serves a basic menu for breakfast, lunch, and dinner.

Calle Adelita, Lote 78, Playa Madera (Apdo. Postal 211), 40880 Zihuatanejo, Gro. ✆ **755/554-2106** or 755/554-3350. Fax 755/554-2149. www.prodigyweb.net.mx/ villasmiramar. 18 units. High season $95 suite, $100 oceanview suite, $135 2-bedroom suite; low season $60 suite, $70 oceanview suite, $106 2-bedroom suite. AE, MC, V. Free enclosed parking. Follow the road leading south out of town toward Playa La Ropa, take the 1st right after the traffic circle, and go left on Adelita. **Amenities:** Restaurant; bar; pool. *In room:* A/C, TV.

PLAYA LA ROPA

Playa La Ropa is a 20- to 25-minute walk south of town on the east side of the bay, or a $2 taxi ride.

Casa Cuitlateca This exclusive B&B is the perfect place for a romantic holiday. It's on the hillside across from La Ropa beach, with stunning views. Rooms are carefully decorated with handicrafts and textiles from all over Mexico, especially from Michoacán, Puebla, and Oaxaca. One suite has a large terrace, another a very nice sitting area and small private garden but no view. Two smaller units have private terraces and sitting areas. The bar, on the first level behind the pool, is open to the public from 4:30 to 8pm. On the top level, there is a sun deck and a hot tub for guests' use. From the entrance, a well-designed yet steep 150-step staircase leads to the B&B. The driveway is also very steep. A hanging bridge connects the parking lot to the house.

Calle Playa La Ropa, Apdo. Postal 124, 40880 Zihuatanejo, Gro. Ⓒ **755/554-2448.** U.S. reservations Ⓒ **877/541-1234** or 406/252-2834. Fax 406/252-4692. www. casacuitlateca.com. 4 suites. $397 double. Extra person $50. Rates include breakfast and round-trip airport transportation. AE, MC, V. Children under 15 not accepted. **Amenities:** Bar; small pool; Jacuzzi. *In room:* A/C.

La Casa Que Canta 𝕲𝕲𝕲 "The House that Sings" opened in 1992 is a member of the Small Luxury Hotels of the world, and is a must-see, even if you're not staying here. It sits on a mountainside overlooking Zihuatanejo Bay, and its striking molded-adobe architecture typifies the rustic-chic style known as Mexican Pacific. Individually decorated rooms have handsome natural-tile floors, unusual painted Michoacán furniture, antiques, and stretched-leather *equipales,* with hand-loomed fabrics throughout. All units have large, beautifully furnished terraces with bay views. Hammocks hang under the thatched-roof terraces. Most of the spacious units are suites, and 10 of them have private pools. Rooms meander up and down the hillside, and while no staircase is terribly long, there are no elevators. An adjacent private villa, El Murmello, holds four suites, all with private plunge pools. A new "well-being" center has been added, offering massage, spa services, and yoga. La Casa Que Canta is on the road leading to Playa La Ropa, but not on any beach. The closest stretch of beach (not Playa La Ropa) is down a steep hill.

Camino Escénico a Playa La Ropa, 40880 Zihuatanejo, Guerrero. Ⓒ **888/523-5050** in the U.S., 755/555-7000, 755/555-7030, or 755/554-6529. Fax 755/554-7900. www. lacasaquecanta.com.mx. 28 units. High season $330–$680 double; low season $290–$525 double. AE, MC, V. Children under 16 not accepted. **Amenities:** Small restaurant; bar; freshwater pool on main terrace; saltwater pool on bottom level; room service; laundry service. *In room:* A/C, minibar.

Sotavento Beach Resort 𝕲𝕲 Perched on a hill above the beach, this hotel is for people who want to relax near the ocean in a beautiful, simple setting without being bothered by televisions or closed up in air-conditioned rooms. A throwback to the style of the 1970s, when Zihua was first being discovered by an international jet set, the Sotavento is made up of two multistory buildings. Quite a variety of rooms are available to choose from—ask to see a few different rooms to find something that suits you. My favorites are the doubles on the upper floors of the Sotavento, which are about three times the size of normal doubles. They are simply and comfortably furnished. Each has an oceanview terrace that is half-sheltered, with hammocks, and half-open, with chaises for taking the sun. Screened windows catch the ocean breezes, and ceiling fans keep the rooms airy. One curious feature of the Sotavento is that the floors are slightly slanted—by design. This hotel is on the side of a hill and is not for people who mind climbing stairs.

Playa La Ropa, 40880 Zihuatanejo, Gro. ℂ **755/554-2032.** Fax 755/554-2975. www.beachresortsotavento.com. 126 units. $60–$110 standard double; $75–$130 terrace suite. AE, DC, MC, V. Take the highway south of Zihuatanejo about a mile, turn right at the hotel's sign, and follow the road. **Amenities:** Restaurant; lobby bar; pool w/whirlpool.

Villa del Sol ⭐⭐⭐ This exquisite inn is known as much for its unequivocal attention to luxurious detail as it is for its exacting German owner, Helmut Leins. A tranquil, magnificently designed spot that caters to guests looking for complete privacy and serenity, it sits on a 180m-long (600-ft.) private beach. Spacious, split-level suites have one or two bedrooms, plus a living area and a large terrace. Some have a private minipool, and all have CD players and fax machines, with satellite TVs or DVD players brought upon request. White netting drapes king-size beds, and comfy lounges and hammocks beckon at siesta time. Standard rooms are smaller and lack TV and telephone, but are appointed with Mexican artistic details. There are nine beachside suites, but I prefer the individually designed original rooms. This is one of only two hotels in Mexico that meet the demanding standards of the French Relais & Châteaux, and is a member of the Small Luxury Hotels of the World. Villa del Sol does not accept children under 12 during high season, and generally has a "no children" and "no excess noise" feel. This may make it less enjoyable for travelers who relish a more welcoming ambience. The meal plan (breakfast and dinner) is mandatory during the winter season.

Playa la Ropa (Apdo. Postal 84), 40880 Zihuatanejo, Gro. ℂ **888/389-2645** in the U.S., or **755/555-5500.** Fax 755/554-2758. www.hotelvilladelsol.com. 45 units. High season $300–$1,000 double; low season $250–$750 double. Meal plan $60 per person, during high season (mandatory) or an optional $45 during summer season.

AE, MC, V. **Amenities:** Open-air beachside restaurant and bar; 3 pools (including 18m/60-ft. lap pool); 2 tennis courts; tour desk; car rental; salon; room service; massage; art gallery; doctor on call. *In room:* A/C, TV, minibar, hair dryer, bathrobes.

Villas San Sebastián   On the mountainside above Playa La Ropa, this nine-villa complex offers great views of Zihuatanejo's bay. The villas surround tropical vegetation and a central swimming pool. Each has a kitchenette and a spacious private terrace, and some have air-conditioning. The personalized service is one reason these villas come so highly recommended; owner Luis Valle, whose family has lived in this community for decades, is always available to help guests with any questions or needs.

Bulevar Escénico Playa La Ropa (across from the Dolphins Fountain). ✆ 755/554-4154. Fax 755/554-3220. 11 units. High season $155 1-bedroom villa, $255 2-bedroom villa; low season $105 1-bedroom villa, $165 2-bedroom villa. No credit cards. **Amenities:** Pool.

PLAYA ZIHUATANEJO
Villa Vera Puerto Mío ✦✦   Located on 10 hectares (25 acres) of beautifully landscaped grounds, this resort sits apart from the rest of the hotels in Zihuatanejo, at the farthest end of the bay, almost directly across from Las Gatas beach. Casa de Mar, the cliff-side mansion near the main entrance, holds most of the rooms. Other units are in the Peninsula area, on the tip of the bay; a more secluded area holds two suites with ample sitting areas, beautiful views, and no TVs. Three suites between Casa de Mar and the Peninsula have private pools; the upper-level unit is largest. All rooms were renovated recently and are nicely decorated with hand-crafted details from around Mexico. They enjoy beautiful views of either Zihuatanejo's bay or the Pacific Ocean. Golf carts provide transportation to areas around the property. The resort accepts children under 16 only during the summer, and recommends that you call in advance to check. The private beach is accessible only through the hotel, and there's a sailboat available for charters.

Paseo del Morro 5, 40880 Zihuatanejo, Gro. ✆ 01-800/021-6566 in Mexico, 755/553-8165, -8166, or -8167. Fax 755/553-8168. 22 units. High season $291 double, $316 suite, $819 top-level suite with pool, $954 master suite; low season $252 double, $252 suite, $670 top-level suite with pool, $819 master suite. AE, MC, V. **Amenities:** 2 restaurants; concierge; tour desk; car rentals; small marina w/sailboat. *In room:* A/C, minibar, safe-deposit box, bathrobes.

IXTAPA
You'll find many beachside resorts along Bahía del Palmar, on Bulevar Ixtapa. **NH Krystal** and **Barceló** are the standouts (below), but you may find better deals and have a similar overall experience next door

at the **Presidente Intercontinental** (© 755/553-0018; www.ixtapa. intercontinental.com), the **Dorado Pacifico** (© 755/553-2025; www.doradopacifico.com), or the **Hotel Emporio Ixtapa** (© 755/ 553-1066), which also offers Temazcal spa treatments.

VERY EXPENSIVE

Las Brisas Ixtapa ✦✦✦ Set above the high-rise hotels of Ixtapa on its own rocky promontory, Las Brisas is the most stunning of Ixtapa's hotels, and the most noted for gracious service. The austere but luxurious public areas, all in stone and stucco, exude an air of exclusivity. Minimalist luxury also characterizes the rooms, which have Mexican-tile floors and private, plant-decked patios with hammocks and lounges. All rooms face the hotel's cove and private beach, which, though attractive, is dangerous for swimming. The six master suites come with private pools, and the 16th floor is reserved for nonsmokers.

Bulevar Ixtapa, 40880 Ixtapa, Gro. © **800/228-3000** in the U.S., or 755/553-2121. Fax 755/553-1091. 423 units. High season $285 deluxe double, $490 Royal Beach Club; low season $196 deluxe double, $230 Royal Beach Club. AE, MC, V. **Amenities:** 5 restaurants; 3 bars (including lobby bar w/live music at sunset); 4 swimming pools (1 for children); 4 lighted tennis courts w/pro on request; fitness center; travel agency; car rental; shopping arcade; salon; room service; massage; babysitting; laundry service; elevator to secluded beach; 3 rooms for those w/limited mobility. *In room:* A/C, TV, minibar, hair dryer, safe-deposit box.

EXPENSIVE

Barceló Ixtapa ✦✦ This grand 12-story resort hotel (formerly the Sheraton) has large, handsomely furnished public areas facing the beach; it's an inviting place to sip a drink and people-watch. Most rooms have balconies with views of the ocean or the mountains. Nonsmoking rooms are available. Gardens surround the large pool, which has a swim-up bar and separate section for children. It's an excellent value and a great choice for families.

Bulevar Ixtapa, 40880 Ixtapa, Gro. © **800/325-3535** in the U.S. and Canada, or 755/553-1858. Fax 755/553-2438. www.barcelo.com. 331 units. High season $245 double all-inclusive, $180 double with breakfast only; low season $225 double all-inclusive. AE, DC, MC, V. **Amenities:** 4 restaurants; nightclub; lobby bar; weekly Mexican fiesta w/buffet and live entertainment; beachside pool; 4 tennis courts; fitness room; concierge; travel agency; car rental; salon; room service; laundry service; pharmacy/gift shop; rooms for those w/limited mobility. *In room:* A/C, TV, minibar.

NH Krystal Ixtapa ✦✦✦ *Kids* Krystal hotels are known in Mexico for quality rooms and service, and this was the original hotel in the chain. It upholds its reputation for welcoming, exceptional service. Many staff members have been with the hotel for its 20-some years of operation, and are on hand to greet return guests. It is probably the best hotel in the area for families. This large, V-shaped hotel has ample grounds and a terrific pool area, expanded in 2004. Each spacious, nicely furnished room has a balcony with an ocean view, game table, and tile bathroom. Master suites have large, furnished, triangular balconies. Some rates include a breakfast buffet. The center of Ixtapa nightlife is here, at Krystal's famed **Christine** dance club.

Bulevar Ixtapa s/n, 40880 Ixtapa, Gro. ℂ **800/231-9860** in the U.S., or 755/553-0333. Fax 755/553-0216. www.nh-hotels.com. 257 units. High season $190 double, $280 suite; low season $170 double, $255 suite. 2 children under 12 stay free in parent's room. Ask about special packages. AE, DC, MC, V. **Amenities:** 5 restaurants; lobby bar; nightclub; pool; tennis court; gym; kids' club; travel agency; car rental; salon; room service; massage; laundry service; racquetball court. *In room:* A/C, TV, minibar.

3 Where to Dine

ZIHUATANEJO

Zihuatanejo's **central market,** on Avenida Benito Juárez about 5 blocks inland from the waterfront, will whet your appetite for cheap and tasty food. It's best at breakfast and lunch, before the market activity winds down in the afternoon. Look for what's hot and fresh. The market area is one of the best on this coast for shopping and people-watching.

The town has several excellent **bakeries.** At **El Buen Gusto,** Guerrero 4, a half-block inland from the museum (ℂ **755/554-3231**), you'll find banana bread, French bread, doughnuts, and cakes. It's open daily from 8:00am to 10pm.

EXPENSIVE

Coconuts ⟨⟨⟨ *Finds* INTERNATIONAL/SEAFOOD   What a find! Not only is the food innovative and delicious, but the restaurant is also in a historic building—the oldest in Zihuatanejo. This popular restaurant in a tropical garden was the weigh-in station for Zihua's coconut industry in the late 1800s. "Fresh" is the operative word on this creative, seafood-heavy menu. Chef Patricia Cummings

---

Tips Beachside Dining That Doesn't Stink

Check out the scene on Playa Principal where the fisherman drag in their catch of the day and prepare it right on the beach—but the odor makes this a foul spot for dining. Head west along the beach, away from the fisherman, or try **Kau Kan** on Playa Madera, or **La Perla** on Playa La Ropa (see listings).

checks what's at the market, then uses only top-quality ingredients in dishes like seafood pâté and grilled filet of snapper Coconuts. The bananas flambé has earned a loyal following, with good reason. Expect friendly, efficient service here.

Augustín Ramírez 1 (at Vicente Guerrero). ✆ **755/554-2518** or 755/554-7980. Main courses $11–$34. AE, MC, V. High season daily 6–11pm. Closed during rainy season.

Kau-Kan ⟨⟨⟨ NUEVA COCINA/SEAFOOD   A stunning view of the bay is one of the many attractions of this refined restaurant. Stucco and whitewashed walls frame the simple, understated furniture. Head chef Ricardo Rodriguez supervises every detail, from the ultra-smooth background music that invites after-dinner conversation to the spectacular presentation of all the dishes. Baked potato with baby lobster and mahimahi *carpaccio* are two of my favorites, but I recommend you consider the daily specials—Ricardo always uses the freshest seafood and prepares it with great care. For dessert, pecan and chocolate cake served with dark chocolate sauce is simply delicious.

Camino a Playa La Ropa. ✆ **755/554-8446**. Main courses $9–$25. AE, MC, V. Daily 5–11:30pm. From downtown on the road to La Ropa, Kau-Kan is on the right side of the road past the 1st curve.

MODERATE

La Perla SEAFOOD   There are many *palapa*-style restaurants on Playa La Ropa, but La Perla, with tables under the trees and thatched roof, is the most popular. Somehow, the long stretch of pale sand and the group of wooden chairs under *palapas* combine with mediocre food and slow service to make La Perla a local tradition. Rumor has it that it is so hard to get the waiters' attention that you can get takeout food from a competitor and bring it here to eat, and they'll never notice. Still, it's considered the best spot for tanning and socializing.

Playa La Ropa. ✆ **755/554-2700**. Breakfast $4–$6.50; main courses $7.50–$24. AE, MC, V. Daily 9am–10pm; breakfast served 10am–noon. Near the southern end of La Ropa Beach, take the right fork in the road; there's a sign in the parking lot.

INEXPENSIVE

Casa Puntarenas MEXICAN/SEAFOOD   A modest spot with a tin roof and nine wooden tables, Puntarenas is one of the best places in town for fried whole fish served with toasted *bolillos* (crusty white-bread miniloaves), sliced tomatoes, onions, and avocado. The place is renowned for chiles rellenos, mild and stuffed with plenty of cheese; the meat dishes are less flavorful. Although it may appear a little too rustic for less experienced travelers, it is very clean, and the food is known for its freshness.

Moments   Dinner With a View At La Casa

La Casa Que Canta (p. 90) is a little gem of a luxury hotel that also serves authentic Mexican food. The menu is a bit pricey, but your jaw *will* drop when you see the view of the bay and the intimate outdoor setting. Make reservations early.

Calle Noria, Col. Lázaro Cárdenas. No phone. Main courses $4.50–$8.50. No credit cards. Daily 6:30–9pm. From the pier, turn left on Alvarez and cross the footbridge on your left. Turn right after you cross the bridge; the restaurant is on your left.

La Sirena Gorda MEXICAN   For one of the most popular breakfasts in town, head to La Sirena Gorda. It serves a variety of eggs and omelets, hotcakes with bacon, and fruit with granola and yogurt. The house specialty is seafood tacos—fish in a variety of sauces, plus lobster—but I consider them overpriced, at $4.50 and $25 respectively. A taco is a taco. I'd recommend something from the short list of daily specials, such as blackened red snapper, steak, or fish kabobs. The food is excellent, and patrons enjoy the casual sidewalk-cafe atmosphere.

Paseo del Pescador. ✆ 755/554-2687. Breakfast $2–$5.50; main courses $4.50–$12. MC, V. Thurs–Tues 7am–10pm. From the basketball court, face the water and walk to the right; La Sirena Gorda is on your right just before the town pier.

Nueva Zelanda MEXICAN   This open-air snack shop serves rich cappuccino sprinkled with cinnamon, fresh-fruit *licuados* (milkshakes), and pancakes with real maple syrup. The mainstays of the menu are *tortas* and enchiladas, and service is friendly and efficient. There's a second location in Ixtapa, in the back section of the Los Patios shopping center (✆ 755/553-0838).

Cuauhtémoc 23 (at Ejido). ✆ 755/554-2340. Tortas $3.50; enchiladas $5; *licuados* $2.50; cappuccino $2.50. No credit cards. Daily 8am–10pm. From the waterfront, walk 3 blocks inland on Cuauhtémoc; the restaurant is on your right.

IXTAPA
VERY EXPENSIVE

Villa de la Selva 🗲 MEXICAN/CONTINENTAL   Clinging to the edge of a cliff overlooking the sea, this elegant, romantic restaurant enjoys the most spectacular sea and sunset view in Ixtapa. The candlelit tables occupy three terraces; try to come early to get one of the best vistas, especially on the lower terrace. The cuisine is delicious, artfully presented, and classically rich. Filet Villa de la Selva is red snapper topped with shrimp and hollandaise sauce. Cold avocado soup or hot lobster bisque makes a good beginning; finish with chocolate mousse or bananas Singapore.

Paseo de la Roca. ℂ 755/553-0362. Reservations recommended during high season. Main courses $15–$44. AE, MC, V. Daily 6–11:30pm.

EXPENSIVE

Beccofino 𝓡𝓡𝓡 NORTHERN ITALIAN   This restaurant is a standout in Mexico. Owner Angelo Rolly Pavia serves the flavorful northern Italian specialties he grew up knowing and loving. The menu is strong on pasta. Ravioli, a house specialty, comes stuffed with seafood (in season). The garlic bread is terrific, and there's an extensive wine list. A popular place in a breezy marina location, the restaurant tends to be loud when it's crowded, which is often. It's also an increasingly popular breakfast spot.

Marina Ixtapa. ℂ 755/553-1770. Breakfast $5–$7; main courses $14–$30. AE, MC, V. Daily 9:30am–midnight.

MODERATE

Golden Cookie Shop 𝓡𝓡 PASTRIES/INTERNATIONAL Although the name is misleading—there are more than cookies here—Golden Cookie's freshly baked goods beg for a detour, and the coffee menu is the most extensive in town. Although prices are high for the area, the breakfasts are noteworthy, as are the deli sandwiches. Large sandwiches on fresh soft bread come with a choice of sliced meats. Chicken curry is among the other specialty items. An air-conditioned area is reserved for nonsmokers.

Los Patios Center. ℂ 755/553-0310. Breakfast $4–$6; sandwiches $4–$6; main courses $6–$8.50. MC, V. Daily 8am–3pm. Walk to the rear of the shopping center as you face Mac's Prime Rib; walk up the stairs, turn left, and you'll see the restaurant on your right.

Ruben's 𝓡𝓡𝓡 (Finds) BURGERS/VEGETABLES   The choices are easy here—you can order either a big, juicy burger made from top sirloin grilled over mesquite, or a foil-wrapped packet of baked potatoes, chayote, zucchini, or sweet corn. Ice cream, beer, and soda fill out the menu, which is posted on the wall by the kitchen. It's

---

Finds **Pozole: Not Just on Thursdays**

The Mexican soup *pozole* is traditionally served on Thursdays, but **Tamales y Atole Any**, Calle Ejido 38 (ℂ755/554-7373), a festive spot for casual lunch or dinner, serves it (red, white or green) Monday through Saturday. See p. 68.

kind of a do-it-yourself place: Patrons snare a waitress and order, grab their own drinks from the cooler, and tally their own tabs. Still, because of the ever-present crowds, it can be a slow process.

Plaza Los Portales. © 755/553-0055 or 755/553-0538. Burgers $4–$5; vegetables $2; ice cream $1.50. No credit cards. Daily noon–midnight.

4 Activities On & Off the Beach

The **Museo de Arqueología de la Costa Grande** (no phone) traces the history of the area from Acapulco to Ixtapa/Zihuatanejo (the Costa Grande) from pre-Hispanic times, when it was known as Cihuatlán, through the colonial era. Most of the museum's pottery and stone artifacts give evidence of extensive trade with far-off cultures and regions, including the Toltec and Teotihuacán near Mexico City, the Olmec on the Pacific and Gulf coasts, and areas known today as the states of Nayarit, Michoacán, and San Luis Potosí. Local indigenous groups gave the Aztec tribute items, including cotton *tilmas* (capes) and *cacao* (chocolate), representations of which can be seen here. This museum, in Zihuatanejo near Guerrero at the east end of Paseo del Pescador, easily merits the half-hour or less it takes to stroll through; signs are in Spanish, but an accompanying brochure is available in English. Admission is $1, and it's open Tuesday through Sunday from 9am to 6pm.

THE BEACHES

IN ZIHUATANEJO   At Zihuatanejo's town beach, **Playa Municipal,** the local fishermen pull their colorful boats up onto the sand, making for a fine photo op. The small shops and restaurants lining the waterfront are great for people-watching and absorbing the flavor of daily village life. **Playa Madera (Wood Beach),** just east of Playa Municipal, is open to the surf but generally peaceful. A number of attractive budget lodgings overlook this area.

South of Playa Madera is Zihuatanejo's largest and most beautiful beach, **Playa La Ropa** 🎏🎏, a long sweep of sand with a great view of the sunset. Some lovely small hotels and restaurants nestle in the hills; palm groves edge the shoreline. Although it's also open to the Pacific, waves are usually gentle. A taxi from town costs $3. The name Playa La Ropa (*ropa* means clothing) comes from an old tale of the sinking of a *galeón* during a storm. The silk clothing that it was carrying back from the Philippines washed ashore on this beach—hence the name.

The nicest beach for swimming, and the best for children, is the secluded **Playa Las Gatas (Cats Beach),** across the bay from Playa La Ropa and Zihuatanejo. The small coral reef just offshore is a nice spot for snorkeling and diving, and a little dive shop on the beach

Tips Beach Safety

All beaches in Zihuatanejo are safe for swimming. Undertow is rarely a problem, and the municipal beach is protected from the main surge of the Pacific. Beaches in Ixtapa are more dangerous for swimming, with frequent undertow problems.

rents gear. Shop owner Jean Claude is a local institution—and the only full-time resident of Las Gatas. He claims to offer special rates for female divers and has a collection of bikini tops on display. The waters at Las Gatas are exceptionally clear, without undertow or big waves. Open-air seafood restaurants on the beach make it an appealing lunch spot. Small *pangas* (launches) with shade run to Las Gatas from the Zihuatanejo town pier, a 10-minute trip; the captains will take you across whenever you wish between 8am and 4pm. Usually the last boat back leaves Las Gatas at 6:30pm, but check to be sure.

Playa Larga is a beautiful, uncrowded beach between Zihuatanejo and the airport, with several small *palapa* restaurants, hammocks, and wading pools.

IN IXTAPA Ixtapa's main beach, **Playa Palmar,** is a lovely white-sand arc on the edge of the Hotel Zone, with dramatic rock formations silhouetted in the sea. The surf can be rough; use caution, and don't swim when a red flag is posted. Several of the nicest beaches in the area are essentially closed to the public. Although by law all Mexican beaches are open to the public, it is common practice for hotels to create artificial barriers (such as rocks or dunes).

Club Med and Qualton Club have largely claimed **Playa Quieta,** on the mainland across from Isla Ixtapa. The remaining piece of beach was once the launching point for boats to Isla Ixtapa, but it is gradually being taken over by a private development. Isla Ixtapa–bound boats now leave from the jetty on **Playa Linda,** about 13km (8 miles) north of Ixtapa. Inexpensive water taxis ferry passengers to Isla Ixtapa. Playa Linda is the primary out-of-town beach, with watersports equipment and horse rentals available. **Playa las Cuatas,** a pretty beach and cove a few miles north of Ixtapa, and **Playa Majahua,** an isolated beach just west of Zihuatanejo, are both being transformed into resort complexes. Lovely **Playa Vista Hermosa** is framed by striking rock formations and bordered by the Las Brisas Hotel high on the hill. All of these are very attractive beaches for sunbathing or a stroll but have heavy surf and strong undertow. Use caution if you swim here.

WATERSPORTS & BOAT TRIPS

Probably the most popular boat trip is to **Isla Ixtapa** for snorkeling and lunch at the El Marlin restaurant, one of several on the island. You can book this outing as a tour through local travel agencies, or go on your own from Zihuatanejo by following the directions to Playa Linda above and taking a boat from there. Boats leave for Isla Ixtapa every 10 minutes between 11:30am and 5pm, so you can depart and return as you like. The round-trip boat ride is $3. Along the way, you'll pass dramatic rock formations and see in the distance **Los Morros de Los Pericos islands,** where a great variety of birds nest on the rocky points jutting out into the blue Pacific. On Isla Ixtapa, you'll find good snorkeling, diving, and other watersports. Gear is available for rent on the island. Be sure to catch the last water taxi back at 5pm, and double-check that time upon arrival on the island.

Local travel agencies can usually arrange day trips to Los Morros de Los Pericos islands for **birding,** though it's less expensive to rent a boat with a guide at Playa Linda. The islands are offshore from Ixtapa's main beach.

Sunset cruises on the sailboat *Nirvana,* arranged through **Yates del Sol** (© 755/554-2694 or 755/554-8270), depart from the Zihuatanejo town pier at Puerto Mío. The cruises cost $49 per person and include an open bar and hors d'oeuvres. There's also a day trip to **Playa Manzanillo** on the very comfortable, rarely crowded sailboat. It begins at 10am, costs $78 per person, and includes an open bar, lunch, and snorkeling gear. Schedules and special trips vary, so call for current information.

You can arrange **fishing trips** with the **boat cooperative** (© 755/554-2056) at the Zihuatanejo town pier. They cost $130 to $300, depending on boat size, trip length, and so on. Most trips last about 7 hours. The cooperative accepts Visa and MasterCard; paying cash saves you 20% tax, but don't expect a receipt. The price includes 10 soft drinks, 10 beers, bait, and fishing gear, but not lunch. You'll pay more for a trip arranged through a local travel agency. The least expensive trips are on small launches called *pangas;* most have shade. Both small-game and deep-sea fishing are offered. The fishing is adequate, though not on par with that of Mazatlán or Baja. Other trips combine fishing with a visit to the near-deserted ocean beaches that extend for miles along the coast. Sam Lushinsky at **Ixtapa Sport-fishing Charters,** 19 Depue Lane, Stroudsburg, PA 18360 (© 570/688-9466; fax 570/688-9554; www.ixtapasportfishing.com), is a noted outfitter. Prices range from $295 to $445 per day, for 8.4 to 13m (28–42 ft.) custom cruisers, fully equipped.

Boating and fishing expeditions from the new **Marina Ixtapa,** a bit north of the Ixtapa Hotel Zone, can also be arranged. As a rule, everything available in or through the marina is more expensive and more "Americanized."

Sailboats, Windsurfers, and other **watersports equipment** rentals are usually available at stands on Playa La Ropa, Playa las Gatas, Isla Ixtapa, and at the main beach, Playa Palmar, in Ixtapa. There's **para-sailing** at La Ropa and Palmar. **Kayaks** are available for rent at hotels in Ixtapa and some watersports operations on Playa La Ropa.

The PADI-certified **Carlo Scuba,** on Los Gatos Beach (① 755/554-6003; www.carloscuba.com), arranges **scuba-diving trips.** Fees start at $55 for a one-tank dive, or $80 for two dives, including all equipment and lunch. This shop has been around since 1962, and is very knowledgeable about the area, which has nearly 30 different dive sites, including walls and caves. Diving takes place year-round, though the water is clearest from May through December, when visibility is 30m (100 ft.) or better. The nearest decompression chamber is in Acapulco. Advance reservations for dives are advised during Christmas and Easter.

Surfing is particularly good at **Petacalco Beach** north of Ixtapa.

LAND SPORTS & ACTIVITIES

In **Ixtapa,** the **Club de Golf Ixtapa Palma Real** (① 755/553-1062 or 755/553-1163), in front of the Sheraton Hotel, has an 18-hole course designed by Robert Trent Jones, Jr. The greens fee is $75; caddies cost $19 for 18 holes, $13 for 9 holes; electric carts are $35; and clubs are $25. Tee times begin at 7am, but the course doesn't take reservations. The **Marina Ixtapa Golf Course** (① 755/553-1410; fax 755/553-0825), designed by Robert von Hagge, has 18 challenging holes. The greens fee is $85 and includes a cart; caddies cost $22, club rental $30. The first tee time is 7am. Call for reservations 24 hours in advance. Both courses accept American Express, MasterCard, and Visa.

In Ixtapa, the **Club de Golf Ixtapa** (① 755/553-1062 or 755/553-1163) and the **Marina Ixtapa Golf Course** (① 755/553-1410; fax 755/553-0825 or 755/553-1400) both have lighted public **tennis courts,** and both rent equipment. Fees are $6 to $20 an hour during the day, $9 to $30 at night. Call for reservations. The **Dorado Pacífico** and most of the other better hotels on the main beach in Ixtapa have courts.

For **horseback riding,** the largest local stable is located on **Playa Linda** (no phone), offering guided trail rides from the Playa Linda beach (about 13km/8 miles north of Ixtapa). It's just next to the pier where the water taxis debark to Isla Ixtapa. Groups of three or more riders can arrange their own tour, which is especially nice around sunset (though you'll need mosquito repellent). Riders can choose to trace the beach to the mouth of the river and back through coconut plantations, or hug the beach for the whole ride (which usually lasts 1–1½ hr.). The fee is around $30, cash only. Travel agencies in either town can arrange your trip but will charge a bit more for transportation. Reservations are suggested in high season. Another good place to ride is in Playa Larga. There is a ranch on the first exit coming from Zihuatanejo (no phone, but you can't miss it—it is the first corral to the right as you drive toward the beach). The horses are in excellent shape. The fee is $30 for 45 minutes. To arrange riding in advance, call Ignacio Mendiola, at © 755/559-8884 (cellphone, so locally, dial 044 before the number).

5 Shopping

ZIHUATANEJO

Zihuatanejo has its quota of T-shirt and souvenir shops, but it's becoming a better place to buy crafts, folk art, and jewelry. Shops are generally open Monday through Saturday from 10am to 2pm and 4 to 8pm. Many better shops close Sunday, but some smaller souvenir stands stay open, and hours vary.

The **artisans' market** on Calle Cinco de Mayo is a good place to start shopping before moving on to specialty shops. There's also a **municipal market** on Avenida Benito Juárez (about 5 blocks inland from the waterfront), but most vendors offer the same things—huaraches, hammocks, and baskets. The market sprawls over several blocks. Spreading inland from the waterfront some 3 or 4 blocks are numerous small shops well worth exploring.

Besides the places listed below, check out **Alberto's,** Cuauhtémoc 12 and 15 (no phone), for jewelry. Also on Cuauhtémoc, 2 blocks down from the Nueva Zelanda Coffee Shop, is a small shop that looks like a market stand and sells beautiful tablecloths, napkins, and other linens, all handmade in Aguascalientes.

Casa Marina This small complex extends from the waterfront to Alvarez near Cinco de Mayo and houses four shops, each specializing in handcrafted wares from all over Mexico. Items include handsome rugs, textiles, masks, colorful woodcarvings, and silver jewelry. Café

Marina, the small coffee shop in the complex, sells shelves and shelves of used paperback books in several languages. Open daily from 9am to 9pm during the high season, 10am to 2pm and 4 to 8pm the rest of the year. Paseo del Pescador 9. ✆ 755/554-2373. Fax 755/554-3533.

Coco Cabaña Collectibles   Located next to Coconuts restaurant, this impressive shop carries carefully selected crafts and folk art from across the country, including fine Oaxacan woodcarvings. Owner Pat Cummings once ran a gallery in New York, and the inventory reveals her discriminating eye. If you make a purchase, she'll cash your dollars at the going rate. Open Monday through Saturday from 10am to 2pm and 4 to 8pm; closed August and September. Guerrero and Alvarez, opposite the Hotel Citali. ✆ 755/554-2518.

Viva Zapatos   This shop carries bathing suits for every taste and shape, great casual and not-so-casual resort wear, sunglasses, and everything else for looking good in and out of the water. The store is three doors down from Amueblados Valle. It's open Monday through Saturday from 10am to 2pm and 5 to 9pm. Vicente Guerrero 33. No phone.

IXTAPA

Shopping in Ixtapa is not especially memorable, with T-shirts and Mexican crafts the usual wares. **Ferroni, Bye-Bye, Aca Joe,** and **Navale** sell brand-name sportswear. All of these shops are in the same area on Bulevar Ixtapa, across from the beachside hotels, and most are open daily from 9am to 2pm and 4 to 9pm.

La Fuente   This terrific shop carries gorgeous Talavera pottery, jaguar-shaped wicker tables, hand-blown glassware, masks, tin mirrors and frames, hand-embroidered clothing from Chiapas, and wood and papier-mâché miniatures. Open daily from 9am to 10pm during high season, daily from 10am to 2pm and 5 to 9pm in low season. Los Patios Center, Bulevar Ixtapa. ✆ 755/553-0812.

6 Zihuatanejo & Ixtapa After Dark

With an exception or two, Zihuatanejo nightlife dies down around 11pm or midnight. For a good selection of dance clubs, hotel fiestas, and fun watering holes with live music and dancing, head for Ixtapa. Note that the shuttle bus stops at 11pm, and a taxi to Zihuatanejo after midnight costs 50% more than the regular price. During the off season (after Easter and before Christmas), hours vary: Some places open only on weekends, while others close completely. The most popular hangout for local residents and expats is **Paccolo,** around the corner from Amueblados Valle.

IXTAPA'S CLUB & MUSIC SCENE

Many dance clubs stay open until the last customers leave, so hours vary. Most have a "ladies' night" (free for women) once a week.

Carlos 'n' Charlie's Knee-deep in nostalgia, bric-a-brac, silly sayings, and photos from the Mexican revolution, this restaurant-nightclub offers party ambience and good food. The eclectic menu includes iguana in season (with Alka-Seltzer and aspirin on the house). Out back by the beach is a partly shaded open-air section with a raised wooden platform for "pier dancing" at night. The restaurant is open daily from 10am to midnight; pier dancing is nightly from 9pm to 3am. Bulevar Ixtapa, just north of the Best Western Posada Real, Ixtapa. ℂ 755/553-0085. Cover (including drink tokens) after 9pm $10. No cover Sun–Fri during off season.

Christine This glitzy street-side dance club is famous for its mid-night light show, which features classical music played on a mega sound system. A semicircle of tables in tiers overlooks the dance floor. No sneakers, sandals, or shorts are allowed, and reservations are recommended during high season. Open daily at 10pm during high season. Off-season hours vary. In the NH Krystal, Bulevar Ixtapa, Ixtapa. ℂ 755/553-0456. Cover free–$20.

Señor Frog's A companion restaurant to Carlos 'n' Charlie's, Señor Frog's has several dining sections and a warehouselike bar with raised dance floors. Large speakers play rock 'n' roll, sometimes even prompting dinner patrons to shimmy by their tables between courses. The restaurant is open daily from 6pm to midnight; the bar is open until 3am. In the La Puerta Center, Bulevar Ixtapa, Ixtapa. ℂ 755/553-2282.

HOTEL FIESTAS & THEME NIGHTS

Many hotels hold Mexican fiestas and other special events that include dinner, drinks, live music, and entertainment for a fixed price (generally $36). The **Barceló Ixtapa** (ℂ 755/555-2000) stages a popular Wednesday night fiesta; the **NH Krystal** (ℂ 755/553-0333) and **Dorado Pacífico** (ℂ 755/553-2025) in Ixtapa also hold good fiestas. Only the Barceló Ixtapa offers them in the off season. Be sure you understand what your reservation price covers (drinks, tax, and tip are not always included).

The Oaxaca Coast: From Puerto Escondido to Huatulco

Coastal towns in Oaxaca are covered in this chapter. **Puerto Escondido,** noted for its celebrated surf break, laid-back village ambience, attractive and inexpensive inns, and nearby nature excursions, is a worthy destination and an exceptional value. It's 6 hours south of Acapulco on coastal Highway 200. Most people fly from Mexico City or drive up from Huatulco.

The **Bahías de Huatulco** encompass a total of nine bays—each lovelier than the last—on a pristine portion of Oaxaca's coast. Development of the area has been gradual and well planned, with great ecological sensitivity. The town of **Huatulco,** 128km (80 miles) south of Puerto Escondido, is emerging as Mexico's most authentic adventure-tourism haven. In addition to an 18-hole golf course and a handful of resort hotels, it offers a growing array of soft adventures that range from bay tours to diving, river rafting, and rappelling. Dining and nightlife remain limited, but the setting is beautiful and relaxing.

1 Puerto Escondido ★★★

368km (230 miles) SE of Acapulco; 240km (150 miles) NW of Salina Cruz; 80km (50 miles) NW of Puerto Angel

I consider Puerto Escondido (*pwer*-toh es-cohn-*dee*-doh) the best overall beach value in Mexico, from hotels to dining. Although it used to be known only as one of the world's top surf sites, today it's broadening its appeal. Think alternative therapies, great vegetarian restaurants, hip nightlife, awesome hotel and dining values, and some of the best coffee shops in Mexico. It's a place for those whose priorities include the dimensions of the surf break (big), the temperature of the beer (cold), the strength of the coffee (espresso), and the "OTA" (beach speak for "optimal tanning angle"). The young and very aware crowd that comes here measures time by the tides, and the pace is relaxed.

The location of "Puerto," as the locals call it, makes it an ideal jumping-off point for ecological explorations of neighboring jungle and estuary sanctuaries, as well as indigenous mountain settlements. Increasingly, it attracts those seeking both spiritual and physical renewal, with abundant massage and bodywork services, yoga classes, and exceptional and varied healthful dining options.

People come from the United States, Canada, and Europe to stay for weeks and even months—easily and inexpensively. Expats have migrated here from Los Cabos, Acapulco, and Puerto Vallarta seeking what originally attracted them to their former homes—stellar beaches, friendly locals, and low prices. Added pleasures include an absence of beach vendors and time-share sales, an abundance of English speakers, and terrific, inexpensive dining and nightlife.

This is a real place, not a produced resort. A significant number of visitors are European travelers, and it's common to hear a variety of languages on the beach and in the bars. Solo travelers will probably make new friends within an hour of arriving. There are still surfers here, lured by the best break in Mexico, but espresso cafes and live music are becoming just as ubiquitous.

The city has been dismissed as a colony of former hippies and settled backpackers, but it's so much more. I have a theory that those who favor "Puerto" are just trying to keep the place true to its name (*escondido* means "hidden") and undiscovered by tourists. Don't let them trick you—visit, and soon, before it, too, changes.

ESSENTIALS
GETTING THERE & DEPARTING
BY PLANE **Aerocaribe** (© 954/582-2023 or 954/582-3676), and **Aerovega** (© 954/582-2024 or -2023) operate daily flights to and from Oaxaca and Mexico City on small planes. Aerocaribe runs a morning and evening flight during high season; the fare is about $140 each way to Oaxaca. Aerovega flies to and from Oaxaca once daily. The price is about $100 each way. **Rodimar Travel** (see "Arriving," below) sells tickets to both.

If flights to Puerto Escondido are booked, you have the (possibly less expensive) option of flying into **Huatulco** on a scheduled or charter flight. This is especially viable if your destination is Puerto Angel, which lies between Puerto Escondido and Huatulco. An airport taxi costs $60 to Puerto Angel, $85 to Puerto Escondido. If you can find a local taxi, rather than a government-chartered cab, you can reduce these fares by about 50%, including the payment of a $5

Puerto Escondido

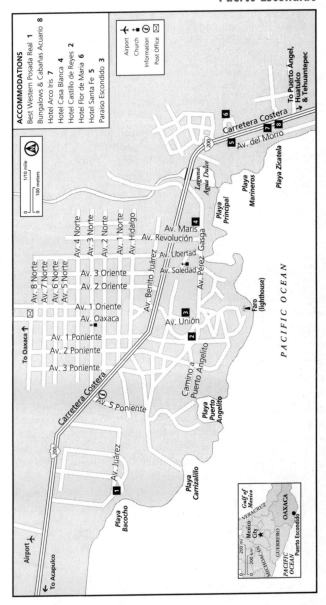

ACCOMMODATIONS

Best Western Posada Real **1**
Bungalows & Cabañas Acuario **8**
Hotel Arco Iris **7**
Hotel Casa Blanca **4**
Hotel Castillo de Reyes **2**
Hotel Flor de María **6**
Hotel Santa Fe **5**
Paraíso Escondido **3**

Airport ✈ Church ⚰ Information ⊙ Post Office ⊠

mandatory airport exit tax. There is frequent bus service between the three destinations. **Budget** (© 958/581-9000) at the Huatulco airport, has cars available for one-way travel to Puerto Escondido, with an added drop charge of about $10. In Puerto Escondido, Budget is at the entrance to Bacocho (© 954/582-0312).

Arriving: The Puerto Escondido **airport** (airport code: PXM) is about 4km (2½ miles) north of the center of town, near Playa Bacocho. The *colectivo* **minibus** to hotels costs $2.25 per person. **Aerotransportes Terrestres** sells *colectivo* tickets to the airport through **Rodimar Travel,** on pedestrian-only Avenida Pérez Gasga (© 954/582-0734; fax 954/582-0737), next to Hotel Casa Blanca. The minibus will pick you up at your hotel.

BY CAR From Oaxaca, Highway 175 via Pochutla is the least bumpy road. The 242km (150-mile) trip takes 5 to 6 hours. Highway 200 from Acapulco is also a good road and should take about 5 hours to travel. However, this stretch of road has been the site of numerous car and bus hijackings and robberies in recent years—travel only during the day.

From Salina Cruz to Puerto Escondido is a 4-hour drive, past the Bahías de Huatulco and the turnoff for Puerto Angel. The road is paved but can be rutty during the rainy season. The trip from Huatulco to Puerto Escondido takes just under 2 hours; you can easily hire a taxi for a fixed rate of about $50 an hour.

BY BUS Buses run frequently to and from Acapulco and Oaxaca, and south along the coast to and from Huatulco and Pochutla, the transit hub for Puerto Angel. Puerto Escondido's several bus stations are all within a 3-block area. For **Gacela** and **Estrella Blanca,** the station is just north of the intersection of the coastal highway and Pérez Gasga. First-class buses go from here to Pochutla, Huatulco, Acapulco, Zihuatanejo, and Mexico City. A block north at Hidalgo and Primera Poniente is **Transportes Oaxaca Istmo,** in a small restaurant. Several buses leave daily for Pochutla, Salina Cruz (5 hr.), and Oaxaca (10 hr. via Salina Cruz). The terminal for **Líneas Unidas, Estrella del Valle,** and **Oaxaca Pacífico** is 2 blocks farther down on Hidalgo, just past Oriente 3. They serve Oaxaca via Pochutla. From Primera Norte 207, **Cristóbal Colón** buses (© 954/582-1073) serve Salina Cruz, Tuxtla Gutiérrez, San Cristóbal de las Casas, and Oaxaca.

Arriving: Minibuses from Pochutla or Huatulco will let you off anywhere, including the spot where Pérez Gasga leads down to the pedestrians-only zone.

VISITOR INFORMATION

The **State Tourist Office, SEDETUR** (© **954/582-0175**), which has a very helpful staff, is about a half-mile from the airport at the corner of Carretera Costera and Bulevar Benito Juárez. It's open Monday through Friday from 9am to 5pm, Saturday from 9am to 2pm. A kiosk at the airport is open for incoming flights during high season; another, near the west end of the paved tourist zone, is open Monday through Saturday from 9am to 1pm.

CITY LAYOUT

Looking out on the Bahía Principal and its beach, to your left you'll see the eastern end of the bay, consisting of a small beach, **Playa Marineros,** followed by rocks jutting into the sea. Beyond this is **Playa Zicatela,** unmistakably the main surfing beach. Zicatela Beach has come into its own as the most popular area for visitors, with restaurants, bungalows, surf shops, and hotels, well back from the shoreline. The west side of the bay, to your right, is about a mile long, with a lighthouse and a long stretch of fine sand. Beaches on this end are not quite as accessible by land, but hotels are overcoming this difficulty by constructing beach clubs reached by steep private roads and jeep shuttles.

The town of Puerto Escondido has roughly an east-west orientation, with the long Zicatela Beach turning sharply southeast. Residential areas behind (east of) Zicatela Beach tend to have unpaved streets; the older town (with paved streets) is north of the Carretera Costera (Hwy. 200). The streets are numbered; Avenida Oaxaca divides east *(oriente)* from west *(poniente),* and Avenida Hidalgo divides north *(norte)* from south *(sur).*

South of this is the original **tourist zone,** through which Avenida Pérez Gasga makes a loop. Part of this loop is a paved pedestrians-only zone, known locally as the *Adoquín,* after the hexagonal bricks used in its paving. Hotels, shops, restaurants, bars, travel agencies, and other services are all here. In the morning, taxis, delivery trucks, and private vehicles may drive here, but at noon it closes to all but foot traffic.

Avenida Pérez Gasga angles down from the highway at the east end; on the west, where the Adoquín terminates, it climbs in a wide northward curve to cross the highway, after which it becomes Avenida Oaxaca.

The beaches—Playa Principal in the center of town and Marineros and Zicatela, southeast of the town center—are connected. It's easy to walk from one to the other, crossing behind the separating rocks.

Puerto Angelito, Carrizalillo, and Bacocho beaches are west of town and accessible by road or water. Playa Bacocho is where you'll find the few more expensive hotels.

GETTING AROUND

Almost everything is within walking distance of the Adoquín. **Taxis** around town are inexpensive; call © **954/582-0990** for service.

It's easy to hire a boat, and possible to walk beside the sea from the Playa Principal to the tiny beach of Puerto Angelito, though it's a bit of a hike.

FAST FACTS: Puerto Escondido

Area Code The telephone area code is **954**.

Currency Exchange Banamex, Bancomer, Bancrear, and Banco Bital all have branches in town, and all will change money during business hours; hours vary, but you can generally find one of the above open Monday through Saturday from 8am to 7pm. Automatic tellers are also available, as are currency-exchange offices.

Hospital **Unidad Médico–Quirúrgica del Sur,** Av. Oaxaca 113 (© **954/582-1288**), offers 24-hour emergency services and has an English-speaking staff and doctors.

Internet Access The restaurant **Un Tigre Azul,** on the Adoquín, has an excellent cybercafe on its second floor (© **954/582-2855**). It charges $2 for 30 minutes, $4 per hour for Internet access. It's open Monday through Friday from 8am to 10pm, Saturday and Sunday from 8 to 10pm. On Zicatela Beach, **Cyber-café** is a small, extremely busy Internet service at the entrance to the Bungalows & Cabañas Acuario, Calle de Morro s/n (© **954/582-0357**). It's open daily from 8am to 9pm and charges just $1.50 for 15 minutes, $3 for a half-hour, $5 per hour.

Pharmacy **Farmacia de Más Ahorro,** Avenida 1 Norte at Avenida 2 Poniente (© **954/582-1911**), is open until 2am.

Post Office The *correo,* on Avenida Oaxaca at the corner of Avenida 7 Norte (© **954/582-0959**), is open Monday through Friday from 8am to 3pm.

Safety Depending on whom you talk to, you need to be wary of potential beach muggings, primarily at night. New lighting at Playa Principal and Playa Zicatela has caused the crime rate to drop considerably. Local residents say most incidents happen after tourists overindulge and then go for a midnight stroll along the beach. Puerto is so casual that it's an easy place to let your guard down. Don't carry valuables, and use common sense and normal precautions.

Also, respect the power of the magnificent waves here. Drownings occur all too frequently.

Seasons Season designations are somewhat arbitrary, but most consider high season to be from mid-December to January, around and during Easter week, July and August, and other school and business vacations.

Telephones Numerous businesses offer long-distance telephone service. Many are along the Adoquín; several accept credit cards. The best bet remains a prepaid Ladatel phone card.

BEACH TIME
BEACHES

Playa Principal, where small boats are available for fishing and tour services, and **Playa Marineros,** adjacent to the town center on a deep bay, are the best swimming beaches. Beach chairs and sun shades rent for about $2, which may be waived if you order food or drinks from the restaurants that offer them. **Playa Zicatela,** which has lifeguards, adjoins Playa Marineros and extends southeast for several kilometers. The surfing part of Zicatela, with large curling waves, is about 2.5km (1½ miles) from the town center. Due to the size and strength of the waves, it's not a swimming beach, and only experienced surfers should attempt to ride Zicatela's powerful waves. Stadium-style lighting has been installed in both of these areas, in an attempt to crack down on nighttime beach muggings. It has diminished the appeal of the Playa Principal restaurants—patrons now look into the bright lights rather than at the sea. Lifeguard service has recently been added to Playa Zicatela.

Barter with one of the fishermen on the main beach for a ride to **Playa Manzanillo** and **Puerto Angelito,** two beaches separated by a rocky outcropping. Here, and at other small coves just west of town, swimming is safe and the overall pace is calmer than in town. You'll also find *palapas,* hammock rentals, and snorkeling equipment. The clear blue water is perfect for snorkeling. Local entrepreneurs cook fresh fish, tamales, and other Mexican dishes right at the beach. Puerto Angelito is also accessible by a dirt road that's a short distance from town, so it tends to be busier. **Playa Bacocho** is on a shallow

Ecotours & Other Adventurous Explorations

An exceptional provider of ecologically oriented tour services is **Ana's Eco Tours** 🌟🌟, in Un Tigre Azul restaurant, on the Adoquín (© 954/582-2001). Ana Marquez was born in the small nearby mountain village of Jamiltepec, and has an intimate knowledge of the customs, people, flora, and fauna of the area. She and her expert guides lead small groups on both eco-adventures and cultural explorations. Tours into the surrounding mountains include a 5-hour horseback excursion up to the jungle region of the Chatino natives' **healing hot springs,** or to **Nopala,** a Chatino mountain village, and a neighboring coffee plantation. An all-day trip to **Jamiltepec** (a small, traditional Mixtex village) offers the opportunity to experience day-to-day life in an authentic village. It includes a stop at a market, church, and cemetery, and visits to the homes of local artisans.

Turismo Dimar Travel Agency, on the landward side just inside the Adoquín (© 954/582-0734; fax 954/582-1551; daily 8am–10pm), is another excellent source of information and can arrange all types of tours and travel. Manager Gaudencio Díaz speaks English and can arrange individualized tours or more organized ones, such as **Michael Malone's Hidden**

cove farther northwest and is best reached by taxi or boat, rather than on foot. It's also the location of Coco's Beach Club at the Posada Real Hotel. A charge of $2.50 gives you access to pools, food and beverage service, and facilities.

SURFING

Zicatela Beach, 2.5km (1½ miles) southeast of Puerto Escondido's town center, is a world-class surf spot. A surfing competition in August and Fiesta Puerto Escondido, held for at least 3 days each November, celebrate Puerto Escondido's renowned waves. The tourism office can supply dates and details. Beginning surfers often start out at Playa Marineros before graduating to Zicatela's awesome waves.

NESTING RIDLEY TURTLES

The beaches around Puerto Escondido and Puerto Angel are nesting grounds for the endangered Ridley turtle. During the summer,

Voyages Ecotours. Malone, a Canadian ornithologist, leads dawn and sunset trips to **Manialtepec Lagoon,** a bird-filled mangrove lagoon about 19km (12 miles) northwest of Puerto Escondido. The tour ($32) includes a stop on a secluded beach for a swim.

One of the most popular all-day tours offered by both companies is to **Chacahua Lagoon National Park,** about 67km (42 miles) west. It costs $38 with Dimar, $25 with Ana's. These are true ecotours—small groups treading lightly. You visit a beautiful sandy spit of beach and the lagoon, which has incredible bird life and flowers, including black orchids. Locals provide fresh barbecued fish on the beach. If you know Spanish and get information from the tourism office, it's possible to stay overnight under a small *palapa,* but bring plenty of insect repellent.

Fishermen keep their colorful *pangas* (small boats) on the beach beside the Adoquín. A **fisherman's tour** around the coastline in a *panga* costs about $39, but a ride to Zicatela or Puerto Angelito beaches is only $5. Most hotels offer or will gladly arrange tours to meet your needs.

tourists can sometimes see the turtles laying eggs or observe the hatchlings trekking to the sea.

Escobilla Beach near Puerto Escondido and **Barra de la Cruz Beach** near Puerto Angel seem to be the favored nesting grounds of the Ridley turtle. In 1991, the Mexican government established the Centro Mexicano la Tortuga, known locally as the **Turtle Museum.** On view are examples of all species of marine turtles living in Mexico, plus six species of freshwater turtles and two species of land turtles. The center (no phone) is on **Mazunte Beach** ⓐ, near the town of the same name. Hours are from 10am to 4:30pm Tuesday through Saturday, from 10am to 2pm Sunday; admission is $2.50. The museum has a unique shop that sells excellent naturally produced shampoos, bath oils, and other personal-care products. All are made and packaged by the local community as part of a project to replace lost income from turtle poaching. Buses go to Mazunte from Puerto

Angel about every half-hour, and a taxi ride is around $5.50. You can fit this in with a trip to Zipolite Beach (see "Puerto Angel: Backpacking Beach Haven," later in this chapter). Buses from Puerto Escondido don't stop in Mazunte; you can cover the 65km (40 miles) in a taxi or rental car.

AN UNUSUAL SPA EXPERIENCE

For terrific massage services—the ideal answer to a day spent in pounding surf—**Espacio Meditativo Temazcalli,** Calle Temazcalli, corner of Av. Infraganti (© **954/582-1023;** www.temazcalli.com), is the place to go. A variety of therapeutic massages range in price from $15 to $32. There are also Body Beauty treatments ($27–$33) and facials ($27), designed to minimize the effects of too much sun. Bioenergetic Balance Techniques and the indigenous Mexican Temazcal steam bath (both individual and group), are added treatments, designed to purify body and soul. The center is a tranquil haven, lushly landscaped, with the sound of the nearby ocean prevalent in the treatment areas. On full-moon nights, they feature a special group Temazcal ceremony, a truly fascinating experience!

SHOPPING

During high season, businesses and shops are generally open all day. During low season, they close between 2 and 5pm.

The Adoquín holds a row of tourist shops selling straw hats, postcards, and T-shirts, plus a few excellent shops featuring Guatemalan, Oaxacan, and Balinese clothing and art. You can also get a tattoo or rent surfboards and boogie boards. Interspersed among the shops, hotels, restaurants, and bars are pharmacies and minimarkets. The largest of these is **Oh! Mar,** Av. Pérez Gasga 502. It sells anything you'd need for a day at the beach, plus phone (Ladatel) cards, stamps, and Cuban cigars, has a mail drop box, and arranges fishing tours.

Highlights along the Adoquín include **Central Surf,** which has a shop on the Adoquín (© **954/582-0568;** www.centralsurfshop.com) and another on Zicatela Beach, Calle del Morro s/n (© **954/582-2285**). They rent and sell surfboards, offer surf lessons, and sell related gear. **Un Tigre Azul,** Av. Pérez Gasga s/n (© **954/582-2954**), is the only true art gallery in town, with quality work and a cafe-bar, plus Internet service upstairs.

Also of interest is **Bazar Santa Fe** *ββ*, Hotel Santa Fe lobby, Calle del Morro s/n, Zicatela Beach (© **954/582-0170**), which sells antiques, including vintage Oaxacan embroidered clothing, jewelry, and religious artifacts. At **Bikini Brazil,** Calle del Morro s/n (no phone), you'll find the hottest bikinis under the sun imported from

Brazil, land of the *tanga* (string bikini). **ego Hardcore Wear,** located on Zicatela Beach, between Bungalows Acali and Hotel Arco Iris, has the hottest selection of surf and babe-wear. It's open daily from 10am to 8pm; no phone. Adjacent to ego is the **360 Surf Shop,** which sells everything for your out-of-town surf needs, as well as sells, trades, and rents boards. Board rentals start at $10 per day, with lessons available for $20. They don't have a phone number, but you can contact them by e-mailing 360@puertoconnection.com. In front of the Rockaway Resort on Zicatela Beach, there's a 24-hour **mini-super** (no phone) that sells the necessities: beer, suntan lotion, and basic food.

WHERE TO STAY
MODERATE

Best Western Posada Real *(Kids)*   On a cliff top overlooking the beach, the expanse of manicured lawn that backs this hotel is one of the most popular places in town for a sunset cocktail. The smallish standard rooms are less enticing than the hotel grounds. A big plus here is Coco's Beach Club, with a half-mile stretch of soft-sand beach, large swimming pool, playground, and bar with occasional live music. A shuttle ride (or a lengthy walk down a set of stairs) will take you there. This is a great place for families, and it's open to the public (nonguests pay $2.50 to enter). The hotel is 5 minutes from the airport and about the same from Puerto Escondido's tourist zone, but you'll need a taxi to get to town.

Av. Benito Juárez 1, Fracc. Bacocho, 71980 Puerto Escondido, Oax. © **800/528-1234** in the U.S., or 954/582-0133. Fax 01-800/719-5236. 100 units. High season $120 double; low season $104 double. AE, MC, V. **Amenities:** 2 restaurants; lobby bar; beach club w/food service; 2 swimming pools; wading pool; putting green; tennis courts; travel agency; car rental; laundry service. *In room:* A/C, TV, hair dryer, safe-deposit box.

Hotel Santa Fe *(Finds)*   If Puerto Escondido is the best beach value in Mexico, then the Santa Fe is without a doubt one of the best hotel values in Mexico. It boasts a winning combination of unique Spanish-colonial style, a welcoming staff, and comfortable rooms. The hotel has grown up with the surfers who came to Puerto in the 1960s and 1970s and nostalgically return today. It's a half-mile southeast of the town center, off Highway 200, at the curve in the road where Marineros and Zicatela beaches join—a prime sunset-watching spot. The three-story hacienda-style buildings have clay-tiled stairs, archways, and blooming bougainvillea. They surround two courtyard swimming pools. The ample but simply stylish rooms feature large tile bathrooms, colonial furnishings, hand-woven fabrics, Guerrero pottery lamps, and both air-conditioning and ceiling fans. Most have a balcony or terrace, with ocean views from upper floors. Bungalows are next to the hotel; each has a living room, kitchen, and bedroom with two double beds. The restaurant (see "Where to Dine," below) is one of the best on the southern Pacific coast.

Calle del Morro (Apdo. Postal 96), 71980 Puerto Escondido, Oax. ✆ 954/582-0170 or 954/582-0266. Fax 954/582-0260. info@hotelsantafe.com.mx. 61 units, 8 bungalows. High season $100 double, $120 bungalow; low season $78 double, $100 bungalow. AE, MC, V. Free parking. **Amenities:** Restaurant; bar; swimming pool; lap pool; tour service; massage; babysitting; laundry. *In room:* A/C, TV, safe-deposit box.

Paraíso Escondido 🌟🌟🌟 *(Finds* This eclectic inn is hidden away on a shady street a couple of short blocks from the Adoquín and Playa Principal. A curious collection of Mexican folk art, masks, religious art, and paintings make this an exercise in Mexican magic realism, in addition to a tranquil place to stay. An inviting pool— surrounded by gardens, Adirondack chairs, and a fountain—affords a commanding view of the bay. The immaculate rooms each have one double and one twin bed, built-in desks, and a cozy balcony or terrace with French doors. The suites have much plusher decor than the rooms, with recessed lighting, desks set into bay windows, living areas, and large private balconies. The penthouse suite has a whirlpool tub and kitchenette, a tile chessboard inlaid in the floor, and murals adorning the walls—it is the owners' former apartment.

Calle Unión 10, 71980 Puerto Escondido, Oax. ✆ 954/582-0444. 25 units. $45–$77 double; $150 suite. No credit cards. Limited free parking. **Amenities:** Restaurant; bar; pool; tour desk. *In room:* A/C.

INEXPENSIVE

Bungalows & Cabañas Acuario 🌟 Facing Zicatela Beach, this surfer's sanctuary offers cheap accommodations plus an on-site gym, surf shop, vegetarian restaurant, and Internet cafe. The two-story hotel and bungalows surround a pool shaded by great palms. Rooms are small and basic; bungalows offer fundamental kitchen facilities but don't have air-conditioning. The cabañas are more open and have hammocks. The adjoining commercial area has public telephones, money exchange, a pharmacy, and a vegetarian restaurant. The well-equipped gym costs an extra $1 per day, $15 per month. If you're traveling during low season, you can probably negotiate a better deal than the rates listed below once you're there.

Calle del Morro s/n, 71980 Puerto Escondido, Oax. ✆ 954/582-0357 or 954/582-1027. 40 units. High season $55 double, $70 double with A/C, $93 bungalow; low season $25 double, $34 double with A/C, $40 bungalow. No credit cards. **Amenities:** Restaurant; gym.

Hotel Arco Iris ⭐ *(Value)*   Rooms at the Arco Iris are in a three-story colonial-style house that faces Zicatela Beach. Each is simple yet comfortable, with a spacious terrace or balcony with hangers for hammocks—all have great views, but the upstairs ones are better. Beds are draped with mosquito nets, and bedspreads are made with beautifully worked Oaxacan textiles. La Galera bar has one of the most popular happy hours in town, daily from 5 to 7pm, with live music during high season. Ample free parking for cars and campers is available.

Calle del Morro s/n, Playa Zicatela, 71980 Puerto Escondido, Oax. ℭ **954/582-0432.** Fax 954/582-2963. www.puertoconnection.com/arco.html. 26 units, 8 bungalows. $42–$46 double; $46–$50 double with kitchen. Extra person $4. Rates 10%–20% higher at Easter and Christmas. MC, V. **Amenities:** Restaurant; bar; pool; wading pool; TV/game room w/foreign channels; tour desk; drugstore; on-call medical services.

Hotel Casa Blanca ⭐ *(Value)*   If you want to be in the heart of the Adoquín, this is your best bet for excellent value and ample accommodations. The courtyard pool and adjacent *palapa* restaurant make great places to hide away and enjoy a margarita or a book from the hotel's exchange rack. The bright, simply furnished rooms offer a choice of bed combinations, but all have at least two beds and a fan. Some rooms have both air-conditioning and a minifridge. The best rooms have a balcony overlooking the action in the street below, but light sleepers should consider a room in the back. Some rooms accommodate up to five ($60). This is an excellent and economical choice for families.

Av. Pérez Gasga 905, 71980 Puerto Escondido, Oax. ℭ **954/582-0168.** 21 units. $29 double; $84 double with A/C. MC, V. **Amenities:** Restaurant; pool; tour desk; car rental; room service; in-room massage; safe-deposit boxes; money exchange. *In room:* TV.

Hotel Castillo de Reyes   Proprietor Don Fernando has a knack for making his guests feel at home. Guests chat around tables on a shady patio near the office. Most of the bright, white-walled rooms have a special touch—perhaps a gourd mask or carved coconut hanging over the bed, plus over-bed reading lights. The rooms are shaded from the sun by palms and cooled by fans. The "castle" is on your left as you ascend the hill on Pérez Gasga, after leaving the Adoquín (you can also enter Pérez Gasga off Hwy. 200). This hotel is on one of Puerto's busiest streets, so traffic noise is a consideration.

Av. Pérez Gasga s/n, 71980 Puerto Escondido, Oax. ℭ **954/582-0442.** 18 units. High season $25 double; low season $15 double. No credit cards. **Amenities:** Safe-deposit box; money exchange.

Hotel Flor de María   Though not right on the beach, this hotel offers a welcoming place to stay. This cheery, three-story hotel faces the ocean, which you can see from the rooftop. Built around a garden courtyard, each room is colorfully decorated with beautiful *trompe l'oeil* still lifes and landscapes. Two rooms have windows with a view, and the rest face the courtyard. All have double beds with orthopedic mattresses. The roof has a small pool, a shaded hammock terrace, and an open-air bar (open 5–9pm during high season) with a TV that receives American channels—all in all, a great sunset spot. The hotel is a third of a mile from the Adoquín, 60m (200 ft.) up a sandy road from Marineros Beach on an unnamed street at the eastern end of the beach.

Playa Marineros, 71980 Puerto Escondido, Oax. ℭ/fax **954/582-0536**. 24 units. $35–$50 double. Ask about off-season long-term discounts. MC, V. **Amenities:** Restaurant; bar; small pool.

WHERE TO DINE

In addition to the places listed below, a Puerto Escondido tradition is the *palapa* restaurants on Zicatela Beach, for early-morning surfer breakfasts or casual dining and drinking at night. One of the most popular is **Los Tíos,** offering very reasonable prices and surfer-size portions. After dinner, enjoy homemade Italian ice cream from **Gelateria Giardino.** It has two locations, on Calle del Morro at Zicatela Beach, and Pérez Gasga 609, on the Adoquín (ℭ **954/582-2243**).

MODERATE

Art & Harry's   SEAFOOD/STEAKS   About 1.2km (¾ mile) southeast of the Hotel Santa Fe, on the road fronting Zicatela Beach, this robust watering hole is great for taking in the sunset, especially if you're having a giant hamburger or grilled shrimp dinner. Late afternoon and early evening here affords the best portrait of Puerto Escondido. Watch surfers, tourists, and the resident cat all slip into lazy silhouette as the sun dips into the ocean.

Av. Morro s/n. No phone. Main courses $4.50–$15. No credit cards. Daily 10am–10pm.

Cabo Blanco ᗱᗱ INTERNATIONAL   "Where Legends are Born" is the logo at this beachside restaurant, and the local crowd craves Gary's special sauces, which top his grilled fish, shrimp, steaks, and ribs. Favorites include dill–Dijon mustard, wine-fennel, and Thai curry sauces. But you can't count on them, because Gary creates based on what's fresh. A bonus is that Cabo Blanco turns into a hot Zicatela Beach bar, with live music Thursday and Saturday after

11pm. Gary's wife, Roxana, and a top-notch team of bartenders keep the crowd well served and well behaved.

Calle del Morro s/n. © **954/582-0337.** Main courses $7–$45. V. Dec–Apr daily 6pm–2am. Closed May–Nov.

Restaurant Santa Fe 🌟🌟🌟 *(Finds)* INTERNATIONAL The atmosphere here is classic and casual, with great views of the sunset and Zicatela Beach. Big pots of palms are scattered around and fresh flowers grace the tables, all beneath a lofty *palapa* roof. The shrimp dishes are a bargain for the rest of the world, at $15, but a little higher-priced than elsewhere in town. Perfectly grilled tuna, served with homemade french-fried potatoes and whole-grain bread, is an incredible meal for under $10. A *nopal* (cactus leaf) salad on the side ($2.50) is a perfect complement. Vegetarian dishes are reasonably priced and creatively adapted from traditional Mexican and Italian dishes. A favorite is the house specialty, chiles rellenos. The bar offers an excellent selection of tequilas.

In the Hotel Santa Fe, Calle del Morro s/n. © **954/582-0170.** Breakfast $4.50–$6; main courses $5–$15. AE, MC, V. Daily 7am–11pm.

INEXPENSIVE

Arte la Galería 🌟🌟 INTERNATIONAL/SEAFOOD At the east end of the Adoquín, La Galería offers a satisfying range of eats in a cool, creative setting. Dark-wood beams tower above, contemporary works by local artists grace the walls, and jazz music plays. Specialties are homemade pastas and brick-oven pizzas, but burgers and steaks are also available. Cappuccino and espresso, plus desserts such as baked pineapples, finish the meal. Two years ago, La Galería opened a second location in Playa Zicatela (next to Arco Iris Hotel, see above; no phone). Beautifully decorated with tiny mosaic tiles on the bar and in the bathrooms, the second Galería serves up the same great fare in a beautiful garden setting.

Av. Pérez Gasga. © **954/582-2039.** Breakfast $2.50–$3; main courses $4–$13. No credit cards. Daily 8am–midnight.

Carmen's Cafecito 🌟🌟 *(Value)* FRENCH PASTRY/SEAFOOD/ VEGETARIAN/COFFEE Carmen's second shop opened a few years ago on Zicatela Beach, with the motto "Big waves, strong coffee!" Featuring all the attractions of Carmen's La Patisserie (below), it also serves lunch and dinner. This restaurant spans two facing corners. The northern corner is set up for coffee or a light snack, with oceanfront bistro-style seating. The southern corner, a more relaxed setting, has wicker chairs and Oaxacan cloth–topped tables under a *palapa* roof. Giant shrimp dinners cost less than $6, and creative daily specials are always a sure bet. An oversize mug of cappuccino is $1.20, and a mango éclair—worth any price—is a steal at $1.

Calle del Morro s/n, Playa Zicatela. © 954/582-0516. Pastries 50¢–$1.50; main courses $2.10–$5.70. No credit cards. Wed–Mon 6am–10pm.

Carmen's La Patisserie 🐦🐦 FRENCH PASTRY/SANDWICHES/ COFFEE   This tiny, excellent cafe and bakery attracts a loyal clientele. Carmen's baked goods are unforgettable and sell quickly, so arrive early for the best selection. She also provides space for an English-speaking AA group. La Patisserie is across the street from the Hotel Flor de María.

Playa Marineros. No phone. Pastries 60¢–$1.50; sandwiches $2.10–$2.70. No credit cards. Mon–Sat 7am–3pm; Sun 7am–noon.

El Jardín 🐦🐦 *Value* VEGETARIAN/COFFEE   Located in front of the Bungalows Acuario, this popular vegetarian restaurant (formerly El Gota Vida) facing Zicatela Beach is generally packed. It's known for its healthy food, ample portions, and low prices. Under a *palapa* roof, it offers an extensive menu that includes fruit smoothies, espresso drinks, herbal teas, and a complete juice bar. The restaurant makes its own tempeh, tofu, pastas, and whole-grain breads. Creative vegetarian offerings are based on Mexican favorites, like chiles rellenos, cheese enchiladas, and bean tostadas. El Jardín also features fresh seafood.

Calle del Morro s/n, Playa Zicatela. No phone. Main courses $1.80–$5.40. No credit cards. Daily 10am–11pm.

Herman's Best *Value* MEXICAN/SEAFOOD   This small restaurant's atmosphere is about as basic as it comes, but clearly Herman's is putting all its attention into the kitchen—offering simply delicious, home-style cooking. The menu changes daily, but generally includes a fresh fish filet, rotisserie chicken, and Mexican staples like enchiladas—all served with beans, rice, and homemade tortillas. Herman's Best is just outside the pedestrian-only zone at the eastern end of the Adoquín.

Av. Pérez Gasga s/n. No phone. Main courses $1.80–$4.20. No credit cards. Mon–Sat 5–10pm.

Un Tigre Azul SANDWICHES/COFFEE/MEXICAN   This place is primarily known for its lower-level art gallery and Internet access, but climb on up to the third floor and enjoy the view overlooking Playa Principal and the ambience of the casual, colorful cafe. It's near the western entrance to the Adoquín. The light fare includes que-sadillas, nachos, fruit smoothies, and sandwiches. There's also excellent coffee and a full bar. Happy hour is every night from 7 to 8pm.

Av. Pérez Gasga s/n. ✆ 954/582-2954. Breakfast $2–$4; sandwiches $2–$5. AE, MC, V. Mon–Fri 11am–11pm; Sat–Sun 3–11pm.

PUERTO ESCONDIDO AFTER DARK

Sunset-watching is a ritual to plan your days around, and good lookout points abound. Watch the surfers at Zicatela and catch up on local gossip at **La Galera,** on the third floor of the Arco Iris hotel. It has a nightly happy hour (with live music during high season) from 5 to 7pm. Other great sunset spots are the **Hotel Santa Fe,** at the junction of Zicatela and Marineros beaches, and the rooftop bar of **Hotel Flor de María.** For a more tranquil, romantic setting, take a cab or walk a half-hour or so west to the cliff-top lawn of the **Hotel Posada Real.**

Puerto's nightlife will satisfy anyone dedicated to late nights and good music. Most nightspots are open until 3am or until the customers leave. **El Son y la Rumba** features live jazz, by its house band, each night from 8 to 11pm. It switches over to DJs playing house music Wednesdays through Saturdays, after 11pm. The cover is $1.20. It's beneath the Un Tigre Azul, on the western end of the Adoquín. Also downtown is **Tequila Sunrise,** a spacious two-story dance club overlooking the beach. It plays Latino, reggae, *cumbia,* tropical, and salsa. It's a half-block from the Adoquín on Avenida Marina Nacional. A small cover charge ($1.20–$2.40) generally applies.

The Adoquín offers an ample selection of clubs. Among the favorites are **BarFly,** and located across the street, **Wipeout,** a multilevel club that packs in the crowds until 4am. **The Blue Iguana** and **Rayos X** cater to a younger surf crowd with alternative and techno tunes. **Montezuma's Revenge** has live bands that usually play contemporary Latin American music. **El Tubo** is an open-air beachside dance club just west of Restaurant Alicia on the Adoquín.

On Zicatela Beach, don't miss **Cabo Blanco** 🅰🅰 (see "Where to Dine," above), where local musicians get together and jam on Thursday and Saturday during high season, alternating with DJs. An added draw are the complimentary snacks with drink purchase, in the style of Mexico's cantina tradition. **Split Coco,** a few doors down, has live music on Tuesday and Friday, and TV sports on other nights. It has one of the most popular happy hours on the beach, and also serves barbecue.

2 Puerto Angel: Backpacking Beach Haven

Eighty kilometers (50 miles) southeast of Puerto Escondido and 48km (30 miles) northwest of the Bays of Huatulco is the tiny fishing port of **Puerto Angel** (*pwer*-toh *ahn*-hehl). Puerto Angel, with its beautiful beaches, unpaved streets, and budget hotels, is popular with the international backpacking set and those seeking an inexpensive and restful vacation. Repeated hurricane damage and the 1999 earthquake took its toll on the village, driving the best accommodations out of business, but Puerto Angel continues to attract visitors. Its small bay and several inlets offer peaceful swimming and good snorkeling. The village's way of life is slow and simple: Fishermen leave very early in the morning and return with their catch before noon. Taxis make up most of the traffic, and the bus from Pochutla passes every half-hour or so.

ESSENTIALS
GETTING THERE & DEPARTING
BY CAR North or south from Highway 200, take coastal Highway 175 inland to Puerto Angel. The road is well marked with signs to Puerto Angel. From Huatulco or Puerto Escondido, the trip should take about an hour.

BY TAXI Taxis are readily available to take you to Puerto Angel or Zipolite Beach for a reasonable price, or to the Huatulco airport or Puerto Escondido.

BY BUS There are no direct buses from Puerto Escondido or Huatulco to Puerto Angel; however, numerous buses leave Puerto Escondido and Huatulco for Pochutla, 11km (7 miles) north of Puerto Angel. Take the bus to Pochutla, then switch to a bus going to Puerto Angel. If you arrive in Pochutla from Huatulco or Puerto Escondido, you may be dropped at one of several bus stations that line the main street; walk 1 or 2 blocks toward the large sign reading POSADA DON JOSE. The buses to Puerto Angel are in the lot just before the sign.

Tips Important Travel Note

Although car and bus hijackings along Highway 200 north to Acapulco have greatly decreased (thanks to improved security measures and police patrols), you're still wise to travel this road only during the day.

ORIENTATION

The town center is only about 4 blocks long, oriented more or less east-west. There are few signs in the village, and off the main street much of Puerto Angel is a narrow sand-and-dirt path. The navy base is toward the west end of town, just before the creek crossing toward Playa Panteón (Cemetery Beach).

Puerto Angel has several public (Ladatel) telephones that use widely available prepaid phone cards. The closest bank is **Bancomer** in Pochutla, which changes money Monday through Friday from 9am to 6pm, Saturday from 9am to 1pm. The **post office** *(correo),* open Monday through Friday from 9am to 3:30pm, is on the curve as you enter town.

BEACHES, WATERSPORTS & BOAT TRIPS

The golden sands and peaceful village life of Puerto Angel are all the reasons you'll need to visit. Playa Principal, the main beach, lies between the Mexican navy base and the pier that's home to the local fishing fleet. Near the pier, fishermen pull their colorful boats onto the beach and unload their catch in the late morning while trucks wait to haul it off to processing plants in Veracruz. The rest of the beach seems light years from the world of work and commitments. Except on Mexican holidays, it's relatively deserted. It's important to note that Pacific Coast currents deposit trash on Puerto Angel beaches. The locals do a fairly good job of keeping it picked up, but the currents are constant.

Playa Panteón is the main swimming and snorkeling beach. Cemetery Beach, ominous as that sounds, is about a 15-minute walk from the center, straight through town on the main street that skirts the beach. The *panteón* (cemetery), on the right, is worth a visit—it holds brightly colored tombstones and equally brilliant blooming bougainvillea.

In Playa Panteón, some of the *palapa* restaurants and a few of the hotels rent snorkeling and scuba gear and can arrange boat trips, but they tend to be expensive. Check the quality and condition of gear—particularly scuba gear—that you're renting.

Playa Zipolite (see-poh-*lee*-teh) and its village are 6km (4 miles) down a paved road from Puerto Angel. Taxis charge less than $2. You can catch a *colectivo* on the main street in the town center and share the cost.

Zipolite is well known as a good surf break and as a nude beach. Although public nudity (including topless sunbathing) is technically illegal, it's allowed here—this is one of only a handful of beaches in

Mexico that permits it. This sort of open-mindedness has attracted an increasing number of young European travelers. Most sunbathers concentrate beyond a large rock outcropping at the far end of the beach. Police will occasionally patrol the area, but they are much more intent on drug users than on sunbathers. The ocean and currents here are quite strong (that's why the surf is so good!), and a number of drownings have occurred over the years—know your limits. There are places to tie up a hammock and a few *palapa* restaurants for a light lunch and a cold beer.

Hotels in Playa Zipolite are basic and rustic; most have rugged walls and *palapa* roofs. Prices range from $10 to $50 a night.

Traveling north on Highway 175, you'll come to another hot surf break and a beach of spectacular beauty: **Playa San Augustinillo.** One of the pleasures of a stay in Puerto Angel is discovering the many hidden beaches nearby and spending the day. Local boatmen and hotels can give details and quote rates for this service.

You can stay in Puerto Angel near Playa Principal in the tiny town, or at Playa Panteón. Most accommodations are basic, older, cement-block style hotels, not meriting a full-blown description. Between Playa Panteón and town are several bungalow and guest-house setups with budget accommodations.

3 Bahías de Huatulco

64km (40 miles) SE of Puerto Angel; 680km (425 miles) SE of Acapulco

Huatulco has the same unspoiled nature and laid-back attitude as its neighbors to the north, Puerto Angel and Puerto Escondido, but with a difference. In the midst of natural splendor, you'll also encounter indulgent hotels and modern roads and facilities.

Pristine beaches and jungle landscapes can make for an idyllic retreat from the stress of daily life—and when viewed from a luxury hotel balcony, even better. Huatulco is for those who want to enjoy the beauty of nature during the day, then retreat to well-appointed comfort by night.

Undeveloped stretches of pure white sand and isolated coves await the promised growth of Huatulco, but it's not catching on as rapidly as Cancún, the previous resort planned by FONATUR, Mexico's Tourism Development arm. FONATUR development of the Bahías de Huatulco is an ambitious project that aims to cover 21,000 hectares (52,000 acres) of land, with over 16,000 hectares

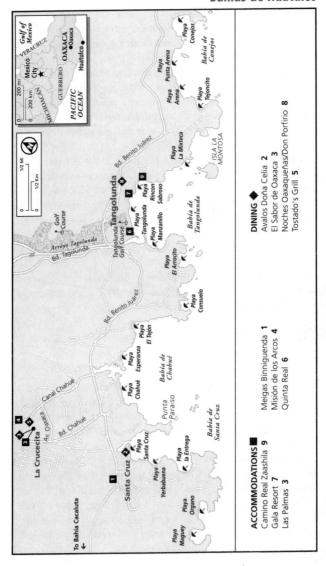

Bahías de Huatulco

ACCOMMODATIONS ■
Camino Real Zaashila **9**
Gala Resort **7**
Las Palmas **3**

Meigas Binniguenda **1**
Misión de los Arcos **4**
Quinta Real **6**

DINING ◆
Avalos Doña Celia **2**
El Sabor de Oaxaca **3**
Noches Oaxaqueñas/Don Porfirio **8**
Tostado's Grill **5**

125

(40,000 acres) to remain ecological preserves. The small local communities have been transplanted from the coast into Crucecita. The area consists of three sections: **Santa Cruz, Crucecita,** and **Tangolunda Bay** (see "City Layout," below).

Though Huatulco has increasingly become known for its ecotourism attractions—including river rafting, rappelling, and hiking jungle trails—it has yet to develop a true personality. There's little shopping, nightlife, or even dining outside the hotels, and what is available is expensive for the quality. However, the service in the area shines.

The planned opening of a new cruise-ship dock in Santa Cruz Bay may change the level of activity in Huatulco, providing the sleepy resort with an important business boost. The new dock's plans call for it to handle up to two 3,000-passenger cruise ships at a time (passengers are currently ferried to shore aboard tenders). Also slated to open soon is a new "ecoarchaeological" park, Punta Celeste. This new development is all being handled with ecological sensitivity in mind.

If you're drawn to snorkeling, diving, boat cruises, and simple relaxation, Huatulco nicely fits the bill. Nine bays encompass 36 beaches and countless inlets and coves. Huatulco's main problem has been securing enough incoming flights. It relies heavily on charter service from the United States and Canada.

ESSENTIALS
GETTING THERE
BY PLANE **Mexicana** flights (© **800/531-7921** in the U.S., 958/587-0223 or 958/587-0260 at the airport) connect Huatulco with Cancún, Chicago, Guadalajara, Los Angeles, Miami, San Antonio, San Francisco, San Jose, and Toronto by way of Mexico City.

From Huatulco's international airport (airport code: HUX; © **958/581-9004** or -9005), about 19km (12 miles) northwest of the Bahías de Huatulco, private **taxis** charge $40 to Crucecita, $42 to Santa Cruz, and $48 to Tangolunda. **Transportes Terrestres** (© **958/581-9014**) *colectivo* minibus fares are $8 to $10 per person. When returning, make sure to ask for a taxi, unless you have a lot of luggage. Taxis to the airport run $40, but unless specifically requested, you'll get a Suburban, which costs $54.

Budget (© **800/322-9976** in the U.S., 958/587-0010, or 958/581-9000) has an office at the airport that is open for flight arrivals. Daily rates run around $71 for a VW sedan, $104 for a Sentra or Geo Tracker, and $123 for a Jeep Ranger. **Dollar** also has rental offices at the Royal, Barceló, and downtown, and offers one-way drop service if you're traveling to Puerto Escondido. Because Huatulco is so spread out and has excellent roads, you may want to consider a rental car, at least for 1 or 2 days, to explore the area.

BY CAR   Coastal Highway 200 leads to Huatulco (via Pochutla) from the north and is generally in good condition. The drive from Puerto Escondido takes just under 2 hours. The road is well maintained, but it's windy and doesn't have lights, so avoid travel after sunset. Allow at least 6 hours for the trip from Oaxaca City on mountainous Highway 175.

BY BUS   There are three bus stations in Crucecita, all within a few blocks, but none in Santa Cruz or Tangolunda. The **Gacela** and **Estrella Blanca** station, at the corner of Gardenia and Palma Real, handles service to Acapulco, Mexico City, Puerto Escondido, and Pochutla. The **Cristóbal Colón** station (© 958/587-0261) is at the corner of Gardenia and Ocotillo, 4 blocks from the Plaza Principal. It serves destinations throughout Mexico, including Oaxaca, Puerto Escondido, and Pochutla. The **Estrella del Valle** station, on Jasmin between Sabali and Carrizal, serves Oaxaca.

VISITOR INFORMATION

The **State Tourism Office,** or Oficina del Turismo (© 958/581-0176; fax 958/581-0177; www.BaysofHuatulco.com.mx), has an information module in Tangolunda Bay, near the Grand Pacific hotel. It's open from 9am to 3pm and 6 to 8pm.

CITY LAYOUT

The overall resort area is called **Bahías de Huatulco** and includes nine bays. The town of Santa María de Huatulco, the original settlement in this area, is 27km (17 miles) inland. **Santa Cruz Huatulco,** usually called Santa Cruz, was the first developed area on the coast. It has a central plaza with a bandstand kiosk, which has been converted into a cafe that serves regionally grown coffee. It also has an artisans' market on the edge of the plaza that borders the main road, a few hotels and restaurants, and a marina where bay tours and fishing trips set sail. **Juárez** is Santa Cruz's 4-block-long main street, anchored at one end by the Hotel Castillo Huatulco and at the other by the Meigas Binniguenda hotel. Opposite the Hotel Castillo is the marina, and beyond it are restaurants in new colonial-style buildings facing the beach. The area's banks are on Juárez. It's impossible to get lost and you can take in almost everything at a glance. This bay will be the site of Huatulco's new cruise-ship dock.

About 3km (1½ miles) inland from Santa Cruz is **Crucecita,** a planned city that sprang up in 1985. It centers on a lovely grassy plaza. This is the residential area for the resorts, with neighborhoods of new stucco homes mixed with small apartment complexes. Crucecita has evolved into a lovely, traditional town where you'll find the area's best, and most reasonably priced, restaurants, plus some shopping and several less expensive hotels.

Until other bays are developed, **Tangolunda Bay,** 5km (3 miles) east, is the focal point of development. Over time, half the bays will have resorts. For now, Tangolunda has an 18-hole golf course, as well as the Las Brisas, Quinta Real, Barceló Huatulco, Royal, Casa del Mar, and Camino Real Zaashila hotels, among others. Small strip centers with a few restaurants occupy each end of Tangolunda Bay. **Chahué Bay,** between Tangolunda and Santa Cruz, is a small bay with a beach club, and other facilities under construction along with houses and a few small hotels.

GETTING AROUND

Crucecita, Santa Cruz, and Tangolunda are too far apart to walk, but **taxis** are inexpensive and readily available. Crucecita has taxi stands opposite the Hotel Grifer and on the Plaza Principal. Taxis are readily available through hotels in Santa Cruz and Tangolunda. The fare between Santa Cruz and Tangolunda is roughly $2.50; between Santa Cruz and Crucecita, $2; between Crucecita and Tangolunda, $3. To explore the area, you can hire a taxi by the hour (about $15 per hour) or for the day.

There is **minibus service** between towns; the fare is 50¢. In Santa Cruz, catch the bus across the street from Castillo Huatulco; in Tangolunda, in front of the Grand Pacific; and in Crucecita, cater-cornered from the Hotel Grifer.

FAST FACTS: Bahías de Huatulco

Area Code The area code is **958.**

Banks All three areas have banks with ATMs, including the main Mexican banks, Banamex and Bancomer. They change money during business hours, Monday through Friday from 9am to 5pm, Saturday from 10am to 1pm. Banks are along Calle Juárez in Santa Cruz, and surrounding the central plaza in Crucecita.

Emergencies **Police emergency** (✆ 060); **local police** (✆ 958/587-0815); **transit police** (✆ 958/587-0186); and **Red Cross,** Bulevar Chahué 110 (✆ 958/587-1188).

Information The **State Tourism Office** (Oficina del Turismo; ✆ **958/581-0176** or -0177; sedetur6@oaxaca.gob.mx) has an information module in Tangolunda Bay near the Grand Pacific hotel, and another inside the Gala Resort.

Internet Access An Internet cafe is located on the ground-floor level of the **Hotel Plaza Conejo,** Av. Guamuchil 208, across from the main plaza (✆ **958/587-0054** or 958/587-0009; www.turismo.conejo.com).

Medical Care **Dr. Ricardo Carrillo** (✆ **958/587-0687** or 958/587-0600) speaks English.

Pharmacy **Farmacia del Carmen,** just off the central plaza in Crucecita (✆ **958/587-0878**), is one of the largest drugstores in town. **Farmacia La Clínica** (✆ **958/587-0591**), Sabalí 1602, Crucecita, offers 24-hour service and delivery.

Post Office The *correo,* at Bulevar Chahué 100, Sector R, Crucecita (✆ **958/587-0551**), is open Monday through Friday from 8am to 3pm, Saturday from 9am to 1pm.

BEACHES, WATERSPORTS & OTHER THINGS TO DO

Attractions around Huatulco concentrate on the nine bays and their watersports. The number of ecotours and interesting side trips into the surrounding mountains is growing. Though it isn't a traditional Mexican town, the community of Crucecita is worth visiting. Just off the central plaza is the **Iglesia de Guadalupe,** with a large mural of Mexico's patron saint gracing the entire ceiling of the chapel. The image of the Virgin is set against a deep-blue night sky, and includes 52 stars—a modern interpretation of Juan Diego's cloak.

You can dine in Crucecita for a fraction of the price in Tangolunda Bay, with the added benefit of some local color. Considering that shopping in Huatulco is generally poor, you'll find the best choices here, in the shops around the central plaza. They tend to stay open late, and offer a good selection of regional goods and typical tourist take-homes, including *artesanía,* silver jewelry, Cuban cigars, and tequila. A small, free trolley train takes visitors on a short tour of the town.

BEACHES

A section of the beach at Santa Cruz (away from the small boats) is an inviting sunning spot. Beach clubs for guests at non-oceanfront hotels are here. In addition, several restaurants are on the beach, and *palapa* umbrellas run down to the water's edge. For about $15 one-way, *pangas* from the marina in Santa Cruz will ferry you to **La Entrega Beach,** also in Santa Cruz Bay. There you'll find a row of *palapa* restaurants, all with beach chairs out front. Find an empty one, and use that restaurant for your refreshment needs. A snorkel-equipment rental booth is about midway down the beach, and there's some fairly good snorkeling on the end away from where the boats arrive.

Between Santa Cruz and Tangolunda bays is **Chahué Bay.** The beach club has *palapas,* beach volleyball, and refreshments for an entrance fee of about $2. However, a strong undertow makes this a dangerous place for swimming.

Tangolunda Bay beach, fronting the best hotels, is wide and beautiful. Theoretically, all beaches in Mexico are public; however, nonguests at Tangolunda hotels may have difficulty entering the hotels to get to the beach.

BAY CRUISES & TOURS

Huatulco's major attraction is its coastline—a magnificent stretch of pristine bays bordered by an odd blend of cactus and jungle vegetation right at the water's edge. The only way to really grasp its beauty is to take a cruise of the bays, stopping at **Organo** or **Maguey Bay** for a dip in the crystal-clear water and a fish lunch at a *palapa* restaurant on the beach.

One way to arrange a bay tour is to go to the **boat-owners' cooperative** (© **958/587-0081**) in the red-and-yellow tin shack at the entrance to the marina. Prices are posted, and you can buy tickets for sightseeing, snorkeling, or fishing. Beaches other than La Entrega, including Maguey and San Agustín, are noted for offshore snorkeling. They also have *palapa* restaurants and other facilities. Several of these beaches, however, are completely undeveloped, so you will need to bring your own provisions. Boatmen at the cooperative will arrange return pickup at an appointed time. Prices run about $15 for 1 to 10 persons at La Entrega, and $35 for a trip to Maguey and Organo bays. The farthest bay is San Agustinillo; that all-day trip will run $80 in a private *panga*.

Another option is to join an organized daylong bay cruise. Any travel agency can easily make arrangements. Cruises are about $30 per person, with an extra charge of $5 for snorkeling-equipment rental and lunch. One excursion is on the *Tequila,* complete with guide, drinks, and on-board entertainment. Another, more romantic option is the *Luna Azul,* a 44-foot sailboat that also offers bay tours and sunset sails. Call © **958/587-2276** for reservations.

Ecotours are growing in both popularity and number throughout the Bays of Huatulco. The mountain areas surrounding the Copalita River are also home to other natural treasures worth exploring, including the **Copalitilla Cascades.** Thirty kilometers (19 miles) north of Tangolunda at 394m (1,300 ft.) above sea level, this group of waterfalls—averaging 20 to 25m (65–80 ft.) in height—form natural whirlpools and clear pools for swimming. The area is also popular for horseback riding and rappelling.

An all-day **Coffee Plantation Tour** takes you into the mountains east of Huatulco, touring various coffee plantations. You'll learn how Oaxacan coffee is cultivated and learn about life on the plantations. Lunch and refreshments are included. Cost for the day is $50; contact Paraíso Tours (© **958/581-0218;** paraisohuatulco@prodigy.net.mx) for reservations.

Guided **horseback riding** through the jungles and to Conejos and Magueyito beach makes for a wonderful way to see the natural beauty of the area. The ride lasts 3½ hours, with departures at 9:45am and 1:45pm, and costs $45. Available through **Caballo del Mar Ranch** (© **958/589-9387**).

For **bird-watchers,** local expert field guide Pedro Gasca will take you to several sites, depending on the season, to view a variety of species from parrots to pygmy owls (www.tomzap.com/h_bird.html). Contact him at © **333/854-7007** or at outdoors_huatulco@hotmail. com. The cost for birding expeditions vary from $20 to $80 depending on the length of the tour and the sites to be visited; each is individually designed for the client's preferences, and includes land or aquatic transportation, a birding list, trip report, and beverages.

Another highly recommended guide is Laura Gonzalez, of **Nature Tours Huatulco** (© **958/583-4047;** lauriycky@hotmail.com), for both **hiking** and bird-watching. Choices include a hike around Punta Celeste with views of the river, open sea, and forest, for sightings of terrestrial and aquatic birds. The 3½-hour tour can be made in the early morning or late afternoon, and costs $45. An 8-hour excursion to the Ventanilla Lagoons takes you by boat through a mangrove to view birds, iguanas, and crocodiles. The cost is $80, and lunch is included. Tours include transportation, binoculars, specialized bird guide, and beverages.

GOLF & TENNIS

The 18-hole, par-72 **Tangolunda Golf Course** (© **958/581-0037**) is adjacent to Tangolunda Bay. It has tennis courts as well. The greens fee is $73, and carts cost $37. Tennis courts are also available at the **Barceló** hotel (© **958/581-0055**).

SHOPPING

Shopping in the area is limited and unmemorable. It concentrates in the **Santa Cruz Market,** by the marina in Santa Cruz, and in the **Crucecita Market,** on Guamuchil, a half-block from the plaza. Both are open daily 10am to 8pm (no phones). Among the proto-typical souvenirs, you may want to search out regional specialties, which include Oaxacan embroidered blouses and dresses, and *barro negro,* pottery made from dark clay exclusively found in the Oaxaca region. Also in Crucecita is the Plaza Oaxaca, adjacent to the central plaza. Its clothing shops include **Poco Loco Club/Coconut's Boutique** (© **958/587-0279**), for casual sportswear; and **Mic Mac** (© **958/587-0565**), for beachwear and souvenirs. **Coconuts** (© **958/ 587-0057**) has English-language magazines, books, and music.

WHERE TO STAY

Moderate- and budget-priced hotels in Santa Cruz and Crucecita are generally more expensive than similar hotels in other Mexican beach resorts. The luxury hotels have comparable rates, especially when they're part of a package that includes airfare. The trend here is toward all-inclusive resorts, which in Huatulco are an especially good option, given the lack of memorable dining and nightlife options. Hotels that are not oceanfront generally have an arrangement with a beach club at Santa Cruz or Chahué Bay, and offer shuttle service. Low-season rates apply August through November only.

EXPENSIVE

Camino Real Zaashila ★★★   One of the original hotels in Tangolunda Bay, the Camino Real Zaashila is on a wide stretch of sandy beach secluded from other beaches by small rock outcroppings. The calm water, perfect for swimming and snorkeling, makes it ideal for families. The white stucco building is Mediterranean in style and washed in colors on the ocean side. The boldly decorated rooms are large and have an oceanview balcony or terrace and a large bathroom with a marble tub/shower combination. Each of the 41 rooms on the lower levels has its own sizable dipping pool. The main pool is a free-form design that spans 121m (400 ft.) of beach, with chaises built into the shallow edges. Well-manicured tropical gardens surround it and the guest rooms.

Bulevar Benito Juárez 5, Bahía de Tangolunda, 70989 Huatulco, Oax. ℂ **800/722-6466** in the U.S., or 958/581-0460. Fax 958/581-0461. www.camino-zaashila.com. 135 units. High season $215 double, $265 Club Room, $460 suite; low season $165 double, $200 Club Room, $350 suite. AE, DC, MC, V. **Amenities:** 3 restaurants (1 Oaxacan); lobby bar w/live music; large pool; lighted tennis court; outdoor whirlpool; beachside watersports center; tour and travel agency services; room service. *In room:* A/C, TV, minibar, safe.

Quinta Real 🌟🌟🌟   Double Moorish domes mark this romantic, relaxed hotel, known for its richly appointed cream-and-white decor and complete attention to detail. From the welcoming reception area to the luxurious beach club below, the staff emphasizes excellence in service. The small groupings of suites are built into the sloping hill to Tangolunda Bay and offer spectacular views of the ocean and golf course. Rooms on the eastern edge of the resort sit above the highway, which generates some traffic noise. Interiors are elegant and comfortable, with stylish Mexican furniture, original art, wood-beamed ceilings, and marble tub/shower combinations with whirlpool tubs. Telescopes grace many of the suites. Balconies have overstuffed seating areas and stone-inlay floors. Eight Grand Class Suites and the Presidential Suite have private pools. The Quinta Real is perfect for weddings, honeymoons, or small corporate retreats.

Bulevar Benito Juárez Lt. 2, Bahía de Tangolunda, 70989 Huatulco, Oax. ℂ **888/561-2817** in the U.S., 958/581-0428, or 958/581-0430. Fax 958/581-0429. www.quintareal.com/huatulco-eng.htm. 28 units. High season $386 Master Suite, $371 Grand Class Suite, $546 suite with private pool; low season $206 Master Suite, $351 Grand Class Suite, $416 suite with private pool. AE, DC, MC, V. **Amenities:** Restaurant (breakfast, dinner); poolside restaurant (lunch); bar w/stunning view; beach club w/2 pools (1 for children); concierge; tour desk; room service; in-room massage; laundry service; dry cleaning; beach *palapas*. *In room:* A/C, TV, dataport, minibar, hair dryer, safe-deposit box, bathrobes.

MODERATE

Gala Resort 🌟 🅺ids   With all meals, drinks, entertainment, tips, and a slew of activities included in the price, the Gala is a value-packed experience. It caters to adults of all ages (married and single) who enjoy both activity and relaxation. An excellent kids' activity program makes it probably the best option in the area for families. Rooms have tile floors and Oaxacan wood trim, large tub/shower combinations, and ample balconies, all with views of Tangolunda Bay.

Bulevar Benito Juárez s/n, Bahía de Tangolunda, 70989 Huatulco, Oax. ℂ **800/GO-MAEVA** in the U.S., or 958/581-0000. Fax 958/581-0220. www.gala-resort-huatulco.com. 290 units. $180–$291 double; $280–$388 junior suite. Child 12–15 an extra

$54–$70; child 7–11 $60. Children under 7 stay free in parent's room. Ask about special promotions. AE, MC, V. **Amenities:** 4 restaurants (buffet, a la carte); 4 bars; 5 swimming pools, including a large free-form pool; 3 lighted tennis courts; full gym; complete beachside watersports center; theme nights. *In room:* A/C, TV, minibar, hair dryer, safe-deposit box.

Hotel Meigas Binniguenda ⊛

Huatulco's first hotel retains the charm and comfort that originally made it memorable. Rooms have Mexican-tile floors, foot-loomed bedspreads, and colonial-style furniture; French doors open onto tiny wrought-iron balconies overlooking Juárez or the pool and gardens. Newer rooms, added during an expansion in 2000, have more modern teak furnishings and are generally much nicer—request this section. A nice shady area surrounds the small pool in back of the lobby. The hotel is away from the marina at the far end of Juárez, only a few blocks from the water. It offers free transportation every hour to the beach club at Santa Cruz Bay.

Bulevar Santa Cruz 201, 70989 Santa Cruz de Huatulco, Oax. ℂ **958/587-0077** or -0078. Fax 958/587-0284. binniguenda@prodigy.net.mx. 165 units. Year-round rates $250 double. Children under 7 stay free in parent's room. AE, MC, V. **Amenities:** Large, *palapa*-topped restaurant; small pool; travel agency; shuttle to beach. *In room:* A/C, TV, safe-deposit box.

INEXPENSIVE

Hotel Las Palmas

The central location and accommodating staff add to the appeal of the bright, basic rooms at Las Palmas. Located a half-block from the main plaza, it's connected to the popular El Sabor de Oaxaca restaurant (see "Where to Dine," below), which offers room service to guests. Rooms have tile floors, cotton textured bedspreads, tile showers, and cable TV.

Av. Guamuchil 206, 70989 Bahías de Huatulco, Oax. ℂ **958/587-0060.** Fax 958/587-0057. www.tomzap.com/huatulco.html. 25 units. High season $45 double; low season $28 double. AE, MC, V. Free parking. **Amenities:** Travel-agency services; tobacco shop; money exchange; safe-deposit boxes. *In room:* A/C, TV.

Misión de los Arcos ⊛⊛ *Finds*

This hotel, just a block from the central plaza, is similar in style to the elegant Quinta Real—but at a fraction of the cost. The hotel is completely white, accented with abundant greenery, giving it a fresh, inviting feel. Rooms continue the theme, washed in white, with cream and beige bed coverings and upholstery. Built-in desks, French windows, and minimal but interesting decorative accents give this budget hotel a real sense of style. At the entrance level, an excellent cafe offers high-speed Internet access, Huatulco's regionally grown coffee, tea, pastries, and ice cream. It's open from 7:30am to 11:30pm. Although there's no pool, the guests have the use of a beach club, to which the hotel provides a complimentary shuttle. The gym offers day passes for nonguests. The hotel is cater-cornered from La Crucecita's central plaza, close to all the shops and restaurants.

Gardenia 902, La Crucecita, 70989 Huatulco, Oaxaca. © 958/587-0165. Fax 958/587-1904. www.misiondelosarcos.com. 13 units. High season $40 double without A/C, $45 double with A/C, $50–$95 suite; low season $30 double without A/C, $35 double with A/C, $40–$85 suite. Rates increase over Christmas and Easter holiday periods. AE, MC, V. **Amenities:** Full gym; tour desk; shuttle to beach club; laundry service. *In room:* TV, safe-deposit box.

WHERE TO DINE

El Sabor de Oaxaca 🐸🐸🐸 OAXACAN   This is the best place in the area to enjoy authentic, richly flavorful Oaxacan food, among the best of traditional Mexican cuisine. This colorful restaurant is a local favorite that also meets the quality standards of tourists. Among the most popular items are mixed grill for two, with a Oaxacan beef filet, tender pork tenderloin, *chorizo* (zesty Mexican sausage), and pork ribs; and the Oaxacan special for two, a generous sampling of the best of the menu, with tamales, Oaxacan cheese, pork *mole,* and more. Generous breakfasts include eggs, bacon, ham, beans, toast, and fresh orange juice. There's lively music, and the restaurant books special group events.

Av. Guamuchil 206, Crucecita. © 958/587-0060. Fax 958/587-0057. Breakfast $3.90; main courses $5–$17. AE, MC, V. Daily 7am–midnight.

Noches Oaxaqueñas/Don Porfirio 🐸 SEAFOOD/OAXACAN   This dinner show presents the colorful, traditional folkloric dances of Oaxaca in an open-air courtyard reminiscent of an old hacienda (but in a modern strip mall). The dancers clearly enjoy performing traditional ballet under the direction of owner Celicia Flores Ramírez, wife of Don Willo Porfirio. The menu includes the *plato oaxaqueño,* a generous, flavorful sampling of traditional Oaxacan fare, with a *tamal,* a *sope,* Oaxacan cheese, grilled filet, pork enchilada, and a chile relleno. Other house specialties include shrimp with *mezcal,* and spaghetti marinara with seafood. Meat lovers can enjoy American-style cuts or a juicy *arrachera* (skirt steak). Groups are welcome.

Bulevar Benito Juárez s/n (across from Royal Maeva), Tangolunda Bay. © 958/581-0001. Show $12. Main courses $12–$35. AE, MC, V. Fri–Sun noon–10pm. Show starts at 8:30 and 10pm Tues, Thurs, and Sat.

Restaurant Avalos Doña Celia SEAFOOD   Doña Celia, an original Huatulco resident, remains in business in the same area where she started her little thatch-roofed restaurant years ago. In a new building at the end of Santa Cruz's beach, she serves the same good eats. Among her specialties are *filete empapelado* (foil-wrapped fish baked with tomato, onion, and cilantro) and *filete almendrado* (fish filet covered with hotcake batter, beer, and almonds). The *ceviche* is terrific—one order is plenty for two—as is *platillo a la huatulqueño* (shrimp and young octopus fried in olive oil with chile and onion, served over white rice). The restaurant is basic, but the food is the reason for its popularity. If you dine here during the day, there are beach chairs and shade, so you can make your own "beach club" in a traditional and accessible part of Huatulco.

Santa Cruz Bay. © 958/587-0128. Breakfast $2.50–$3.50; seafood $4–$25. MC, V. Daily 8:30am–11pm.

Tostado's Grill MEXICAN This traditional family-oriented Mexican restaurant serves typical Mexican fare, in a casual, friendly atmosphere. It's the place to dine if you're looking for a dose of local color with your meal, and want something authentically Mexican. Especially delectable is their Aztec soup (tortilla soup), and their beef is known for its tenderness. It is one of the few restaurants in La Crucecita that is open late during low season.

Flamboyan 306. Located in front of La Crucecita's central plaza. © 958/587-1697. Prices vary $2.20–$20. AE, MC, V. Daily 7pm–midnight.

HUATULCO AFTER DARK

There's a very limited selection of dance clubs around Huatulco—meaning that's where everyone goes. Huatulco seems to have the least consistent nightlife of any resort in Mexico, and clubs seem to change ownership—and names—almost annually. The current hot spot is **La Crema,** in Crucecita (about 4 blocks south of the *zócalo,* at the corner of Bugambilia and La Ceiba), playing predominantly reggae, but also a mix of dance tunes from the '60s and '70s. With bamboo-covered walls and batik hangings, it has a "just back from the beach" vibe to it. Nearby is **Café Dublin,** Carrizal 504 (1 block east and a half-block south from the *zócalo*), an Irish pub with a book exchange. On the east side of the *zócalo* is **Bar La Iguana,** playing rock music and featuring televised sports. During the high season, La Iguana has live tropical music. The bar is open from noon to 4am.

In Tangolunda, closer to the resort hotels, you'll find **Savage,** this area's hottest nightspot. It's across from the Barcelo hotel, and draws a more sophisticated crowd—meaning the T-shirts worn don't generally have advertising on them. The club plays techno dance music, with an impressive multimedia and light show. Each Wednesday, the Barcelo Resort hosts its **Fiesta Mexicana** from 7 to 11pm, featuring folkloric dances, mariachi music, and a buffet of Mexican food and drinks.

Inland to Old Mexico: Taxco & Cuernavaca

It may seem as if the small towns in this region of Mexico are trying to capitalize on recent trends in travel toward spas and self-exploration, but in reality, they've helped define them. From the restorative properties of thermal waters and earth-based spa treatments to the mystical and spiritual properties of gemstones and herbs, the treasures and knowledge in these towns have existed for years—and, in some cases, for centuries.

This is only a sampling of towns south and west of Mexico City. They are fascinating in their diversity, history, and mystery, and make for a unique travel experience, either on their own or combined. They vary in character from mystical villages to sophisticated spa towns, with archaeological and colonial-era attractions in the mix. And with their proximity to Mexico City, all are within easy reach by private car or taxi—or by inexpensive bus—in under a few hours.

The legendary silver city of **Taxco,** on the road between Acapulco and Mexico City, is renowned for its museums, picturesque hillside colonial-era charm, and, of course, its silver shops. North of Taxco and southwest of Mexico City, over the mountains, are the venerable thermal spas at **Ixtapan de la Sal,** as well as their more modern counterparts in **Valle de Bravo.** Verdant **Cuernavaca,** known as the land of eternal spring, has gained a reputation for its exceptional spa facilities and its wealth of cultural and historic attractions. Finally, **Tepoztlán,** with its enigmatic charms and legendary pyramid, captivates the few travelers who find their way there.

1 Taxco: Cobblestones & Silver ★★

178km (111 miles) SW of Mexico City; 80km (50 miles) SW of Cuernavaca; 296km (185 miles) NE of Acapulco

In Mexico and around the world, the town of Taxco de Alarcón—most commonly known simply as Taxco (*tahs*-koh)—is synonymous with silver. The town's geography and architecture are equally precious: Taxco sits at nearly 1,515m (5,000 ft.) on a hill among hills, and almost any point in the city offers fantastic views.

Hernán Cortez discovered Taxco as he combed the area for treasure, but its rich caches of silver weren't fully exploited for another 2 centuries. In 1751, the French prospector Joseph de la Borda—who came to be known locally as José—commissioned the baroque Santa Prisca Church that dominates Taxco's *zócalo* (Plaza Borda) as a way of giving something back to the town. In the mid-1700s, Borda was considered the richest man in New Spain.

The fact that Taxco has become Mexico's most renowned center for silver design, even though it now mines only a small amount of silver, is the work of an American, William Spratling. Spratling arrived in the late 1920s with the intention of writing a book. He soon noticed the skill of the local craftsmen and opened a workshop to produce handmade silver jewelry and tableware based on pre-Hispanic art, which he exported to the United States in bulk. The workshops flourished, and Taxco's reputation grew.

Today, most of the residents of this town are involved in the silver industry in some way. Taxco is home to hundreds (some say up to 900) of silver shops and outlets, ranging from sleek galleries to small stands in front of stucco homes. You'll find silver in all of its forms here—the jewelry basics, tea sets, silverware, candelabras, picture frames, and napkin holders.

The tiny one-man factories that line the cobbled streets all the way up into the hills supply most of Taxco's silverwork. "Bargains" are relative, but nowhere else will you find this combination of diversity, quality, and rock-bottom prices. Generally speaking, the larger shops that most obviously cater to the tourist trade will have the highest prices—but they may be the only ones to offer "that special something" you're looking for. For classic designs in jewelry or other silver items, shop around, and wander the back streets and smaller venues.

You can get an idea of what Taxco is like by spending an afternoon, but there's much more to this picturesque town of 120,000 than just the Plaza Borda and the shops surrounding it. Stay overnight, wander its steep cobblestone streets, and you'll discover little plazas, fine churches, and, of course, an abundance of silversmiths' shops.

The main part of town is relatively flat. It stretches up the hillside from the highway, and it's a steep but brief walk up. White VW minibuses, called *burritos,* make the circuit through and around town, picking up and dropping off passengers along the route, from

Taxco

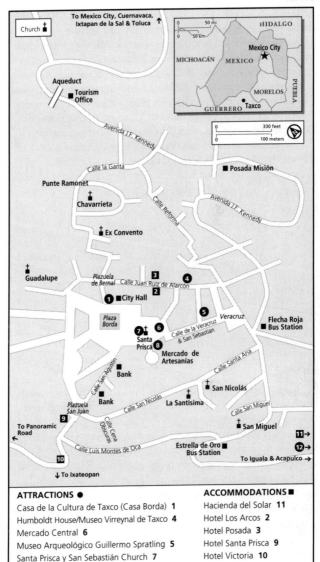

ATTRACTIONS ●

Casa de la Cultura de Taxco (Casa Borda) **1**

Humboldt House/Museo Virreynal de Taxco **4**

Mercado Central **6**

Museo Arqueológico Guillermo Spratling **5**

Santa Prisca y San Sebastián Church **7**

Wholesale Silver Market **8**

Workshops: Los Castillo & Spratling **12**

ACCOMMODATIONS ■

Hacienda del Solar **11**

Hotel Los Arcos **2**

Hotel Posada **3**

Hotel Santa Prisca **9**

Hotel Victoria **10**

about 7am until 9pm. These taxis are inexpensive (about 50¢), and you should use them even if you arrive by car, because parking is practically impossible. Also, the streets are so narrow and steep that most visitors find them nerve-racking. Find a secured parking lot for your car or leave it at your hotel, and forget about it until you leave.

Warning: Self-appointed guides will undoubtedly approach you in the *zócalo* (Plaza Borda) and offer their services—they get a cut (up to 25%) of all you buy in the shops they take you to. Before hiring a guide, ask to see his SECTUR (Tourism Secretary) credentials. The Department of Tourism office on the highway at the north end of town can recommend a licensed guide.

ESSENTIALS
GETTING THERE & DEPARTING

BY CAR   From Mexico City, take Paseo de la Reforma to Chapultepec Park and merge with the Periférico, which will take you to Highway 95D on the south end of town. From the Periférico, take the Insurgentes exit and merge until you come to the sign for Cuernavaca/Tlalpan. Choose either CUERNAVACA CUOTA (toll) or CUERNAVACA LIBRE (free). Continue south around Cuernavaca to the Amacuzac interchange, and proceed straight ahead for Taxco. The drive from Mexico City takes about 3½ hours.

From Acapulco you have two options: Highway 95D is the toll road through Iguala to Taxco, or you can take the old two-lane road (Hwy. 95) that winds more slowly through villages; it's in good condition.

BY BUS   From Mexico City, buses depart from the Central de Autobuses del Sur station (Metro: Taxqueña) and take 2 to 3 hours, with frequent departures.

Taxco has two bus stations. Estrella de Oro buses arrive at their own station on the southern edge of town. Estrella Blanca service, including *Futura* executive-class buses, and Flecha Roja buses arrive at the station on the northeastern edge of town on Avenida Los Plateros ("Avenue of the Silversmiths," formerly Av. Kennedy). Taxis to the *zócalo* cost around $2.

VISITOR INFORMATION

The **State of Guerrero Dirección de Turismo** (©/fax **762/622-6616** or 762/622-2274) has offices at the arches on the main highway at the north end of town (Av. de los Plateros 1), which is useful if you're driving into town. The office is open Monday through Friday from 8am to 3:30pm, and Saturday from 8am to noon. To get there from the Plaza Borda, take a ZOCALO-ARCOS *combi* and get off at the arch over the highway. As you face the arches, the tourism office is on your right.

CITY LAYOUT

The center of town is the tiny **Plaza Borda,** shaded by perfectly manicured Indian laurel trees. On one side is the imposing twin-towered, pink-stone **Santa Prisca Church;** whitewashed, red-tile buildings housing the famous silver shops and a restaurant or two line the other sides. Beside the church, deep in a crevice of the mountain, is the **wholesale silver market**—absolutely the best place to begin your silver shopping, to get an idea of prices for more standard designs. You'll be amazed at the low prices. Buying just one piece is perfectly acceptable, and buying in bulk can lower the per-piece price. One of the beauties of Taxco is that its brick-paved and cobblestone streets are completely asymmetrical, zigzagging up and down the hillsides. The plaza buzzes with vendors of everything from hammocks and cotton candy to bark paintings and balloons.

FAST FACTS

The telephone area code is **762.** The main post office, Benito Juárez 6, at the City Hall building (© **762/622-8596**), is open Monday through Friday from 9am to 3pm. The older branch of the post office (© **762/622-0501**) is on the outskirts, on the highway to Acapulco. It's in a row of shops with a black-and-white CORREO sign.

EXPLORING TAXCO

Shopping for jewelry and other items is the major pastime for tourists. Prices for silver jewelry at Taxco's shops are about the best in the world, and everything is available, from $1 trinkets to artistic pieces costing hundreds of dollars.

In addition, Taxco is the home of some of Mexico's finest stone sculptors and is a good place to buy masks. However, beware of so-called "antiques"—there are virtually no real ones for sale.

Viajes Sibely, Miguel Hidalgo 24 (©/fax **762/622-8080** or 762/622-3808), offers daily tours to the Cacahuamilpa Caves and the ruins of Xochicalco for $59, including transportation, ticket, and the services of a guide. It also sells bus tickets to Acapulco, Chilpancingo, Iguala, and Cuernavaca. The agency is to the left of La Hamburguesa. Another agency offering similar services is **Turismo Garlum,** next to the Santa Prisca Church (© **762/622-3021** or 762/627-3500). It offers daily tours to the Cacahuamilpa Caves and the Santa Prisca

Church for $18, which includes transportation, ticket, and the services of a guide. Both agencies are open Monday through Friday from 9am to 7pm and Saturday from 9am to 2pm.

SPECIAL EVENTS & FESTIVALS

January 18 marks the annual celebration in honor of Santa Prisca, with public festivities and fireworks displays. **Holy Week** 𝄞𝄞 in Taxco is one of the most poignant in the country, beginning the Friday a week before Easter with processions daily and nightly. The most riveting, on Thursday evening, lasts almost 4 hours and includes villagers from the surrounding area carrying statues of saints, followed by hooded members of a society of self-flagellating penitents, chained at the ankles and carrying huge wooden crosses and bundles of thorny branches. On Saturday morning, the Plaza Borda fills for the **Procession of Three Falls,** reenacting the three times Christ stumbled and fell while carrying the cross.

Taxco's **Silver Fair** starts the last week in November and continues through the first week in December. It includes a competition for silver works and sculptures among the top silversmiths. At the same time, **Jornadas Alarconianas** features plays and literary events in honor of Juan Ruiz de Alarcón (1572–1639), a world-famous dramatist who was born in Taxco—and for whom Taxco de Alarcón is named. Art exhibits, street fairs, and other festivities are part of the dual celebration.

SIGHTS IN TOWN

Casa de la Cultura de Taxco (Casa Borda)   Diagonally across from the Santa Prisca Church and facing Plaza Borda is the home José de la Borda built for his son around 1759. Now the Guerrero State Cultural Center, it houses classrooms and exhibit halls where period clothing, engravings, paintings, and crafts are on display. The center also books traveling exhibits.

Plaza Borda 1. ⓒ **762/622-6617** or 762/622-6632. Fax 762/662-6634. Free admission. Tues–Sun 10am–5pm.

Humboldt House/Museo Virreinal de Taxco   Stroll along Ruiz de Alarcón (the street behind the Casa Borda) and look for the richly decorated facade of the Humboldt House, where the renowned German scientist and explorer Baron Alexander von Humboldt (1769–1859) spent a night in 1803. The museum houses 18th-century memorabilia pertinent to Taxco, most of which came from a secret room discovered during the recent restoration of the Santa Prisca Church. Signs with detailed information are in Spanish and English. As you enter, to the right are very rare *tumelos* (three-tiered funerary paintings). The bottom two were painted in honor of Charles III of Spain; the top one, with a carved phoenix on top, was supposedly painted for the funeral of José de la Borda.

Another section presents historical information about Don Miguel Cabrera, Mexico's foremost 18th-century artist. Fine examples of clerical garments decorated with gold and silver thread hang in glass cases. Excellently restored Cabrera paintings hang throughout the museum. And, of course, a small room is devoted to Humboldt and his sojourns through South America and Mexico.

Calle Juan Ruiz de Alarcón 12. © 762/622-5501. Admission $2 adults, $1.50 students and teachers with ID. Tues–Sat 10am–5pm; Sun 10am–3pm.

Mercado Central   Located to the right of the Santa Prisca Church, behind and below Berta's, Taxco's central market meanders deep inside the mountain. Take the stairs off the street. In addition to a collection of wholesale silver shops, you'll find numerous food stands, always the best place for a cheap meal.

Plaza Borda. Shops daily 10am–8pm; food stands daily 7am–6pm.

Museo Arqueológico Guillermo Spratling   A plaque in Spanish explains that most of the collection of pre-Columbian art displayed here, as well as the funds for the museum, came from William Spratling. You'd expect this to be a silver museum, but it's not—for Spratling silver, go to the Spratling Ranch Workshop (see "Nearby Attractions," below). The entrance floor and the one above display a good collection of pre-Columbian statues and implements in clay, stone, and jade. The lower floor holds changing exhibits.

Calle Porfirio A. Delgado 1. © 762/622-1660. Admission $3 adults, free for children under 12; free to all Sun. Tues–Sat 9am–6pm; Sun 9am–3pm. Leaving Santa Prisca Church, turn right and right again at the corner; continue down the street, veer right, then immediately left. The museum will be facing you.

Santa Prisca y San Sebastián Church ★★   This is Taxco's centerpiece parish church; it faces the pleasant Plaza Borda. José de la Borda, a French miner who struck it rich in Taxco's silver mines, funded the construction. Completed in 1758, it's one of Mexico's most impressive baroque churches. The ultracarved facade is eclipsed by the interior, where the intricacy of the gold-leafed saints and cherubic angels is positively breathtaking. The paintings by Miguel Cabrera, one of Mexico's most famous colonial-era artists, are the pride of Taxco. The sacristy (behind the high altar) contains more Cabrera paintings.

Guides, both children and adults, will approach you outside the church offering to give a tour. Make sure the guide's English is passable, and establish whether the price is per person or per tour.

Plaza Borda. ℂ 762/622-0184. Free admission. Daily 6:30am–8pm.

Silver Museum   The Silver Museum, operated by a local silversmith, is a relatively recent addition to Taxco. After entering the building next to Santa Prisca (upstairs is Sr. Costilla's restaurant; p. 148), look for a sign on the left; the museum is downstairs. It's not a traditional public museum; nevertheless, it does the much-needed job of describing the history of silver in Mexico and Taxco, as well as displaying some historic and contemporary award-winning pieces. Time spent here seeing quality silver work will make you a more discerning shopper. At press time, it was in the process of upgrading the exhibits.

Plaza Borda 1. ℂ 762/622-0658. Admission $1. Daily 10am–5:30pm.

NEARBY ATTRACTIONS

The impressive **Grutas de Cacahuamilpa** ✪, known as the Cacahuamilpa Caves or Grottoes (ℂ 734/346-1716), are 20 minutes north of Taxco. Hourly guided tours run daily at the caverns, which are truly sensational and well worth the visit. To see them, you can join a tour from Taxco (see "Exploring Taxco," above) or take a *combi* from the Flecha Roja terminal in Taxco; the one-way fare is $2.50. For more information, see "Sights near Tepoztlán," later in this chapter.

Los Castillo   Don Antonio Castillo was one of hundreds of young men to whom William Spratling taught silversmithing in the 1930s. He was also one of the first to branch out with his own shops and line of designs, which over the years have earned him a fine reputation. Castillo has shops in several Mexican cities. Now, his daughter Emilia creates her own noteworthy designs, including decorative pieces with silver fused onto porcelain. Emilia's work is for sale on the ground floor of the Posada de los Castillo, just below the Plazuela Bernal.

8km (5 miles) south of town on the Acapulco Hwy. Also at Plazuela Bernal, Taxco. ℂ 762/622-1016 or ℂ/fax 762/622-1988 (workshop). Free admission. Workshop Mon–Fri 8am–2pm and 3–6pm; open to groups at other hours by appointment only.

Spratling Ranch Workshop   William Spratling's hacienda-style home and workshop on the outskirts of Taxco still bustles with busy hands reproducing unique designs. A trip here will show you what distinctive Spratling work was all about, for the designs crafted today show the same fine work. Although the prices are higher than at other outlets, the designs are unusual and considered collectible.

There's no store in Taxco, and unfortunately, most of the display cases hold only samples. With the exception of a few jewelry pieces, most items are by order only. Ask about U.S. outlets.

10km (6 miles) south of town on the Acapulco Hwy. No phone. Free admission. Mon–Sat 9am–5pm. The *combi* to Iguala stops at the ranch; fare is 70¢.

WHERE TO STAY

Taxco is an overnight visitor's dream: charming and picturesque, with a respectable selection of pleasant, well-kept hotels. Hotel prices tend to rise at holiday times (especially Easter week).

MODERATE

Hacienda del Solar 🐵🐵   This hotel comprises several Mexican-style cottages, all on a beautifully landscaped hilltop with magnificent views of the surrounding valleys and the town. The decor is slightly different in each cottage, but most contain lots of beautiful handicrafts, red-tile floors, and bathrooms with handmade tiles. Several rooms have vaulted tile ceilings and private terraces. Others come equipped with more modern amenities, like televisions. Standard rooms have no terraces and only showers in the bathrooms; deluxe rooms have sunken tubs (with showers) and terraces. Junior suites are the largest and most luxurious accommodations. All rooms are priced the same, so if you want one of the larger ones (suites), make sure to ask for it when you check in.

Paraje del Solar s/n (Apdo. Postal 96), 40200 Taxco, Gro. ⓒ/fax 762/622-0587. 22 units. $120 double. MC, V. Take Hwy. 95 toward Acapulco 4km (2½ miles) south of the town center; look for signs on the left and go straight down a narrow road until you see the hotel entrance. **Amenities:** Restaurant (w/spectacular city view; see "Where to Dine," below); heated outdoor pool; tennis court; travel desk; room service; laundry service.

INEXPENSIVE

Hotel los Arcos 🐵   Los Arcos occupies a converted 1620 monastery. The handsome inner patio is bedecked with Puebla pottery surrounding a central fountain. The rooms are nicely but sparsely appointed, with natural tile floors and colonial-style furniture. You'll feel immersed in colonial charm and blissful quiet. To find the hotel from the Plaza Borda, follow the hill down (with Hotel Agua Escondida on your left) and make an immediate right at the Plazuela Bernal; the hotel is a block down on the left, opposite the Hotel Posada (see below).

Juan Ruiz de Alarcón 4, 40200 Taxco, Gro. ⓒ **762/622-1836.** Fax 762/622-7982. 21 units. $35 double; $40 triple; $45 quad; $50 junior suite. No credit cards. **Amenities:** Tour desk.

Hotel Posada Emilia Castillo ☙ Each room in this delightful small hotel is simply but beautifully appointed with handsome carved doors and furniture; bathrooms have either tubs or showers. The manager, Don Teodoro Contreras Galindo, is a true gentleman and a fountain of information about Taxco.

Juan Ruiz de Alarcón 7, 40200 Taxco, Gro. ☎/fax 762/622-1396. 15 units. $30 double; $40 double with TV. MC, V. From the Plaza Borda, go downhill a short block to the Plazuela Bernal and make an immediate right; the hotel is a block farther on the right, opposite the Hotel los Arcos (see above). *In room:* TV.

Hotel Santa Prisca ☙☙ *Value* The Santa Prisca, 1 block from the Plaza Borda on the Plazuela San Juan, is one of the older and nicer hotels in town. Rooms are small but comfortable, with standard bathrooms (showers only), tile floors, wood beams, and a colonial atmosphere. For longer stays, ask for a room in the adjacent new addition, where the rooms are sunnier, quieter, and more spacious. There is a reading area in an upstairs salon overlooking Taxco, as well as a lush patio with fountains.

Cenaobscuras 1, 40200 Taxco, Gro. ☎ **762/622-0080** or 762/622-0980. Fax 762/622-2938. 34 units. $46 double; $52 superior double; $64 suite. AE, MC, V. Limited free parking. **Amenities:** Dining-room-style restaurant and bar; room service; laundry service; safe-deposit boxes.

Hotel Victoria ☙☙ The Victoria clings to the hillside above town, with stunning views from its flower-covered verandas. It exudes the charm of old-fashioned Mexico. The comfortable furnishings, though slightly run-down, evoke the hotel's 1940s heyday. In front of each standard room, a table and chairs sit out on the tiled common walkway. Each deluxe room has a private terrace; each junior suite has a bedroom, a nicely furnished large living room, and a spacious private terrace overlooking the city. Deluxe rooms and junior suites have TVs. Even if you don't stay here, come for a drink in the comfortable bar and living room, or sit on the terrace to take in the fabulous view. Formerly known as Rancho Taxco Victoria, the hotel underwent a change in management in 2002.

Carlos J. Nibbi 5 and 7 (Apdo. Postal 83), 40200 Taxco, Gro. ☎ **762/622-0004.** Fax 762/622-0010. 63 units. $55 standard double; $89 deluxe double; $100 junior suite. AE, MC, V. Free parking. From the Plazuela San Juan, go up Carlos J. Nibbi, a narrow, winding cobbled street. The hotel is at the top of the hill. **Amenities:** Restaurant; bar; small outdoor pool.

WHERE TO DINE

Taxco gets a lot of day-trippers, most of whom choose to dine close to the Plaza Borda. Prices in this area are high for what you get. Just a few streets back, you'll find some excellent, simple *fondas* (taverns) or restaurants.

VERY EXPENSIVE

Toni's ⋌ STEAKS/SEAFOOD   High on a mountaintop, Toni's is an intimate, classic restaurant enclosed in a huge, cone-shaped *palapa* with a panoramic view of the city. Eleven candlelit tables sparkle with crystal and crisp linen. The menu, mainly shrimp or beef, is limited, but the food is superior. Try tender, juicy prime roast beef, which comes with Yorkshire pudding, creamed spinach, and baked potato. Lobster is sometimes available. To reach Toni's, it's best to take a taxi. Note that it's open for dinner only.

In the Hotel Monte Taxco. ✆ 762/622-1300. Reservations recommended. Main courses $14–$22. AE, MC, V. Mon–Sat 7pm–1am.

MODERATE

Café Sasha ⋌⋌ INTERNATIONAL/VEGETARIAN   One of the cutest places to dine in town, Café Sasha is very popular with locals, and offers a great array of vegetarian options—like falafel and vegetarian curries, as well as Mexican and international classics. Try their Thai chicken or a hearty burrito. Open for breakfast, lunch, and dinner, it's also a great place for a cappuccino and pastry, or an evening cocktail. The music is hip, and the atmosphere inviting and chic. Local artists often exhibit here.

Calle Juan Ruiz de Alarcón 1, just down from Plazuela de Berna. No phone. cafe sasha@hotmail.com. Breakfast $2–$7; main courses $5–$15. No credit cards. Daily 8am–11:30pm.

La Terraza Café-Bar INTERNATIONAL   One of two restaurants at the Hotel Agua Escondida (on the *zócalo*), the rooftop La Terraza is a popular place for lunch, with wonderful views and tasty food. The menu is ample—there's something for every taste—as well as classic Mexican dishes. You can get anything from soup to roast chicken, enchiladas, tacos, steak, and dessert, as well as frosty margaritas or a great cappuccino. During the day, cafe umbrellas shade the sun, but you can stargaze at night here.

Plaza Borda 4. ✆ 762/622-0663. Main courses $7.50–$14. MC, V. Daily noon–10pm.

La Ventana de Taxco ⋌ ITALIAN   The spectacular view of the city from this restaurant makes it one of the best places to dine in Taxco. The changing menu of standard Italian fare is also quite good. The pasta dishes are the most recommendable. Lasagna is a big favorite, and Sicilian steak is also popular.

In the Hacienda del Solar hotel, Paraje del Solar s/n. ✆/fax **762/622-0587.** Breakfast $3–$7; main courses $10–$20. MC, V. Daily 8–11am and 1–10:30pm.

Sotavento Restaurant Bar Galería ★★ ITALIAN/INTERNA-TIONAL   Paintings decorate the walls of this stylish restaurant, and a variety of linen colors dot the tables. The menu features many Italian specialties—try deliciously fresh spinach salad and large pepper steak for a hearty meal, or Spaghetti Barbara, with poblano peppers and avocado, for a vegetarian option.

Juárez 8, next to City Hall. No phone. Main courses $3–$8. No credit cards. Tues–Sun 1pm–midnight. From the Plaza Borda, walk downhill beside the Hotel Agua Escondida, then follow the street as it bears left (don't go right on Juan Ruiz de Alarcón) about 1 block. The restaurant is on the left just after the street bends left.

Sr. Costilla's MEXICAN/INTERNATIONAL   The offbeat decor at "Mr. Ribs" includes a ceiling decked out with an assortment of cultural curios. Several tiny balconies hold a few minuscule tables that afford a view of the plaza and church, and they fill up long before the large dining room does. The menu is typical of Carlos Anderson chain restaurants, with Spanglish sayings and a large selection of everything from soup, steaks, sandwiches, and spareribs to desserts and coffee. The restaurant serves wine, beer, and drinks.

Plaza Borda 1 (next to Santa Prisca, above Patio de las Artesanías). ✆/fax **762/622-3215.** Main courses $8–$20. MC, V. Daily noon–midnight.

INEXPENSIVE

Fonda Ethel MEXICAN/INTERNATIONAL   This family-run place is opposite the Hotel Santa Prisca, 1 block from the Plaza Borda. It has colorful cloths on the tables and a tidy, homey atmosphere. The hearty *comida corrida* consists of soup or pasta, meat (perhaps a small steak), dessert, and good coffee.

Plazuela San Juan 14. ✆ **762/622-0788.** Breakfast $4.45–$5.55; main courses $5.15–$6.30; *comida corrida* (served 1–5pm) $5.80. No credit cards. Daily 9am–9pm.

TAXCO AFTER DARK

Paco's (no phone) is the most popular place overlooking the square for cocktails, conversation, and people-watching, all of which continue until midnight daily. Taxco's version of a dance club, **Windows,** is high up the mountain in the **Hotel Monte Taxco** (✆ **762/622-1300**). The whole city is on view, and music runs the gamut from the hit parade to hard rock. For a cover of $7, you can dance away Saturday night from 10pm to 3am.

Completely different in tone is **Berta's** (no phone), next to the Santa Prisca Church. Opened in 1930 by a lady named Berta, who made her fame on a drink of the same name (tequila, soda, lime, and honey), it's the traditional gathering place of the local gentry and more than a few tourists. Spurs and old swords decorate the walls. A Berta (the drink, of course) costs about $2; rum, the same. It's open daily from 11am to around 10pm.

National drinks (not beer) are two-for-one nightly between 6 and 8pm at the terrace bar of the **Hotel Victoria** (© **762/622-0004**), where you can also drink in the fabulous view. The gay-friendly **Aztec Disco** (© **762/627-3833**) features drag shows and dancing. It's located on Av. de los Plateros 184, and is open from 10pm until late.

2 Cuernavaca: Land of Eternal Spring ★★★

102km (64 miles) S of Mexico City; 80km (50 miles) N of Taxco

Often called the "land of eternal spring," Cuernavaca is known these days as much for its rejuvenating spas and spiritual sites as it is for its perfect climate and flowering landscapes. Spa services are easy to find, but more than that, Cuernavaca exudes a sense of deep connection with its historical and spiritual heritage. Its palaces, walled villas, and elaborate haciendas are home to museums, spas, and extraordinary guesthouses.

Wander the traditional markets and you'll see crystals, quartz, onyx, and tiger's-eye, in addition to tourist trinkets. These stones come from the Tepozteco Mountains—for centuries considered an energy source—which cradle Cuernavaca to the north and east. This area is where Mexico begins to narrow, and several mountain ranges converge. East and southeast of Cuernavaca are two volcanoes, also potent symbols of earth energy, Ixaccihuatl (the Sleeping Woman) and the recently active Popocatépetl (the Smoking Mountain).

Cuernavaca, capital of the state of Morelos, is also a cultural treasure, with a past that closely follows the history of Mexico. So divine are the landscape and climate that both the Aztec ruler Moctezuma and colonial Emperor Maximilian built private retreats here. Today, the roads between Mexico City and Cuernavaca are jammed almost every weekend, when city residents seek the same respite. Cuernavaca even has a large American colony, plus many students attending the numerous language and cultural institutes.

Emperor Charles V gave Cuernavaca to Hernán Cortez as a fief, and in 1532 the conquistador built a palace (now the Museo de Cuauhnahuac), where he lived on and off for half a dozen years before returning to Spain. Cortez introduced sugar-cane cultivation to the area, and African slaves were brought in to work in the cane fields, by way of Spain's Caribbean colonies. His sugar hacienda at the edge of town is now the impressive Hotel de Cortez.

After Mexico gained independence from Spain, powerful landowners from Mexico City gradually dispossessed the remaining small landholders, imposing virtual serfdom on them. This condition led to the rise of Emiliano Zapata, the great champion of agrarian reform, who battled the forces of wealth and power, defending the small farmer with the cry of "*¡Tierra y Libertad!*" (Land and Liberty!) during the Mexican revolution following 1910.

Today, Cuernavaca's popularity has brought an influx of wealthy foreigners and industrial capital. With this commercial growth, the city has also acquired the less desirable by-products of increased traffic, noise, and air pollution.

ESSENTIALS
GETTING THERE & DEPARTING
BY CAR   From Mexico City, take Paseo de la Reforma to Chapultepec Park and merge with the Periférico, which will take you to Highway 95D, the toll road on the far south of town that goes to Cuernavaca. From the Periférico, take the Insurgentes exit and continue until you come to signs for Cuernavaca/Tlalpan. Choose either the CUERNAVACA CUOTA (toll) or CUERNAVACA LIBRE (free) road on the right. The free road is slower and very windy, but is more scenic.

BY BUS   *Important note:* Buses to Cuernavaca depart directly from the Mexico City airport. (See "Getting There," in chapter 1, for details.) The trip takes an hour. The Mexico City Central de Autobuses del Sur exists primarily to serve the Mexico City–Cuernavaca–Taxco–Acapulco–Zihuatanejo route. Pullman has two stations in Cuernavaca: downtown, at the corner of Abasolo and Netzahualcoyotl (© **777/318-0907** or 777/312-6063), 4 blocks south of the center of town; and Casino de la Selva (© **777/ 312-9473**), less conveniently located at Plan de Ayala 14, near the railroad station.

Autobuses Estrella Blanca, Elite, Futura, and Flecha Roja also depart from the Central del Sur (© **777/312-2626**), with 33 buses daily from Mexico City. They arrive in Cuernavaca at Morelos 329, between Arista and Victoria, 6 blocks north of the town center. Here, you'll find frequent buses to Toluca, Chalma, Ixtapan de la Sal, Taxco, Acapulco, the Cacahuamilpa Caves, Querétaro, and Nuevo Laredo.

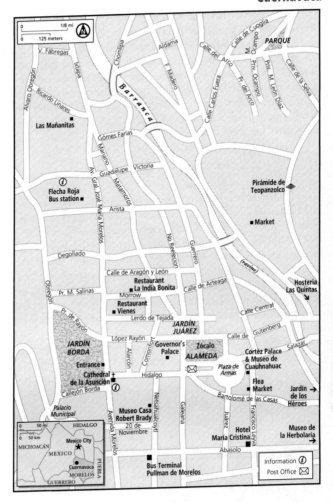

Estrella de Oro (© 777/312-3055), Morelos 900, serves Iguala, Chilpancingo, Acapulco, and Taxco.

Estrella Roja (© 777/318-5934), a second-class station at Galeana and Cuauhtemotzin in Cuernavaca, about 8 blocks south of the town center, serves Cuautla, Yautepec, Oaxtepec, and Izúcar de Matamoros.

VISITOR INFORMATION

Cuernavaca's **State Tourist Office** is at Av. Morelos Sur 187, between Jalisco and Tabasco (© **777/314-3881;** ©/fax 777/314-3872 or 777/314-3920; www.morelostravel.com), half a block north of the Estrella de Oro bus station and about a 15- to 20-minute walk south of the cathedral. It's open Monday through Friday from 8am to 5pm. There's also a **City Tourism kiosk** (© **777/318-7561** or 777/318-6498), on Morelos beside the El Calvario Church. It's open daily from 8am to 5pm.

CITY LAYOUT

In the center of the city are two contiguous plazas. The smaller and more formal, across from the post office, has a Victorian gazebo (designed by Gustave Eiffel, of Eiffel Tower fame) at its center. This is the **Alameda.** The larger, rectangular plaza with trees, shrubs, and benches is the **Plaza de Armas.** These two plazas are known collectively as the *zócalo* and form the hub for strolling vendors selling balloons, baskets, bracelets, and other crafts from surrounding villages. It's all easy-going, and one of the great pleasures of the town is hanging out at a park bench or table in a nearby restaurant. On Sunday afternoons, orchestras play in the gazebo. At the eastern end of the Alameda is the **Cortez Palace,** the conquistador's residence, now the Museo de Cuauhnahuac.

Note: The city's street-numbering system is extremely confusing. It appears that the city fathers, during the past century or so, imposed a new numbering system every 10 or 20 years. An address given as "no. 5" may be in a building that bears the number "506," or perhaps "Antes no. 5" (former no. 5).

FAST FACTS: Cuernavaca

American Express The local representative is **Viajes Marín,** Edificio las Plazas, Loc. 13 (© **777/314-2266** or 777/318-9901; fax 777/312-9297). It's open daily from 9am to 2pm and 4 to 7pm.

Area Code The telephone area code is **777.**

Banks Bank tellers (9am–3 or 5pm, depending on the bank), ATMs, and *casas de cambio* change money. The closest bank to the *zócalo* is **Bancomer,** Matamoros and Lerdo de Tejada, cater-cornered to Jardín Juárez (across López Rayón from the Alameda). Most banks are open until 6pm Monday through Friday and a half-day on Saturday.

Elevation Cuernavaca sits at 1,533m (5,058 ft.).

Hospital **Clínica Londres,** Calle Cuauhtémoc 305, Col. Lomas de la Selva (© **777/311-2482,** -2483, or -2484).

Internet Access **Café Internet Net-Conn,** on Morelos Norte, 360-A Col. Carolina (© **777/317-9496**), offers high-speed access for $2.50 per hour, as well as color laser printers, webcams, scanners, and other equipment. They also serve coffee, and have an adjoining bookstore. It's open Monday through Saturday from 8am to 11pm, closed Sunday.

Pharmacy **Farmacias del Ahorro** (© **777/322-2277**) offers hotel delivery service, but you must ask the front desk of your hotel to place the order, because the pharmacy requires the name of a hotel employee. It has 12 locations around the city, but the individual pharmacies have no phone. They are open daily from 7am to 8pm.

Population Cuernavaca has 400,000 residents.

Post Office The *correo* (© **777/312-4379**) is on the Plaza de Armas, next door to Café los Arcos. It's open Monday through Friday from 8am to 6pm, Saturday from 9am to 1pm.

Spanish Lessons Cuernavaca is known for its Spanish-language schools. Generally, the schools will help students find lodging with a family or provide a list of places to stay. Rather than make a long-term commitment in a family living situation, try it for a week, then decide. Contact the **Center for Bilingual Multicultural Studies,** San Jerónimo 304 (Apdo. Postal 1520), 62000 Cuernavaca, Morelos (© **777/317-1087** or 777/317-2488; www.spanish.com.mx); **Instituto de Idioma y Cultura en Cuernavaca** (© **777/317-8947;** fax 777/317-0455); or **Universal Centro de Lengua y Comunicación Social A.C. (Universal Language School),** J. H. Preciado 171 (Apdo. Postal 1-1826), 62000 Cuernavaca, Morelos (© **777/318-2904** or 777/312-4902; www. universal-spanish.com). Note that the whole experience, from classes to lodging, can be quite expensive; the school may accept credit cards for the class portion.

EXPLORING CUERNAVACA

On weekends, the whole city (including the roads, hotels, and restaurants) fills with people from Mexico City. This makes weekends more hectic, but also more fun. You can spend 1 or 2 days sightseeing pleasantly enough. If you've come on a day trip, you may not have time to make all the excursions listed below, but you'll have enough time to see the sights in town. Also notable is the traditional *mercado* (**public market**) adjacent to the Cortez Palace. It's open daily from 10am to 10pm, and the colorful rows of stands are a lively place for testing your bargaining skills as you purchase pottery, silver jewelry, crystals, and other trinkets. Note that the Cuauhnahuac museum is closed on Monday.

Catedral de la Asunción de María 👉 *Moments*

Construction on the church began in 1529, a mere 8 years after Cortez conquered Tenochtitlán (Mexico City) from the Aztec, and was completed in 1552. The churchmen could hardly trust their safety to the tenuous allegiance of their new converts, so they built a fortress as a church. The skull and crossbones above the main door is a symbol of the Franciscan order, which had its monastery here. The monastery is still here, in fact, and open to the public; it's on the northwest corner of the church property. Also visible on the exterior walls of the main church are inlaid rocks, placed there in memory of the men who lost their lives during its construction.

Once inside, wander through the sanctuaries and the courtyard, and pay special attention to the impressive frescoes painted on the walls, in various states of restoration. The frescoes date from the 1500s and have a distinct Asian style.

The main church sanctuary is stark, even severe, with an incongruous modern feeling (it was refurbished in the 1960s). Frescoes on these walls, discovered during the refurbishing, depict the persecution and martyrdom of St. Felipe de Jesús and his companions in Japan. No one is certain who painted them. In the churchyard, you'll see gravestones marking the tombs of the most devout—or wealthiest—of the parishioners. Being buried on the church grounds was believed to be the most direct route to heaven.

At the corner of Hidalgo and Morelos (3 blocks southwest of the Plaza de Armas). Free admission. Daily 8am–2pm and 4–10pm.

Jardín Borda

Across Morelos Street from the cathedral is the Jardín Borda (Borda Gardens). José de la Borda, the Taxco silver magnate, ordered a sumptuous vacation house built here in the late 1700s. When he died in 1778, his son Manuel inherited the land and transformed it into a botanical garden. The large enclosed garden next to the house was a huge private park, laid out in Andalusian style, with kiosks and an artificial pond. Maximilian took it over as his private summer house in 1865. He and Empress Carlota entertained lavishly in the gardens and held frequent concerts by the lake.

The gardens were completely restored and reopened in 1987 as the Jardín Borda Centro de Artes. In the gateway buildings, several galleries hold changing exhibits and large paintings showing scenes from the life of Maximilian and from the history of the Borda Gardens. One portrays the initial meeting between Maximilian and La India Bonita, a local maiden who became his lover.

On your stroll through the gardens, you'll see the little man-made lake on which Austrian, French, and Mexican nobility rowed small boats in the moonlight. Ducks have taken the place of dukes, however. There are rowboats for rent. The lake is now artfully adapted as an outdoor theater, with seats for the audience on one side and the stage on the other. A cafe serves refreshments and light meals, and a weekend market inside the *jardín* sells arts and crafts.

Morelos 271, at Hidalgo. *©* 777/318-1038 or 777/318-1052. Fax 777/318-3706. Admission $1.50; free Sun. Tues–Sun 10am–5:30pm.

Jardín Botánico y Museo de Medicina Tradicional y Herbolaria *★★*

This museum of traditional herbal medicine, in the south Cuernavaca suburb of Acapantzingo, occupies a former resort residence built by Maximilian, the Casa del Olvido. During his brief reign, the Austrian-born emperor came here for trysts with La India Bonita, his Cuernavacan lover. The building was restored in 1960, and the house and gardens now preserve the local wisdom of folk medicine. The shady gardens are lovely to wander through, and you shouldn't miss the 200 orchids growing near the rear of the property.

Matamoros 14, Acapantzingo. *©* 777/312-5955, 777/312-3108, or 777/314-4046. www.inah.gob.mx Free admission. Daily 9am–4:30pm. Take a taxi, or catch *combi* no. 6 at the *mercado* on Degollado. Ask to be dropped off at Matamoros near the museum. Turn right on Matamoros and walk 1½ blocks; the museum will be on your right.

Museo Casa Robert Brady *★★*

This museum in a private home contains more than 1,300 works of art. Among them are pre-Hispanic and colonial pieces; oil paintings by Frida Kahlo and Rufino Tamayo; and handicrafts from America, Africa, Asia, and India. Robert Brady, an Iowa native with a degree in fine arts from the Art Institute of Chicago, assembled the collections. He lived in Venice for 5 years before settling in Cuernavaca in 1960. The wildly colorful rooms are exactly as Brady left them. Admission includes a guide in Spanish; English and French guides are available if requested in advance.

Calle Netzahualcoyotl 4 (between Hidalgo and Abasolo). *©* 777/318-8554. Fax 777/314-3529. www.geocities.com/bradymuseum/bradyspanish.html. Admission $3. Tues–Sun 10am–6pm.

Museo de Cuauhnahuac   The museum is in the Cortez Palace, the former home of the greatest of the conquistadors, Hernán Cortez. Construction started in 1530 on the site of a Tlahuica Indian ceremonial center and was finished by the conquistador's son Martín. The palace later served as the legislative headquarters for the state of Morelos.

In the east portico on the upper floor is a large Diego Rivera mural commissioned by Dwight Morrow, U.S. ambassador to Mexico in the 1920s. It depicts the history of Cuernavaca from the coming of the Spaniards to the rise of Zapata (1910). On the lower level, the excellent bookstore is open daily from 10am to 8pm. Tour guides in front of the palace offer their services in the museum, and for other sights in Cuernavaca, for about $10 per hour. Make sure you see official SECTUR (Tourism Secretary) credentials before hiring one of these guides. This is also a central point for taxis in the downtown area.

In the Cortez Palace, Leyva 100. (℗ 777/312-8171. www.morelostravel.com/cultura/museo7.html. Admission $3.30; free Sun. Tues–Sun 9am–6pm.

ACTIVITIES & EXCURSIONS
GOLF

With its perpetually springlike climate, Cuernavaca is an ideal place for golf. The **Tabachines Golf Club and Restaurant,** Km 93.5 Carretera Mexico-Acapulco (℗ 777/314-3999), the city's most popular course, is open for public play. Percy Clifford designed this 18-hole course, surrounded by beautifully manicured gardens blooming with bougainvillea, gardenias, and other flowers. The elegant restaurant is a popular place for breakfast, lunch, and especially Sunday brunch. Greens fees are $80 during the week and $160 on weekends. American Express, Visa, and MasterCard are accepted. It's open Tuesday through Sunday from 7am to 6pm; tee times are available from 7am to 2pm.

Also in Cuernavaca is the **Club de Golf Hacienda San Gaspar,** Avenida Emiliano Zapata, Col. Cliserio Alanis (℗ 777/319-4424), an 18-hole golf course designed by Joe Finger. It's surrounded by more than 3,000 trees and has two artificial lagoons, plus beautiful panoramic views of Cuernavaca, the Popocatépetl and Iztacihuatl volcanoes, and the Tepozteco Mountains. Greens fees are $45 on weekdays, $89 on weekends; carts cost an additional $28 for 18 holes, and a caddy is $17 plus tip. American Express, Visa, and MasterCard are accepted. Additional facilities include a gym with whirlpool and sauna, pool, four tennis courts, and a restaurant and snack bar. It's open Wednesday through Monday from 7am to 7pm.

LAS ESTACAS

Either a side trip from Cuernavaca or a destination on its own, Las Estacas, Km 6.5 Carretera Tlaltizapán–Cuautla, Morelos (© **777/ 312-4412** or 777/312-7610 in Cuernavaca, or 734/345-0350 or 734/ 345-0159; www.lasestacas.com) is a natural water park. Its clear spring waters reputedly have healing properties. In addition to the crystal-clear rivers, Las Estacas has two pools, wading pools for children, horseback riding, and a *balneario* (traditional-style spa), open daily from 8am to 6pm. Several restaurants serve such simple food as quesadillas, fruit with yogurt, sandwiches, and *tortas*. Admission is $19 for adults, $12 for children under 4 feet tall. A small, basic hotel charges $91 to $140 for a double room; rates include the entrance fee to the *balneario* and breakfast. Cheaper lodging options are available, including a trailer park; you can rent an adobe or straw hut with two bunk beds for $15. Visit the website for more information. MasterCard and Visa are accepted. On weekends, the place fills with families. Las Estacas is 36km (23 miles) east of Cuernavaca. To get there, take Highway 138 to Yautepec, then turn right at the first exit past Yautepec.

PYRAMIDS OF XOCHICALCO ®

This beautiful ceremonial center provides clues to the history of the whole region. Artifacts and inscriptions link the site to the mysterious cultures that built Teotihuacán and Tula, and some of the objects found here would indicate that residents were also in contact with the Mixtec, Aztec, Maya, and Zapotec. The most impressive building in Xochicalco is the Pirámide de la Serpiente Emplumada (Pyramid of the Plumed Serpent), with its magnificent reliefs of plumed serpents twisting around seated priests. Underneath the pyramid is a series of tunnels and chambers with murals on the walls. There is also an observatory, where from April 30 to August 15 you can follow the trajectory of the sun as it shines through a hexagonal opening. The pyramids (© **777/314-3920** for information) are 36km (23 miles) southwest of Cuernavaca. They're open daily from 6am to 5pm. Admission is $3.80.

WHERE TO STAY

Because so many residents of Mexico City come down for a day or two, tourist traffic at the hotels may be heavy on weekends and holidays. Reservations during these times are recommended.

EXPENSIVE

Camino Real Sumiya ☆☆   About 11km (7 miles) south of Cuernavaca, this unusual resort, whose name means "the place of peace, tranquillity, and longevity," was once the home of Woolworth heiress Barbara Hutton. Using materials and craftsmen from Japan, she constructed the estate in 1959 for $3.2 million on 12 wooded hectares (30 acres). The main house, a series of large connected rooms and decks, overlooks the grounds and contains restaurants and the lobby. Sumiya's charm is in its relaxing atmosphere, which is best midweek (escapees from Mexico City tend to fill it on weekends). The guest rooms, which cluster in three-story buildings bordering manicured lawns, are simple in comparison to the striking Japanese architecture of the main house. Rooms have subtle Japanese accents, with austere but comfortable furnishings and scrolled wood doors. Hutton built a Kabuki-style theater and exquisite Zen meditation garden, which are now used only for special events. The theater contains vividly colored silk curtains and gold-plated temple paintings protected by folding cedar and mahogany screens. Strategically placed rocks in the garden represent the chakras, or energy points of the human body.

Cuernavaca is an inexpensive taxi ride away. Taxis to the Mexico City airport cost $112 one-way.

Interior Fracc. Sumiya s/n, Col. José Parres, 62550 Jiutepec, Mor. ⓒ 01-800/ 901-2300 or 777/329-9888. Fax 777/329-9889. www.caminoreal.com/sumiya. 163 units. $200 double; $385 suite. Low-season packages and discounts available. AE, DC, MC, V. Free parking. From the freeway, take the Atlacomulco exit and follow signs to Sumiya. Ask directions in Cuernavaca if you're coming from there; the route is complicated. **Amenities:** 2 restaurants; poolside snack bar; outdoor pool; golf privileges nearby; 10 tennis courts; business center; room service; convention facilities w/simultaneous translation capabilities. *In room:* A/C, TV, minibar, dual-line phones w/dataport, hair dryer, iron, safe, ceiling fans.

Las Mañanitas *Overrated*   This has been Cuernavaca's most renowned luxury lodging for years. Although it is impeccably maintained, Las Mañanitas has an overly formal feeling to it, which may take away from some guests' comfort. The rooms are formal in a style that was popular 15 years ago, with gleaming polished molding and brass accents, large bathrooms, and rich fabrics. Rooms in the original mansion, called terrace suites, overlook the restaurant and inner lawn; the large rooms in the patio section each have a secluded patio; and those in the luxurious, expensive garden section each have a patio overlooking the pool and emerald lawns. Thirteen rooms have fireplaces, and the hotel also has a heated pool in the private garden. The hotel is one of only two in Mexico associated with the prestigious Relais & Châteaux chain. Transportation to and from the Mexico City airport can be arranged through the hotel for $240 round-trip. The restaurant overlooking the gardens is one of the country's premier dining places (see "Where to Dine," below). It's open to nonguests for lunch and dinner only.

Ricardo Linares 107 (5½ long blocks north of the Jardín Borda), 62000 Cuernavaca, Mor. ✆ **777/314-1466** or 777/312-4646. Fax 777/318-3672. www.lasmananitas. com.mx. 20 units. Weekday $190–$390 double; weekend $220–$425 double. Rates include breakfast. AE, MC, V. Free valet parking. **Amenities:** Restaurant; outdoor pool; concierge; room service; laundry service. *In room:* TV upon request, hair dryer.

Misión Del Sol Resort & Spa ★★★ *(Finds)*   This adults-only hotel and spa offers an experience that rivals any in North America or Europe—and is an exceptional value. You feel a sense of peace from the moment you enter the resort, which draws on the mystical wisdom of the ancient cultures of Mexico, Tibet, Egypt, and Asia. Guests and visitors are encouraged to wear light-hued clothes to contribute to the harmonious flow of energy.

Architecturally stunning adobe buildings that meld with the natural environment house the guest rooms, villas, and common areas. Streams border the extensive gardens. Such group activities as reading discussions, chess club, and painting workshops take place in the salon, where films are shown on weekend evenings. Rooms are large and peaceful; each looks onto its own garden or stream and has three channels of ambient music. Some have air-conditioning. Bathrooms are large, with sunken tubs, and the dual-headed showers have river rocks set into the floor, as a type of reflexology treatment. Beds contain magnets for restoring proper energy flow. Villas have two separate bedrooms, plus a living/dining area and a meditation room. The spa has a menu of 32 services, with an emphasis on water-based treatments. Elegant relaxation areas are interspersed among the treatment rooms and whirlpool. Airport transfers from Mexico City are available for $180 one-way.

Av. General Diego Díaz González 31, Col. Parres, 62550 Cuernavaca, Mor. ✆ **01-800/999-9100** toll-free inside Mexico, or 777/321-0999. Fax 777/320-7981. www.misiondelsol.com.mx. 42 units, plus 12 villas. $262 deluxe double; $551 villa (up to 4 persons); $610 Villa Magnolia (up to 4 persons). Special spa and meal packages available. AE, MC, V. Free parking. Children under 13 not accepted. **Amenities:** Restaurant; 2 tennis courts; well-equipped gym; spa services, including massages, body wraps, scrubs, facial treatments, *temazcal* (pre-Hispanic sweat lodge), Janzu, phototherapy; daily meditation, yoga, Tai Chi classes/sessions; Ping-Pong table. *In room:* Safe-deposit box; bathrobes.

MODERATE

Hotel Posada María Cristina ✦✦   The María Cristina's high walls conceal many delights: a small swimming pool, lush gardens with fountains, a good restaurant, and patios. Guest rooms vary in size; all are exceptionally clean and comfortable, with firm beds and colonial-style furnishings. Bathrooms have inlaid Talavera tiles and skylights. Suites are only slightly larger than normal rooms; junior suites have Jacuzzis. La Calandria, the handsome little restaurant on the first floor, overlooks the gardens and serves excellent meals based on Mexican and international recipes. Even if you don't stay here, consider having a meal. The Sunday brunch ($13 per person) is especially popular. The hotel is half a block from the Palacio de Cortez.

Leyva 20, at Abasolo (Apdo. 203), 62000 Cuernavaca, Mor. ✆ 777/318-6984 or 777/318-5767. Fax 777/312-9126 or 777/318-2981. www.maria-cristina.com. 19 units. $110 double; $135–$160 suite or cabaña. AE, MC, V. Free parking. **Amenities:** Restaurant; bar; outdoor pool; concierge; tour desk. *In room:* A/C, TV, hair dryer, ceiling fan.

INEXPENSIVE

Hotel Juárez   Low rates and a prime location (downtown, 1 block from the Casa Borda) make the Juárez a good choice for those intent on exploring the town's cultural charms. Each of the simple rooms is old-fashioned but well kept.

Netzahualcoyotl 19, 62000 Cuernavaca, Mor. ✆ 777/314-0219. 12 units. $30 double. No credit cards. Limited street parking. From the Cathedral, go east on Hidalgo, then turn right on Netzahualcoyotl. The hotel is 1 block down on the left. **Amenities:** Outdoor pool; tour desk. *In room:* TV, fan.

WHERE TO DINE
VERY EXPENSIVE

Restaurant Las Mañanitas *Overrated* MEXICAN/INTERNATIONAL   Las Mañanitas has set the standard for sumptuous, leisurely dining in Cuernavaca, but lately its reputation has surpassed the reality. The setting is exquisite and the service superb, but the food is not as noteworthy as one would expect. Tables are on a shaded terrace with a view of gardens, strolling peacocks, and softly playing violinists or a romantic trio. Service is extremely attentive. The cuisine is Mexican with an international flair, drawing on seasonal fruits and vegetables and offering a full selection of fresh seafood, beef, pork, veal, and fowl, but in standard preparations. Try cream of watercress soup, filet of red snapper in curry sauce, and black-bottom pie, the house specialty.

In Las Mañanitas hotel, Ricardo Linares 107 (5½ long blocks north of the Jardín Borda). ✆ 777/314-1466 or 777/312-4646. www.lasmananitas.com.mx. Reservations recommended. Main courses $16–$32. AE, MC, V. Daily 1–5pm and 7–11pm.

MODERATE

Casa Hidalgo ✸✸✸ GOURMET MEXICAN/INTERNA-TIONAL   In a beautifully restored colonial building across from the Palacio de Cortez, this is a relatively recent addition to Cuernavaca dining. The food is more sophisticated and innovative than that at most places in town. Specialties include cream of Brie soup, smoked rainbow trout, and the exquisite Spanish-inspired filet Hidalgo—breaded and stuffed with serrano ham and *manchego* cheese. There are always daily specials, and bread is baked on the premises. Tables on the balcony afford a view of the action in the plaza below. The restaurant is accessible by wheelchair.

Calle Hidalgo 6. ✆ 777/312-2749. Reservations recommended on weekends. Main courses $13–$20. AE, MC, V. Mon–Thurs 1:30–11pm; Fri–Sat 1:30pm–midnight; Sun 1:30–11:30pm. Valet parking available.

Restaurant La India Bonita ✸✸ MEXICAN   Housed among the interior patios and portals of the restored home of former U.S. Ambassador Dwight Morrow, La India Bonita is a gracious haven where you can enjoy the setting as well as the food. Specialties include *mole poblano* (chicken with a sauce of bitter chocolate and fiery chiles) and *fillet a la parrilla* (charcoal-grilled steak). There are also several daily specials. A breakfast mainstay is *desayuno Maximiliano*, a gigantic platter featuring enchiladas.

Morrow 15 (between Morelos and Matamoros), Col. Centro, 2 blocks north of the Jardín Juárez. ✆ 777/318-6967 or 777/312-5021. Breakfast $4.15–$6.50; main courses $6.70–$14. AE, MC, V. Tues–Sat 9am–9pm; Sun–Mon 9am–5pm.

INEXPENSIVE

La Universal ✸✸ *Value* MEXICAN/PASTRIES   This is a busy place, partly because of its great location (overlooking both the Alameda and Plaza de Armas), partly because of its traditional Mexican specialties, and partly because of its reasonable prices. It's open to the street and has many outdoor tables, usually filled with older men discussing the day's events or playing chess. These tables are perfect for watching the parade of street vendors and park life. The specialty is a Mexican grilled sampler plate, including *carne asada*, enchilada, pork cutlet, green onions, beans, and tortillas, for $10. A full breakfast special ($4) is served Monday through Friday from 9:30am to noon. There's also a popular happy hour on weekdays from 8 to 10pm.

Guerrero 2. ✆ 777/318-6732 or 777/318-5970. Breakfast $4–$7.50; main courses $4–$15; *comida corrida* $8.90. AE, MC, V. Daily 9:30am–midnight.

CUERNAVACA AFTER DARK

Cuernavaca has a number of cafes right off the Jardín Juárez where people gather to sip coffee or drinks till the wee hours. The best are **Café de La Parroquia**, Jesus 11 (© 777/152-3161), and **La Universal** (see above). There are band concerts in the Jardín Juárez on Thursday and Sunday evenings.

A recent—and welcome—addition is **La Plazuela,** a short, pedestrian-only stretch across from the Cortez Palace. Here, coffee shops alternate with tattoo parlors and live-music bars. It's geared toward a 20-something, university crowd.

3 Tepoztlán ✶✶

72km (45 miles) S of Mexico City; 45km (28 miles) NE of Cuernavaca

Tepoztlán is one of the strangest and most beautiful towns in Mexico. Largely undiscovered by foreign tourists, it occupies the floor of a broad, lush valley whose walls were formed by bizarrely shaped mountains that look like the work of some abstract expressionist giant. The mountains are visible from almost everywhere in town; even the municipal parking lot has a spectacular view.

Tepoztlán is small and steeped in legend and mystery—it is adjacent to the alleged birthplace of Quetzalcoatl, the Aztec serpent god—and comes about as close as you're going to get to an unspoiled, magical mountain hideaway. Though the town is tranquil during the week, escapees from Mexico City overrun it on the weekends, especially Sunday. Most Tepoztlán residents, whether foreigners or Mexicans, tend to be mystically or artistically oriented—although some also appear to be just plain disoriented.

Aside from soaking up the ambience, two things you must do are climbing up to the Tepozteco pyramid and hitting the weekend crafts market. In addition, Tepoztlán offers a variety of treatments, cures, diets, massages, and sweat lodges. Some of these are available at hotels; for some, you have to ask around. Many locals swear that the valley possesses mystical curative powers.

If you have a car, Tepoztlán provides a great starting point for traveling this region of Mexico. Within 90 minutes are Las Estacas, Taxco, las Grutas de Cacahuamilpa, and Xochicalco (some of the prettiest ruins in Mexico). Tepoztlán is 20 minutes from Cuernavaca and only an hour south of Mexico City, which—given its lost-in-time feel—seems hard to believe.

ESSENTIALS
GETTING THERE & DEPARTING

BY CAR   From Mexico City, the quickest route is Highway 95 (the toll road) to Cuernavaca; just before the Cuernavaca city limits, you'll see the clearly marked turnoff to Tepoztlán on 95D and Highway 115. The slower, free federal Highway 95D, direct from Mexico City, is also an option, and may be preferable if you're departing from the western part of the city. Take 95D south to Km 71, where the exit to Tepoztlán on Highway 115 is clearly indicated.

BY BUS   From Mexico City, buses to Tepoztlán run regularly from the Terminal de Sur and the Terminal Poniente. The trip takes an hour.

In addition, you can book round-trip transportation to the Mexico City airport through **Marquez Sightseeing Tours** (℡ 777/320-9109 and 777/315-5875; marqueztours@hotmail.com) and two hotels: the **Posada del Tepozteco** (℡ 739/395-0010), and **Casa Iccemayan** (℡ 739/395-0899). The round-trip cost varies between $125 and $200.

EXPLORING TEPOZTLAN

Tepoztlán's **weekend crafts market** is one of the best in central Mexico. More crafts are available on Sunday, but if you can't stand the multitudes, Saturday is quite good, too. Vendors sell all kinds of ceramics, from simple fired clay works resembling those made with pre-Hispanic techniques, to the more commercial versions of Majolica and pseudo-Talavera. There are also puppets, carved wood figures, and some textiles, especially thick wool Mexican sweaters and jackets made out of *jerga* (a coarse cloth). Very popular currently is the "hippie"-style jewelry that earned Tepoztlán its fame in the '60s and '70s. The market is also remarkable for its variety of food stands.

The other primary activity is hiking up to **Tepozteco pyramid.** The climb is steep but not difficult. Dense vegetation shades the trail (actually a long natural staircase), which is beautiful from bottom to top. Once you arrive at the pyramid you are treated to remarkable views and, if you are lucky, a great show by a family of *coatis* (tropical raccoons), who visit the pyramid most mornings to beg for food; they especially love bananas. The pyramid is a Tlahuica construction that predates the Náhuatl (Aztec) domination of the area. It was the site of important celebrations in the 12th and 13th centuries. The main street in Tepoztlán, Avenida 5 de Mayo, takes you to the path that leads you to the top of the

Tepozteco. The trail begins where the name of Avenida 5 de Mayo changes to Camino del Tepozteco. The hike is about an hour each way, but if you stop and take in the scenery and really enjoy the trail, it can take up to 2 hours each way.

Also worth visiting is the **former convent Dominico de la Navidad,** just east of the main plaza. Built between 1560 and 1588, it is now a museum.

SIGHTS NEAR TEPOZTLAN

Many nearby places are easily accessible by car. One good tour service is **Marquez Sightseeing Tours,** located in Cuernavaca (© **777/320-9109** or 777/315-5875). Marquez has four- and seven-passenger vehicles, very reasonable prices, and a large variety of set tours. The dependable owner, Arturo Marquez Diaz, speaks better than passable English and will allow you to design your own tour. He also offers transportation to and from Mexico City airport for approximately $150.

Two tiny, charming villages, **Santo Domingo Xocotitlán** and **Amatlán,** are only a 20-minute drive from Tepoztlán and can be reached by minibuses, which depart regularly from the center of town. There is nothing much to do in these places except wander around absorbing the marvelous views of the Tepozteco Mountains and drinking in the magical ambience.

Las Grutas de Cacahuamilpa ⊛, known as the Cacahuamilpa Caves or Grottoes (© **555/150-5031**), is an unforgettable system of caverns with a wooden walkway for easy access. As you pass from chamber to chamber you'll see spectacular illuminated rock formations. Admission for 2 hours is $3.50; a guide for groups, which can be assembled on the spot, costs an additional $8. The caverns are open daily from 10am to 5pm, and are 90 minutes from Tepoztlán.

About 40 minutes southeast of Tepoztlán is **Las Estacas,** an ecological resort with a cold-water spring that is said to have curative powers (p. 157). The ruins of **Xochicalco** (see "Cuernavaca: Land of Eternal Spring," earlier in this chapter), and the colonial town of **Taxco** (earlier in this chapter) are easily accessible from Tepoztlán.

WHERE TO STAY

The town gets very busy on the weekends, so if your stay will include Friday or Saturday night, make reservations well in advance. In addition to the choices noted below, consider two other excellent options just outside of town. **Casa Bugambilia** ⊛⊛⊛, Callejón de Tepopula 007, Valle de Atongo (© **739/395-0158;** www.casabugambilia.com)

is a new 11-room hotel property not far from *el Telón*, the local dance club (don't confuse this with *Posada* Bugambilia, a modest hotel in town). The spacious rooms are elegantly furnished with high-end carved Mexican furniture, and every room has a fireplace. Doubles average $180 to $250. And **Las Golondrinas** ⟨⟩⟨⟩⟨⟩, Callejón de Terminas 4 (© **739/395-0649;** homepage.mac.com/marisolfernandez/ LasGolondrinas), is a B&B so off the beaten track that even cab drivers have trouble finding the place—in the area behind Ixcatepec church. But owner Marisol Fernandez has imbued the house with her tranquil, down-to-earth charm; three of the four guest rooms open onto a wraparound terrace that overlooks the garden, a small pool, and the Tepozteco Mountains beyond. Doubles are $109, including breakfast.

Hotel Nilayam ⟨⟩   Formerly Hotel Tepoztlán, this holistic-oriented retreat is in a colonial building, but the decor has been brightened up considerably. Suites, with hydromassage tubs and terraces, are the most spacious option. Stays here encourage self-exploration: The gracious, helpful staff offers complete detox programs and a full array of services, including yoga, reflexology, spinal-column exercises, meditation, music therapy, and more. The hotel has a great view of the mountain. The restaurant features a creative menu of vegetarian cuisine.

Industrias 6, 62520 Tepoztlán, Mor. © **739/395-0522.** Fax 739/395-0522. www. nilayam.com 36 units. $85 double; $175 suite. AE, MC, V. **Amenities:** Restaurant; pool; tennis court; spa services; private *temazcal* (pre-Hispanic sweat lodge). *In room:* TV.

Posada del Tepozteco ⟨⟩⟨⟩   This property looks out over the town and down the length of the spectacular valley; the views from just about anywhere are superb. Rooms are tastefully furnished in rustic Mexican style. All but the least expensive have terraces and views. All suites have small whirlpool tubs. The grounds are exquisitely landscaped, and the atmosphere intimate and romantic.

Paraíso 3 (2 blocks from the town center), 62520 Tepoztlán, Mor. © **739/395-0010.** Fax 739/395-0323. www.posadadeltepozteco.com. 20 units. $145–$225 double. Rates include breakfast. AE, MC, V. Free parking. **Amenities:** Restaurant w/stunning view; small outdoor pool.

WHERE TO DINE

In addition to the two choices listed below, El Chalchi restaurant at the **Hotel Nilayam** (see above) offers some of the best vegetarian fare in the area. It's 3 blocks from the main square, with main courses priced around $5.

Moments **Tepoznieves: A Taste of Heaven**

Don't leave town without a stop at **Tepoznieves,** av. 5 de Mayo 21 (© **739/395-3813**), the sublime local ice-cream shop. The store's slogan, *Nieve de Dioses* (Ice Cream of the Gods), doesn't exaggerate. More than 120 types of all-natural ice cream and sorbet, come in flavors familiar (vanilla, bubble gum), exotic (tamarind, mango studded with chile piquin), and off the wall (beet? lettuce? corn?).

El Ciruelo Restaurant Bar ℛ MEXICAN GOURMET   This picturesque restaurant, surrounded by beautiful flowering gardens and adobe walls, offers a sampling of Tepoztlán's essence in one place. The service is positively charming, and the food divine. House specialties include chalupas of goat cheese, chicken with *huitlacoche,* and a regional treat: milk candies.

Zaragoza 17, Barrio de la Santísima, in front of the church. © **739/395-1203**. Dinner $7.50–$25. AE. Sun–Thurs 1–7pm; Fri–Sat 1pm–midnight.

Restaurant Axitla ℛℛℛ *Finds* GOURMET MEXICAN/INTER-NATIONAL   Axitla is not only the best restaurant in Tepoztlán, but also one of the finest in Mexico for showcasing the country's cuisine. Gourmet Mexican delicacies are made from scratch using the freshest local ingredients. Specialties include chicken breast stuffed with wild mushrooms in a *chipotle chile* sauce, *chiles en nogada,* and exceptional *mole.* There are also excellent steaks and fresh seafood. As if the food weren't enough—and believe me, it is—the setting will make your meal even more memorable. The restaurant is at the base of the Tepozteco Pyramid, surrounded by 1.2 hectares (3 acres) of junglelike gardens that encompass a creek and lily ponds. The views of the Tepozteco Mountains are magnificent. Memo and Laura, the gracious owners, speak excellent English and are marvelous sources of information about the area.

Av. del Tepozteco, at the foot of the trail to the pyramid. © **739/395-0519**. Lunch $5–$10; dinner $5–$20. MC, V. Wed–Sun 10am–7pm.

Appendix:
Useful Terms & Phrases

1 Basic Vocabulary

For more Spanish words and phrases, see the inside back cover of this book.

ENGLISH-SPANISH PHRASES

English	Spanish	Pronunciation
Good day	**Buen día**	bwehn *dee*-ah
Good morning	**Buenos días**	*bweh*-nohss *dee*-ahss
How are you?	**¿Cómo está?**	*koh*-moh ehss-*tah?*
Very well	**Muy bien**	mwee byehn
Thank you	**Gracias**	*grah*-syahss
You're welcome	**De nada**	deh *nah*-dah
Goodbye	**Adiós**	ah-*dyohss*
Please	**Por favor**	pohr fah-*vohr*
Yes	**Sí**	see
No	**No**	noh
Excuse me	**Perdóneme**	pehr-*doh*-neh-meh
Give me	**Déme**	*deh*-meh
Where is . . . ?	**¿Dónde está . . . ?**	*dohn*-deh ehss-*tah?*
the station	**la estación**	lah ehss-tah-*syohn*
a hotel	**un hotel**	oon oh-*tehl*
a gas station	**una gasolinera**	*oo*-nah gah-soh-lee-*neh*-rah
a restaurant	**un restaurante**	oon res-tow-*rahn*-teh
the toilet	**el baño**	el *bah*-nyoh
a good doctor	**un buen médico**	oon bwehn *meh*-dee-coh
the road to . . .	**el camino a/hacia . . .**	el cah-*mee*-noh ah/*ah*-syah
To the right	**A la derecha**	ah lah deh-*reh*-chah

English	Spanish	Pronunciation
To the left	A la izquierda	ah lah ees-*kyehr*-dah
Straight ahead	Derecho	deh-*reh*-choh
I would like	Quisiera	key-*syeh*-rah
I want	Quiero	*kyeh*-roh
to eat	comer	koh-*mehr*
a room	una habitación	*oo*-nah ah-bee-tah-*syohn*
Do you have . . . ?	¿Tiene usted . . . ?	tyeh-neh oo-*sted?*
a book	un libro	oon *lee*-broh
a dictionary	un diccionario	oon deek-syow-*nah*-ryo
How much is it?	¿Cuánto cuesta?	*kwahn*-toh *kwehss*-tah?
When?	¿Cuándo?	*kwahn*-doh?
What?	¿Qué?	keh?
There is (Is there . . . ?)	(¿)Hay (. . . ?)	eye?
What is there?	¿Qué hay?	keh eye?
Yesterday	Ayer	ah-*yer*
Today	Hoy	oy
Tomorrow	Mañana	mah-*nyah*-nah
Good	Bueno	*bweh*-noh
Bad	Malo	*mah*-loh
Better (best)	(Lo) Mejor	(loh) meh-*hohr*
More	Más	mahs
Less	Menos	*meh*-nohss
No smoking	Se prohibe fumar	seh proh-*ee*-beh foo-*mahr*

MORE USEFUL PHRASES

English	Spanish	Pronunciation
Do you speak English?	¿Habla usted inglés?	*ah*-blah oo-*sted* een-*glehs?*
Is there anyone here who speaks English?	¿Hay alguien aquí que hable inglés?	eye *ahl*-gyehn ah-*kee* keh *ah*-bleh een-*glehs?*

English	Spanish	Pronunciation
I speak a little Spanish.	**Hablo un poco de español.**	*ah*-bloh oon *poh*-koh deh ehss-pah-*nyohl*
I don't understand Spanish very well.	**No (lo) entiendo muy bien el español.**	noh (loh) ehn-*tyehn*-doh mwee byehn el ehss-pah-*nyohl*
The meal is good.	**Me gusta la comida.**	meh *goo*-stah lah koh-*mee*-dah
What time is it?	**¿Qué hora es?**	keh *oh*-rah ehss?
May I see your menu?	**¿Puedo ver el menú (la carta)?**	*pueh*-do vehr el meh-*noo* (lah *car*-tah)?
The check, please.	**La cuenta, por favor.**	lah *quehn*-tah pohr fa-*vorh*
What do I owe you?	**¿Cuánto le debo?**	*kwahn*-toh leh *deh*-boh?
What did you say?	**¿Mande?** (formal) **¿Cómo?** (informal)	*mahn*-deh? *koh*-moh?
I want (to see) . . .	**Quiero (ver) . . .**	*kyeh*-roh vehr
a room	**un cuarto** or **una habitación**	oon *kwar*-toh, *oo*-nah ah-bee-tah-*syohn*
for two persons	**para dos personas**	*pah*-rah dohss pehr-*soh*-nahs
with (without) bathroom.	**con (sin) baño.**	kohn (seen) *bah*-nyoh
We are staying here only	**Nos quedamos aquí solamente**	nohs keh-*dah*-mohss ah-*kee* soh-lah-*mehn*-teh
one night	**una noche**	*oo*-nah *noh*-cheh
one week	**una semana**	*oo*-nah seh-*mah*-nah

English	Spanish	Pronunciation
We are leaving	**Partimos (Salimos)**	pahr-*tee*-mohss (sah-*lee*-mohss)
tomorrow	**mañana**	mah-*nya*-nah
Do you accept . . . ?	**¿Acepta usted . . . ?**	ah-*sehp*-tah oo-*sted*
. . . traveler's checks?	**. . . cheques de viajero?**	*cheh*-kehss deh byah-*heh*-roh?
Is there a laundromat?	**¿Hay una lavandería?**	eye *oo*-nah lah-*vahn*-deh-ree-ah
. . . near here?	**. . . cerca de aquí?**	*sehr*-kah deh ah-*kee*
Please send these clothes to the laundry.	**Hágame el favor de mandar esta ropa a la lavandería.**	ah-gah-meh el fah-*vohr* deh mahn-*dahr* ehss-tah roh-pah a lah lah-*vahn*-deh-*ree*-ah

NUMBERS

1 **uno** (*ooh*-noh)
2 **dos** (dohss)
3 **tres** (trehss)
4 **cuatro** (*kwah*-troh)
5 **cinco** (*seen*-koh)
6 **seis** (sayss)
7 **siete** (*syeh*-teh)
8 **ocho** (*oh*-choh)
9 **nueve** (*nweh*-beh)
10 **diez** (dyess)
11 **once** (*ohn*-seh)
12 **doce** (*doh*-seh)
13 **trece** (*treh*-seh)
14 **catorce** (kah-*tohr*-seh)
15 **quince** (*keen*-seh)
16 **dieciseis** (dyess-ee-*sayss*)
17 **diecisiete** (dyess-ee-*syeh*-teh)
18 **dieciocho** (dyess-ee-*oh*-choh)
19 **diecinueve** (dyess-ee-*nweh*-beh)
20 **veinte** (*bayn*-teh)
30 **treinta** (*trayn*-tah)
40 **cuarenta** (kwah-*ren*-tah)
50 **cincuenta** (seen-*kwen*-tah)
60 **sesenta** (seh-*sehn*-tah)
70 **setenta** (seh-*tehn*-tah)
80 **ochenta** (oh-*chehn*-tah)
90 **noventa** (noh-*behn*-tah)
100 **cien** (syehn)
200 **doscientos** (do-*syehn*-tohs)
500 **quinientos** (kee-*nyehn*-tohs)
1,000 **mil** (meel)

TRANSPORTATION TERMS

English	Spanish	Pronunciation
Airport	**Aeropuerto**	ah-eh-roh-*pwehr*-toh
Flight	**Vuelo**	*bweh*-loh
Rental car	**Arrendadora de autos**	ah-rehn-da-doh-rah deh ow-tohs

English	Spanish	Pronunciation
Bus	**Autobús**	ow-toh-*boos*
Bus or truck	**Camión**	ka-*myohn*
Lane	**Carril**	kah-*reel*
Nonstop	**Directo**	dee-*rehk*-toh
Intercity	**Foraneo**	foh-rah-*neh*-oh
Luggage storage area	**Guarda equipaje**	gwar-dah eh-kee-*pah*-heh
Arrival gates	**Llegadas**	yeh-*gah*-dahss
Originates at this station	**Local**	loh-*kahl*
Originates elsewhere	**De paso**	deh *pah*-soh
Stops if seats available	**Para si hay lugares**	*pah*-rah see eye loo-*gah*-rehs
First class	**Primera**	pree-*meh*-rah
Second class	**Segunda**	seh-*goon*-dah
Nonstop	**Sin escala**	seen ess-*kah*-lah
Baggage claim area	**Recibo de equipajes**	reh-see-boh deh eh-kee-*pah*-hehss
Toilets	**Sanitarios**	sah-nee-*tah*-ryohss
Ticket window	**Taquilla**	tah-*kee*-yah

2 Menu Glossary

Achiote Small red seed of the *annatto* tree.

Achiote preparado A Yucatecan prepared paste made of ground *achiote*, wheat and corn flour, cumin, cinnamon, salt, onion, garlic, and oregano.

Agua fresca Fruit-flavored water, usually watermelon, cantaloupe, chia seed with lemon, hibiscus flour, rice, or ground melon-seed mixture.

Antojito Typical Mexican supper foods, usually made with *masa* or tortillas and having a filling or topping such as sausage, cheese, beans, and onions; includes such things as *tacos, tostadas, sopes,* and *garnachas.*

Atole A thick, lightly sweet, hot drink made with finely ground corn and usually flavored with vanilla, pecan, strawberry, pineapple, or chocolate.

Botana An appetizer.

Buñuelos   Round, thin, deep-fried crispy fritters dipped in sugar.

Carnitas   Pork deep-cooked (not fried) in lard, and then simmered and served with corn tortillas for tacos.

Ceviche   Fresh raw seafood marinated in fresh lime juice and garnished with chopped tomatoes, onions, chiles, and sometimes cilantro.

Chayote   A vegetable pear or mirliton, a type of spiny squash boiled and served as an accompaniment to meat dishes.

Chiles rellenos   Usually poblano peppers stuffed with cheese or spicy ground meat with raisins, rolled in a batter, and fried.

Churro   Tube-shaped, breadlike fritter, dipped in sugar and sometimes filled with *cajeta* (milk-based caramel) or chocolate.

Cochinita pibil   Pork wrapped in banana leaves, pit-baked in a *pibil* sauce of *achiote,* sour orange, and spices; common in the Yucatán.

Enchilada   A tortilla dipped in sauce, usually filled with chicken or white cheese, and sometimes topped with *mole* (*enchiladas rojas* or *de mole*), or with tomato sauce and sour cream (*enchiladas suizas*—Swiss enchiladas), or covered in a green sauce *(enchiladas verdes),* or topped with onions, sour cream, and guacamole *(enchiladas potosinas).*

Frijoles refritos   Pinto beans mashed and cooked with lard.

Garnachas   A thickish small circle of fried *masa* with pinched sides, topped with pork or chicken, onions, and avocado, or sometimes chopped potatoes and tomatoes, typical as a *botana* in Veracruz and Yucatán.

Gorditas   Thick, fried corn tortillas, slit and stuffed with choice of cheese, beans, beef, chicken, with or without lettuce, tomato, and onion garnish.

Horchata   Refreshing drink made of ground rice or melon seeds, ground almonds, cinnamon, and lightly sweetened.

Huevos mexicanos   Scrambled eggs with chopped onions, hot green peppers, and tomatoes.

Masa   Ground corn soaked in lime; the basis for tamales, corn tortillas, and soups.

Mixiote   Rabbit, lamb, or chicken cooked in a mild chile sauce (usually chile *ancho* or *pasilla*), and then wrapped like a tamal and steamed. It is generally served with tortillas for tacos, with traditional garnishes of pickled onions, hot sauce, chopped cilantro, and lime wedges.

Papadzules   Tortillas stuffed with hard-boiled eggs and seeds (pumpkin or sunflower) in a tomato sauce.

Pibil   Pit-baked pork or chicken in a sauce of tomato, onion, mild red pepper, cilantro, and vinegar.

Poc chuc Slices of pork with onion marinated in a tangy sour orange sauce and charcoal-broiled; a Yucatecan specialty.

Pozole A soup made with hominy in either chicken or pork broth.

Quesadilla Corn or flour tortillas stuffed with melted white cheese and lightly fried.

Rompope Delicious Mexican eggnog, invented in Puebla, made with eggs, vanilla, sugar, and rum.

Salsa verde An uncooked sauce using the green tomatillo and puréed with spicy or mild hot peppers, onions, garlic, and cilantro; on tables countrywide.

Sopa de lima A tangy soup made with chicken broth and accented with fresh lime; popular in Yucatán.

Sopa de tortilla A traditional chicken broth–based soup, seasoned with chiles, tomatoes, onion, and garlic, served with crispy fried strips of corn tortillas.

Sope Pronounced "*soh*-peh." An *antojito* similar to a *garnacha*, except spread with refried beans and topped with crumbled cheese and onions.

Tamal Incorrectly called a tamale (*tamal* singular, *tamales* plural). A meat or sweet filling rolled with fresh *masa*, wrapped in a corn husk or banana leaf, and steamed.

Tikin xic Also seen on menus as "tik-n-xic" and "tikik chick." Charbroiled fish brushed with *achiote* sauce.

Index

See also Accommodations, and Restaurant indexes below.

FROMMER'S® COMPLETE TRAVEL GUIDES

Alaska
Alaska Cruises & Ports of Call
American Southwest
Amsterdam
Argentina & Chile
Arizona
Atlanta
Australia
Austria
Bahamas
Barcelona
Beijing
Belgium, Holland & Luxembourg
Bermuda
Boston
Brazil
British Columbia & the Canadian
  Rockies
Brussels & Bruges
Budapest & the Best of Hungary
Calgary
California
Canada
Cancún, Cozumel & the Yucatán
Cape Cod, Nantucket & Martha's
  Vineyard
Caribbean
Caribbean Ports of Call
Carolinas & Georgia
Chicago
China
Colorado
Costa Rica
Cruises & Ports of Call
Cuba
Denmark
Denver, Boulder & Colorado Springs
Edinburgh & Glasgow
England
Europe
Europe by Rail
European Cruises & Ports of Call
Florence, Tuscany & Umbria

Florida
France
Germany
Great Britain
Greece
Greek Islands
Halifax
Hawaii
Hong Kong
Honolulu, Waikiki & Oahu
India
Ireland
Italy
Jamaica
Japan
Kauai
Las Vegas
London
Los Angeles
Madrid
Maine Coast
Maryland & Delaware
Maui
Mexico
Montana & Wyoming
Montréal & Québec City
Munich & the Bavarian Alps
Nashville & Memphis
New England
Newfoundland & Labrador
New Mexico
New Orleans
New York City
New York State
New Zealand
Northern Italy
Norway
Nova Scotia, New Brunswick &
  Prince Edward Island
Oregon
Ottawa
Paris
Peru

Philadelphia & the Amish Country
Portugal
Prague & the Best of the Czech
  Republic
Provence & the Riviera
Puerto Rico
Rome
San Antonio & Austin
San Diego
San Francisco
Santa Fe, Taos & Albuquerque
Scandinavia
Scotland
Seattle
Seville, Granada & the Best of
  Andalusia
Shanghai
Sicily
Singapore & Malaysia
South Africa
South America
South Florida
South Pacific
Southeast Asia
Spain
Sweden
Switzerland
Texas
Thailand
Tokyo
Toronto
Turkey
USA
Utah
Vancouver & Victoria
Vermont, New Hampshire & Maine
Vienna & the Danube Valley
Virgin Islands
Virginia
Walt Disney World® & Orlando
Washington, D.C.
Washington State

FROMMER'S® DOLLAR-A-DAY GUIDES

Australia from $50 a Day
California from $70 a Day
England from $75 a Day
Europe from $85 a Day
Florida from $70 a Day
Hawaii from $80 a Day

Ireland from $80 a Day
Italy from $70 a Day
London from $90 a Day
New York City from $90 a Day
Paris from $90 a Day
San Francisco from $70 a Day

Washington, D.C. from $80 a Day
Portable London from $90 a Day
Portable New York City from $90
  a Day
Portable Paris from $90 a Day

FROMMER'S® PORTABLE GUIDES

Acapulco, Ixtapa & Zihuatanejo
Amsterdam
Aruba
Australia's Great Barrier Reef
Bahamas
Berlin
Big Island of Hawaii
Boston
California Wine Country
Cancún
Cayman Islands
Charleston
Chicago
Disneyland®
Dominican Republic

Dublin
Florence
Frankfurt
Hong Kong
Las Vegas
Las Vegas for Non-Gamblers
London
Los Angeles
Los Cabos & Baja
Maui
Miami
Nantucket & Martha's Vineyard
New Orleans
New York City
Paris

Phoenix & Scottsdale
Portland
Puerto Rico
Puerto Vallarta, Manzanillo &
  Guadalajara
Rio de Janeiro
San Diego
San Francisco
Savannah
Vancouver Island
Venice
Virgin Islands
Washington, D.C.
Whistler

FROMMER'S® NATIONAL PARK GUIDES

Algonquin Provincial Park
Banff & Jasper
Family Vacations in the National Parks

Grand Canyon
National Parks of the American West
Rocky Mountain

Yellowstone & Grand Teton
Yosemite & Sequoia/Kings Canyon
Zion & Bryce Canyon

FROMMER'S® MEMORABLE WALKS

Chicago
London

New York
Paris

San Francisco

FROMMER'S® WITH KIDS GUIDES

Chicago
Hawaii
Las Vegas
New York City

Ottawa
San Francisco
Toronto

Vancouver
Walt Disney World® & Orlando
Washington, D.C.

SUZY GERSHMAN'S BORN TO SHOP GUIDES

Born to Shop: France
Born to Shop: Hong Kong, Shanghai & Beijing

Born to Shop: Italy
Born to Shop: London

Born to Shop: New York
Born to Shop: Paris

FROMMER'S® IRREVERENT GUIDES

Amsterdam
Boston
Chicago
Las Vegas
London

Los Angeles
Manhattan
New Orleans
Paris
Rome

San Francisco
Seattle & Portland
Vancouver
Walt Disney World®
Washington, D.C.

FROMMER'S® BEST-LOVED DRIVING TOURS

Austria
Britain
California
France

Germany
Ireland
Italy
New England

Northern Italy
Scotland
Spain
Tuscany & Umbria

THE UNOFFICIAL GUIDES®

Beyond Disney
California with Kids
Central Italy
Chicago
Cruises
Disneyland®
England
Florida
Florida with Kids
Inside Disney

Hawaii
Las Vegas
London
Maui
Mexico's Best Beach Resorts
Mini Las Vegas
Mini Mickey
New Orleans
New York City
Paris

San Francisco
Skiing & Snowboarding in the West
South Florida including Miami & the Keys
Walt Disney World®
Walt Disney World® for Grown-ups
Walt Disney World® with Kids
Washington, D.C.

SPECIAL-INTEREST TITLES

Athens Past & Present
Cities Ranked & Rated
Frommer's Best Day Trips from London
Frommer's Best RV & Tent Campgrounds in the U.S.A.
Frommer's Caribbean Hideaways
Frommer's China: The 50 Most Memorable Trips
Frommer's Exploring America by RV
Frommer's Gay & Lesbian Europe

Frommer's NYC Free & Dirt Cheap
Frommer's Road Atlas Europe
Frommer's Road Atlas France
Frommer's Road Atlas Ireland
Frommer's Wonderful Weekends from New York City
Retirement Places Rated
Rome Past & Present

THE NEW TRAVELOCITY GUARANTEE

EVERYTHING YOU BOOK WILL BE RIGHT, OR WE'LL WORK WITH OUR TRAVEL PARTNERS TO MAKE IT RIGHT, RIGHT AWAY.

*To drive home the point,
we're going to use the word "right" in every single sentence.*

Let's get right to it. Right to the meat! Only Travelocity guarantees everything about your booking will be right, or we'll work with our travel partners to make it right, right away. Right on!

Here's a picture taken smack dab right in the middle of Antigua, where the guarantee also covers you.

The guarantee covers all but one of the items pictured to the right.

For example, what if the ocean view you booked actually looks out at a downright ugly parking lot? You'd be right to call – we're there for you. And no one in their right mind would be pleased to learn the rental car place has closed and left them stranded. Call Travelocity and we'll help get you back on the right track.

Now, you may be thinking, "Yeah, right, I'm so sure." That's OK; you have the right to remain skeptical. That is until we mention help is always right around the corner. Call us right off the bat, knowing that our customer service reps are there for you 24/7. Righting wrongs. Left and right.

Now if you're guessing there are some things we can't control, like the weather, well you're right. But we can help you with most things – to get all the details in righting,* visit **travelocity.com/guarantee**.

*Sorry, spelling things right is one of the few things not covered under the guarantee.

I'd give my right arm for a guarantee like this, although I'm glad I don't have to.

travelocity

You'll never roam alone.